QUALITY OF WORKLIFE IN ISLAMIC CULTURE

QUALITY OF WORKLIFE IN ISLAMIC CULTURE

DR. MOHAMMED GALIB HUSSAIN
Associate Professor and Head, Department of Corporate Secretaryship
Islamiah College, Vaniyambadi (T.N.)

and

DR. S. SHAMSUDDIN
Associate Professor, Department of Commerce
C. Abdul Hakeem College, Melvisharam (T.N.)

DEEP & DEEP PUBLICATIONS PVT. LTD.
F-159, Rajouri Garden, New Delhi - 110 027

QUALITY OF WORKLIFE IN ISLAMIC CULTURE

ISBN 978-81-8450-298-5

Printed in India at MAYUR ENTERPRISES
WZ Plot No. 3, Gujjar Market, Tihar Village, New Delhi - 110 018

Published by DEEP & DEEP PUBLICATIONS PVT. LTD.,
F-159, Rajouri Garden, New Delhi - 110 027 • Phone : 25435369, 25440916
E-mail : ddpubs@gmail.com • ddpbooks@yahoo.co.in
Showroom :
2/13, Ansari Road, Daryaganj, New Delhi - 110 002 • Telefax : 23245122

DEDICATED

TO

Mom :
ZIAUNNISA

Wife :
NASEEMA

Children :
MUJADDID,
FAYIZA,
MUJAHID,
MUSAID,
NABEEL
and
NASHITA

By
Mohammed Galib Hussain

Dad :
S. SHAHABUDDIN

Mom :
S. BEGUM SHARIF

Wife :
SHIRA

Children :
SAIFUDDIN,
AMMERUDDIN
and
AYESHA

By
S. Shamsuddin

Contents

Preface

The *Quality of Worklife* movement which originated in the western organizations has an avowed objective of humanizing work situation. It addresses the question of what people want from their work situation so that their needs, not just as employees but as human beings are met. Restless and alienated blue collar workers want meaningful work. Factory employees need to have jobs with altered content to give them task variety, task significance, challenge, responsibility, a sense of accomplishment/achievement and reliable feed-back. Engineers and scientists are increasingly concerned about technical obsolescence. As human beings they should be provided work -life balance; career demands should not be such as to reduce their leisure and family time. Separation of planning and implementation has led to fractionalization of work. The work need to be designed in such a way the worker can use his skills to the optimum extent. The organizational culture shall have to be designed in such a way personal privacy, tolerance of diversity of individual cultures should be valued. Man has lost the meaning of life; the work milieu should allow him to regain the paradise lost.

Islam is a revealed thought for the entire humanity. It does not stand for a few rituals, certain ceremonies, dogmas and specified beliefs. The entire metaphysics, beliefs, culture, civilization, values, mores, standards, morality and ethos are derived from divine guidance. This guidance is contained in two prime sources: the Quran and Sunnah. Muslims believe the

Quran is the word of divinity and Sunnah is the divine inspired precepts and practices of Prophet Muhammad.

Drawing on these pristine sources, an attempt has been made to articulate the meaning of life for employees, an exposition of motivational basis in Islamic paradigm is made. Stress inoculation through Islamic metaphysics and devotional methods, stress busters and coping mechanism are described. Conflict resolution methods in Islamic framework and Islamic Shariah are discussed in this study.

Though the concepts of enrichment of quality of job life presented in this book are culture-specific, it should not be misunderstood as to mean that this new paradigm holds good only in Muslim organizations. Some of the ideas can be used by way of cultural intervention strategies in any organization for improving the psychological health of the members as well as organizational effectiveness. Surely, the path-breaking philosophical underpinnings of Islam articulated can be employed in non-Muslim organizations as well.

The authors wish to express their sincere gratitude to all those writers whose works have been consulted. Their contributions to the development of thought in this book have been acknowledged by way of citations where ever needed. It is quite possible that some of the ideas, views and conclusions of some authorities on Islam might have influenced, albeit subconsciously, the thinking of the authors. To all of them, heartfelt thanks are expressed.

The managements, the former as well as the present Secretaries, the Principals—current and the past—of Islamiah College, Vaniyambadi and C. Abdul Hakeem College, Melvisharam have shown keen interest in the project. Janab S. Ziauddin Saheb, Chairman, Melvisharam Muslim Educational Society, Melvisharam and Janab C. Khaiser Ahmed Saheb, Secretary and Correspondent, Islamiah College, Vaniyambadi have taken personal interest in the study. The authors would ever remain indebted to all of them.

Mr. G.S. Bhatia and his team at Deep and Deep Publications Pvt. Ltd. certainly need to be congratulated for bringing out the book in such an excellent form.

DR. MOHAMMED GALIB HUSSAIN
DR. S. SHAMSUDDIN

1

Introduction

The word 'Quality' gains an importance, in the industrial world due to 'Quality culture'. The 'Quality' movement represents a change in the management view. It gives importance to people's issues rather than the technical issues.[1]

Quality is everyone's responsibility in any organization. Quality demands that one should perform the best. It assumes a goal or an objective or a priority. But work of quality cannot be achieved easily. Performing quality work is an accountability of every employee. It is nothing but the result of the intelligent and aesthetic work.

When organizations have addressed the issue of quality of working life, they have always achieved great productivity breakthrough (Jerome M. Rosow).[2] Therefore, organizations gradually began experimenting with work designs that provide effective human results along with high efficiency. The purpose is to develop a better quality of work life for employees and higher productivity for the employer.

Quality of work life (QWL) refers to favourableness or unfavourableness of a job environment for people.[3] The aim is to develop work environments that are excellent for people as well as for the economic health of the organization. QWL programmes usually emphasize employee skill development, the reduction of occupational stress, and the development of more cooperative labour management relations.[4] QWL programs and new socio-technical systems in Greenfield sites have better results than redesign of existing systems.[5]

QWL is a large step forward from the traditional job design of scientific management, which focused mostly on specialization and efficiency. As it evolved, it used full division of labour, rigid hierarchy and standardization of labour to reach its objectives of efficiency. The idea was to lower costs by using unskilled, repetitive labour that could be trained easily to do a small part of a job. A large hierarchy that strictly enforced controlled Job performance.

HUMANIZED WORK

QWL produces a more humanized work environment. It serves the higher-order needs of employees as well as their more basic needs. It seeks to employ the higher skills of employees and to provide an environment that encourages them to improve their skills. The idea is that employees are human resources that are to be developed rather than simply used. Further, the work should not have excessively negative conditions. It should not put employees under undue stress. It should not damage or degrade their humanness. It should not be threatening or unduly dangerous. Finally, it should contribute to or at least leave unimpaired, employees abilities to perform in other life roles, such as citizen, spouse and parent. That is, work should contribute to general social advancement.

The basic assumption of humanized work is that, work is most advantageous when it provides a "best fit" among employees, jobs, technology and the environment.

Quality of work life (QWL) is the overall satisfaction felt by an employee. It can be described as nature of work, coping-up with working conditions, such as stress, conflicts, motivation, etc. which the employee experience in the work.[6] There are white-collar jobs, which provide satisfaction due to unique characters such as human relations activity, intellectual effort, and managerial responsibility.[7] This is the western view of quality of work life. The aim is to humanize the work situation is the root of the quality of work life movements. The basic problem with western quality of work life movement is that it has failed to generate the practical results for the business managers. The more the job enrichment programme such as building autonomy in the work situation, communicating the task significance, a changing the work situation in such a way that it brings task variety, the more are the dissatisfied employees. An average employee in western organization has lost meaning of work. The net result is that both the management and the employees are disillusion with quality of work life movement. There is a need to examine the QWL concept from altogether a new angle; paradigmatic shift in the approach is needed.

One such effort was made by S.K. Chakraborthy. 'Sacrifice' is the quality of work life given by S.K. Chakraborthy. The employee and the employer have to sacrifice their pleasure and maintaining the quality of work. We have the examples of M.K. Gandhi, Vivekananda, and Rabindrannath Tagore who had sacrificed their pleasure and a lot more.[8]

The basic problem is all the above conceptualizations be it western or Hindu are all the products of human intellect. Human thinking cannot be relied totally for understanding the human nature, and human behaviour. There is a need to examine the whole gamut of QWL in the light of Diving guidance.

CRITICISM OF JOB-ENRICHMENT

The Western view of quality of work life developed through an emphasis on Job-enrichment. The term was coined by Frederick Herzberg based on his research with motivators and maintenance factors. Job-enrichment means that additional motivators are added to a job to make it more rewarding, although the term has come to apply to almost any effort to humanize jobs. Job enrichment is an expansion of an earlier concept of Job-enlargement, which sought to give employees a wide variety of duties in order to reduce monotony.

It is more appropriate for some situations than for others and in certain situations it may not be appropriate at all.[9] Some employees do not want increased responsibility and other employees do not adapt to group interaction that is sometimes required. In other words, enrichment is contingent on attitudes of employees and their capability to handle enriched tasks.

It can be argued that employees should accept job enrichment because it is "good", but it is more consistent with human values to recognize and respect individual differences of employees.

Pay Relationships

Job enrichment may upset pay relationships. Management typically assumes that the intrinsic rewards of the enriched job are sufficient. Employees however may become unhappy because they think they are not paid in proportion to their increased duties. They want more money, but a pay increase adds to costs and may upset comparative pay relationships.

Union Attitudes

Job-enrichment may upset existing job classifications, thereby causing union resistance. In some instances enrichment may create jurisdictional disputes between the territories of two unions. Likely places for this problem are maintenance work and construction work. Distinction between jobs may be so narrow and rules so rigid that unions will not tolerate some changes.

Other Costs

There are other costs in addition to pay. Equipment and floor space may need to be redesigned. In some instance more space and tools will be needed so that teams can work independently. Even work-in-progress inventory may have to be increased so that individual employees or team can have enough supplies. In addition, there are substantial training costs in order to prepare employees for their new patterns of work. They are likely to be temporary quality and output problems during the period of change because existing teamwork among employees is disrupted. Some employees even resign.

Contingency Factors

Job enrichment does not apply to all types of situations.[10] It appears to suit higher level jobs compared with lower-level ones. This is more so if the lower-level jobs are dictated by the technological process. If the technology is stable and highly automated the cost of job enrichment may be too great in relation to the rewards. Some organizations have such huge investment in equipment that they cannot afford to make substantial changes until the equipment is replaced. When difficult technological conditions are combined with negative attitudes toward job-enrichment, then it becomes inappropriate until the environment for it can be changed.

Results of the Socio-technical Experiments

One of the earliest, at Non-linear system was discarded when the firm's product leadership declined and productivity failed to keep pace with that of competitors.[11] Despite numerous behavioural innovations, the participative system proved too cumbersome to respond to quickly needed changes and the firm was forced to return to a more traditional work system to survive.

Some employees object when other team members earn more after learning additional tasks. Some employees prefer to work as traditional tasks and avoid the extra group work and added responsibility. Both team leaders and entire work teams occasionally become autocratic, exerting excessive peer pressure for conformity to group norms. Role confusion can occur.

This study is a humble beginning in understanding the various aspects of QWL in the light of uncorrupted, pure and God's sent guidance in pristine form.

The word 'Quality' refers to satisfaction, which is the greatest gate of God. Whoever is the greatest gate of God and the paradise of this world knows that the servant will not approach being satisfied with God (May He exalted) until God is satisfied with him, because God Most High says,

> "God is well pleased with them and they are well pleased with God".
>
> (Quran, 98 : 8)

> "God does not accept belief,
> if it is not expressed in deed;
> and does not accept deed,
> if it does not confirm to belief".

"The Quran is essentially a code of human conduct. That is the claim which the Book itself advances".

(Quran, 2 : 5)

It is meant to offer guidance to those who seek it. The Quran is to be endorsed in action by a rational approach to it, and is an account of a subject of consideration even by those who may not believe in any established religion but who dislike in thought and action and recognize the need for some standard of conduct to govern their working life. To such, it may be told that the essential purpose of the Quran is to develop in an employee's mind the primary functions of which is to enable him to live in peace with himself and in peace with his external world and in so doing he is to serve a deeper purpose as well. This wider applicability is beyond the purview of abstract ethics or of any exclusively secular concept of life. The Quran postulates that death is not the end of life, but on the other hand, it is a gateway to a new sphere of life marking a further stage in the making of an employee.

"From state to state, shall ye, assuredly, be carried forward". (Q 84 : 19)

The ultimate purpose is perfection of an employee. It is this purpose, which has to govern the character of the life one has to live in the present. The mind, which the Quran aims to build, is to view in one sweep the entire course of working life in the present and what is to follow, and adjust accordingly.

"Your creation and your resurrection are but like a single soul". (Q 31 : 27)

The cultural process recommended by the Quran is single directive:

"Believe and work for the pleasure of God", this line of action suggests that the employee has to grow conscious of certain basic realities or truths of life and see that the work life should be in confirmative with them. This introductory chapter is devoted to a statement of these basic truths.

They are expressed in the form of doctrinal beliefs, which every Muslim employee has to prefer and attempt to implement it in his working life.

This is the fundamental belief that each Muslim employee has to express in his working life. At the cultural plane or in the process of implementing in working life, these beliefs to explained later on, are to develop in Muslim employee a living sense of God both in thought and action and equip him to work for a life of peace—peace within and peace external, peace in one's self, and peace in one's relation with the world around him.

States the Quran:

> "Those who believe and those whose hearts find rest in the thought of God—indeed, it is the thought of God that the heart (an employee) doth really find rest—those who believe and work for pleasure of God, joy is for them and a blissful home to return to". (Q : 14-29)

BELIEF IN THE UNITY OF GOD

The basic concept into which the Quran desires to initiate an employee's mind is the concept of the unity of God. This is called '*Tawheed*' in Islamic terminology.

The very basic creed which every Muslim employee has to profess runs in the following words :

> "I affirm that there is none worthy of worship except God, that is one, with none to associate with, and I affirm that Prophet Muhammad (SAW) is His messenger".

A disciple asked his master "does the servant know if God is pleased with him? The answer was no; how could he know that when His pleasure is hidden?" The disciple protested, but he did know that! The master asked the disciple "how do you know whether God is pleased with you or not". He replied, "If I find my heart pleased with God Most High, I know that he is pleased with me. Then the master remarked, well have you spoken, young man".

It is said that Moses (upon whom be peace) prayed, "O my God, direct me to a deed which performance would please you". He was told, "you would not be able to do that". Moses fell down to prostrate Him. So God Most High revealed to him, "O son of Imran, My pleasure is your pleasure with my decree".[12]

Therefore, for an employee or worker or manager or owner, quality of work life is the pleasure of God. 'RAZA-YE-ILAHI' (pleasure of God) is the only objective which will satisfy all.

The relationship between an employer and an employee is given in the following Hadeeths :

> The best of livelihood is that of a labourer provided he discharges his obligations to his employer in the spirit of good-will towards him.
>
> —Ahmed : Majm'a al-Zawaid
>
> Said the Prophet (SAW): "Pay the wages of the labourer before his perspiration dries up".
>
> —Ibn Maja
>
> Abu Say'id Qhudri : Narrates that the Prophet (SAW) "forbade the forcing of a labourer to take up his work before settling his wages".
>
> —Baihaqi
>
> God looks upon a labourer as His friend.
>
> —Baihaqi
>
> Narrates Anas bin Malik : When Sayid al Ansari met the Prophet (SAW) during the campaign of Tabuk, the Prophet (SAW) shook hands with him and asked him why his hands were so full of scars. Ansari replied saying that the scars were wrought on his hands by the heavy hammer and the rough rope, which he had to employ in a quarry to earn the lively bread for his family. The Prophet (SAW) kissed both his hands and said: 'Fire can never tough these hands".
>
> —Asad Al Ghabah
>
> Once a person came to the Prophet (SAW) and asked of him as to how far he should forgive his servant. The Prophet (SAW) kept silence. The man again asked him: How many times should he forgive his servant? The

Prophet (SAW) said : Seventy times. (In the Arabic idiom, it means many times).

—Tirmizi

Said the Prophet (SAW): To reduce the promised wages of a labourer is a major sin.

—Kunuzul Haqaiq

Said the Prophet (SAW) : I shall remonstrate with three types of people on the day of judgment and will make them feel ashamed of themselves. One of them is he who having taken work out of a labourer declines to pay him adequately.

—Baihaqi

Said the Prophet (SAW) : Those who happen to be your bondsmen or your own brothers. God has placed them under your authority. It is meant that he who is in authority over his brother should feed him with the food that he himself eats, and cloth him with the stuff that he himself wears. Do not ask him to do a thing, which is not physically possible for him to do; and if such a thing is to be done, do assist him in his task.

—Bukhari

Said the Prophet (SAW) : When your servant prepares food for you, if you do not choose to ask him to partake of it at the same table, at least offer him a morsel of it, for, he has borne the heat of the kitchen and cooked the food for you.

—Bukhari

According to the Quran, employee has a dual responsibility to discharge. One is in relation to God, i.e. Pleasure of God (RAZA-YE-ILAHI) the other is in relation to his external world, i.e. relation to superior, relation to subordinate, relation to co-workers. The one is to acknowledge in thought and action what is pleasure to God. The two types of responsibilities are one and the same attitudes towards working life of the same activity proceeding from it and signify the character of the mind an employee has to develop. It is this mind, which matters in determining responsibility for every human action. "Action rest on motives says the prophet because motive is the index to the mind or to the manner in which the mind chooses to exercise. It is why every stress is laid on purity of motives. And this purity is promoted by proper exercise of the balance aiming at a harmonious with God and others. This is in the interest of the organization. This is called one of the qualities of work life.

The culture of Islam is an expression of this process. The directive inspiring the process is summed up in the words of the prophet "Respect the ways of God and be affectionate to the family of God". The entire organization is a family of God. All the employees has to respect the ways of Allah and follow it with others.

Quality of work in the context of "Believe and work" is for the pleasure of God has no other meaning for an employee except to bear this distinction in mind in all activity, whether it concerns his own self or his relations with his own self or his relations with his fellow beings or superiors or co-workers. An employee has to follow the qualities like kindliness, purity, chastity, love, affection, truth, respect, forbearance, forgiveness, trustworthiness, justice and mercy towards other employees.

Such quality of work helps an employee to live in peace with himself and in peace with his fellow-beings and the rest of the creation. The duty of an employee is to see that every action is to confirm the law of harmonious living.

> "Verily my prayers, and my sacrifice
> And my life and my death are
> All for Allah". (Q : 6 : 163)

Thus work life viewed, every action of an employee assumes a spiritual significance. It is this significance, which distinguish from every other form of employee's activity. The spirit underlying it, whatever the result of a relation of twin spiritual faculties in employees the sense of God, and the sense of fellow being.

Prayed the Prophet both for himself and his followers:

> "O Allah! Make us guides in the path of life, and keep us guided ourselves therein—neither going astray, nor leading astray".
>
> —Hisn-in Hisin

"O Allah! I seek they refuge from misleading others, and from being misled by others; from betraying others into error and from being betrayed into error by others; from doing any wrong to others; and from being wronged by others; and from drawing others into ignorance, and from being drawn into ignorance by other".

—Hisn-Hisin

"O Allah! I seek they refuge from any wrong that I may do to others, and from any wrong that others may do to me; from any harshness that I may show to others, and from any harshness that others may show to me; and from any sin that thou may not forgive".

—*Ibid.*

An employee should pray to God that he should maintain good relation with all in the organizations.

The following are some of the verses from Quran:

"I ask of thee qualities which more. They grace forgiveness. I ask of thy protection from doing harm to any one and I ask of thee the enhance of doing well to every one".

—*Ibid.*

"O Allah! I ask of thee steadfastness in every pursuit. I ask of thee the intent for good action and the power to thank thee for thy benevolence and to render devoted service. I ask of Thee the tongue that speaks truth and the mind that erred not and the gift of true fellow-feeling. I seek that thou know; and I ask of Thee the good that lie in everything that Thou know; and I seek they refuse from every sin of which than refuge from every sin of which than hast knowledge, and verily, thou know all that we cannot know".

—*Ibid.*

The following are some of the Hadeeth which are related to relationship:

1. Said the prophet : O Lord! Lord of my life and of everything in the Universe! I affirm that all human beings are brothers unto one another".

—Ahmed Abu Dawud

2. "All creatures of God from the family of God and he is the best loved of God who love best His creatures".
—Baihaqi : Kitabul Iman, Shuabul Iman
3. "Mankind is a fold every member of which is a shepherd into every other, and will be accountable for the welfare of the entire fold".
—Bukhari : Kitabul-Imam
4. "Islam demands a united life for man".
—Kunuzul Haqaiq
5. "Said the prophet : Unity is bliss : Disunity is misery".
—Kunuzul Haqaiq
6. "In loving devotion to God, you ought to live a united life as brothers into each other". —Kunuzul Haqaiq
7. One believer is for another believer what the foundation is to the building, supporting the other. Then joining the fingers of both his hands in a grip said "They are joined together like this".
—Bukhari Kitabul Adab
8. Said prophet : Whosoever loves another for the sake of God in reality has expressed his love for God.
—Ahmed : Musnad
9. I have heard the prophet sayings; "God says : It is obligatory on we to love those who for my sake love each others and meet together and spend on each other out of what they have.
—Malik : Mutta
10. God says: If you wish to receive graciousness from me, show graciousness to those whom I have created.
—Kunuzul Haqaiq
11. Said the Prophet : a believer is truly the centre and embodiment of live and affection. There is no goodness in him who does not show affection for others and for whom others do not show affection.
—Musnad and Baihaqi
12. "God says", related the prophet, "Love becomes obligatory on my part who for my sake love one another, and live together and who for my sake greet each other with a goodly cheer, and who for my sake spend a what they earn for the good of one another".
—Malik : Muatta

13. None among you is a believer in God, unless he wishes for his brother what he wishes for his brother what he wishes for himself. —Bukhari-Kitabul -Imam
14. Said the prophet: Be faithful to God and be brothers to one another.

    —Bukhari
15. Said the prophet: Of all human actions, the one which pleases God is that expression of love which is expressed for the sake of God and that expression of dislike which is expressed for the sake of God.

    —Abu Dawud
16. He who, for the sake of God, has loved another human being, that person verily has extolled the glory of God.

    —Ahmed : Musnad
17. Said the prophet: Shall I tell you what is better than prayer and fasting and the highest form of charity? It is to resolve internal dissensions and bring about concord between contending parties? It is internal dissension that primarily ruins a society.

    —Ibn Maia, Tirmizi-Ahmed
18. Live together, do not turn against each other, make things easy for the other and do not put obstacles in each other's way.

    —Kunuzul-Haqaiq
19. Abu Huraira narrates that the apostle of God said, "He who believes in God and the Day of recompense will never harm his neighbour, will be hospitable to his guests, and speak to others in a gentle tone or remain silent. —Bukhari
20. The believer in God is he who is not a danger to life and property of any other.

    —Tirmizi Nisai and Bukhari
21. A true believer in God does not curse others or taunts at them: nor does he indulge in slander or abusive language.

    —Tirmzi and Baihaqi
22. Wisdom lies in loving each other without depriving the other of his rights.

    —Kunuzul Haqiaq

23. The Apostle of God said : Tenderness always lends beauty to one who displays it in one's relations with others. On the other hand, a lack of it lends ugliness.
—Taisirul Usul : Kitabul Iman

From the above, it has been concluded that an organization is like a family of God. In an organization employer, supervisor, employee and others are the members of a family. They are all brothers and sisters. They should love and be affectionate with each other for the pleasure of God. They should help each other. This type of relationship in an organization will only long last and all will happy for the sake of God. There will not be stress among them. The employer should respect, love and be affectionate with all the employees of the organization. The supervisor should respect love and be affectionate with his employer, his subordinates and colleagues of the organization. An employee should respect, love and be affectionate with supervisor, his subordinates and his co-worker and all others in the organization. Their aim is only to satisfy God.

Unity among the employees, supervisors and employer is important for the organization live a united life as brothers and sisters in an organization, which is said by God. Patience should be maintained among the members of the organization for the sake of Allah. This will give a better relationship among them. An organization is like a human body. All parts are like employees. If any part (employee) is affected, the body will be affected. Therefore, all the employees should be united and work for the organization for the RAZA-YE-ILAHI (pleasure of God).

IMPORTANCE OF THE STUDY

Human behaviour is everyone's concern. Management is concerned about the lack of commitment from the employees. Employees are dissatisfied with their work. Unions are unable to solve the employee's problem. Supervisors are not happy with the employees. When the employees are well remunerated in an organization, they indulge in strikes or some other forms of protest. The assumption that a well-paid employee is supposed to be motivated enough to carryout the responsibilities entrusted to him/her and he/she should be happy with the job is shattered in the present day organization.

The traditional methods of motivating human beings with in the established institution have become ineffective. Modern technology gives importance to higher production, it does have a negative impact on the working environment. These changes in the new forms of work organization led to formation of Quality of work life concept.

Quality of work life is a generic phrase that covers an employee's feelings about every dimensions of work including economic rewards and benefits, security, working conditions, organizational and interpersonal relationships and the intrinsic meaning of work to a person.[13]

Since classical designs also gave inadequate attention to quality of work life, many difficulties were developed. There was excessive division of labour and over dependence on rules, procedures and hierarchy. Specialized employees became socially isolated from their colleagues because their highly specialized work weakened their community of interest in the whole product. Many employees were so deskilled that they lost pride in their work. The result was higher turnover and absenteeism. Quality declined and workers became alienated. Conflict arose as employees tried to improve their conditions. Due to conflict, stress among many employees leads to health problems like headache, ulcers, Diabetics, etc.

Management response to this situation was to tight controls, to increase supervision and to organize more rigidly. These actions were intended to improve the situation, but they only made it worse, because they further dehumanized the work. Management made a common error by treating the symptoms rather than the cause of the problems. The real cause was that in many instance the job itself simply was not satisfying. The odd condition developed for some employees that the more they worked, the less they were satisfied. Hence, the desire to work declined.

A factor contributing to the problem was that the employees themselves were changing. They became more educated, more affluent and more independent. They began reducing for higher-order needs, something more than merely earning their bread. Perhaps classical design was best for a poor, uneducated, often illustrate work force that lacked skills, but it was less appropriate for the new work force. Design of jobs and organizations had failed to keep up with widespread changes in employee's aspirations and attitudes.

This study is a paradigmatic shift in the conceptualization of various dimensions of the QWL. The new paradigm is developed on the basis of Divine guidance given to entire mankind—not just to Muslims alone. Islam is a religion for the entire humanity. The delineation of various dimensions of QWL in the light of Quran and Sunnah will contribute to the knowledge in the field of QWL. Further Islam claims that the Divine guidance given that God has universal application. Therefore, the ideas developed in the thesis will have universal application.

STATEMENT OF THE PROBLEM

Marx's concept of labour alienation from his output, led many social scientists and management theorists in the west to think about the quality of work life. The human-relation school of thirties, the socio-technical school of the fifties, the job-enrichment/enlargement school of the sixties, the software industries of twenty-first centuries have all been deeply concerned with the organizing of the social and technical component of the work in order to harness energies of a total man at work. The aim of all these efforts is humanization at work.

Those planning job-enrichment for QWL programs need to ask such questions as the following about employee needs and attitudes.

- Can the employee tolerate responsibility?
- How strong employee growth and achievement are need?
- What is the employee's attitude towards working with the group?
- Can the employee work with more complexity?
- How strong are the employee's drives for security and stability?
- Will the employees view the job changes as significant?

All these theories emphasize that human beings are given importance with certain set of needs, such as work autonomy, task significance task variety, etc. Even the humanization of work environment has failed to produce necessary results. When employees have been provided with job autonomy, task variety, task significance, more and more demands are cropping up from them. Evidently Western theorizing about human behaviour in so far it relates to QWL is at fault. Even the Herzberg two factor theory has failed to produce the desired result when applied to different organizations across the globe. There is a need to examine the concept of work as well as meaning of work on the basis of Divine guidance.

OBJECTIVES OF THE STUDY

The following are the specific objectives of the study :

1. To understand the various dimensions of quality of work-life from Islamic point of view.
2. To understand the stress-inoculation methods of Islam.
3. To identify the conflict resolution mechanism in Islamic culture.
4. To examine the Islamic basis of employee motivation.
5. To delineate the effect of Tawheed on quality of work-life.

RESEARCH METHODOLOGY

The above study is based on the insights of Quran and Hadeeth, which are divine sources. The Quran is the basis of all Islamic principles, knowledge, behaviour and action. The second important source of divine guidance is Hadeeth. The Hadeeth means the literature, which consists of the narrations of the life of the Prophet (SAW) and the things approved by him.

This is a descriptive study, no effort is made to test it empirically. The empiricism is not only way of knowing the phenomena. More particularly in social sciences empirical method cannot be relied. Therefore, this study relies on Divine guidance for describing the various aspects of QWL.

SCOPE OF THE STUDY

The religion of Islam has originated from the creator. It claims that it is a perfect religion. It is a religion for entire mankind and for all times to come. Therefore, the findings of this study have Universal validity. Irrespective of the nature place of the organization the findings hold good for all the organizations.

USES OF QWL IN ORGANIZATIONS AND SOCIETY

If an employee is trained in Islamic ways, his motivation will be increased; performance will improve, thus providing both a more human and a more productive job. Negative effects also tend to be reduced, such as turnover, absence, grievance and idle time. In this manner both an employee and society will be benefited. The employee performs better, has more job satisfaction and is more self-actualized, thus being able to participate in all life roles more effectively. Society benefits from the more effectively functioning person as well as better job-performance.

LIMITATIONS OF THE STUDY

Though this study claims to rely on Quran and sunnah for understanding various dimensions of QWL, the element of researcher's thinking in drawing inferences cannot be denied. To that extent it is a product of human-mind.

However, this does not detract the value of the study. The researcher did not allow his mind to run a riot; he dutifully interpreted the various ayahs of Quran and traditions of prophet Mohammed (SAW). On the basis of consensus opinion of the various authorities on Quran and sunnah. It is not creation of researcher's creativity.

CHAPTER ARRANGEMENTS

Chapter I : Introduction

This chapter presents the background of the study and sets out the objectives of the study.

Chapter II : Methodology of the Study

This chapter presents the procedure and methodology of this study and for the collection and analysis of the data.

Chapter III : Review of Literature

This chapter provides a brief review of literature related to the present study. A classified review of literature in the western and Indian philosophy is presented.

Chapter IV : Tawheed and Quality of Work Life

This chapter deals with the Tawheed and Quality of Work Life.

Chapter V : Motivational Basis in Islamic Paradigm

This chapter deals with the relationship between the motivation and QWL from Islamic point of view.

Chapter VI : Stress Inoculation in Islam

This chapter deals with the relationship between the stress and QWL from Islamic point of view.

Chapter VII : Conflict and their Resolution in Islam

This chapter deals with the conflict resolution mechanism from Islamic point of view.

Chapter VIII: Summary and Conclusions

The last chapter provides the summary of the report.

Notes and References

1. Robert, L. Dodson, Speeding the way of Total Quality, *Training and Development Journal*, June 1991, p. 40.
2. Jerome, M. Rosow, in Karew, E. Debats (ed.,), "The Continuing Personnel Challenge", *Personnel Journal*, May 1982, p. 344.
3. David, A. Nadler and Edward, E. Lawler, IV, "Quality of work-life: Perspectives and Directions", Organizational Dynamics, Winter 1983, 20-30.
4. George Burstein, "Enhancing the Quality of work life", Business Forum, California State University, Los Angels, Winter 1987, pp. 23-27.
5. Daniel, A. On rack and Martin, G. Evans, Job Enrichment and Job Satisfaction in Greenfield and Redesign QWL sites", Group and organization studies, March 18, 1987, p. 19. A Greenfield site for a quality

of work life program is a location where an organization constructs a totally new operation and therefore it has no prior job designs or systems in place.

6. R. Singh, Participation and consultative mechanics QWL, Quality of work life and productivity, New Delhi, NPC 1991, p. 62.
7. Sayles and Straus, Human behaviour in organizations, London : Prentice Hall, 1966, p. 70.
8. S.K. Chakraborty, Managerial effectiveness and quality of working life: Indian insights, New Delhi: Tata McGraw Hill, 1990, p. 141.
9. The need to balance internal and external factors is presented in Randall B. Dunham, Jon L. Pierce and John W. Newstrom, "Job context and Job content: A conceptual perspective", *Journal of Management*, Fall Winter 1983, pp. 1870-202, mixed results from a literature review are in Richard E. Kopelman, "Job Redesign and productivity : A Review of the Evidence", *National Productivity Review*, Summer 1985, pp. 237-55.
10. Four different Job design approaches for different situations are described in Michael, A. Campion and Paul, W. Thayer, "Job Design: Approaches, outcomes and Trade-offs", *Organizational Dynamics*, Winter 1987, pp. 66-79.
11. A discussion of this early failure is presented in Erwin L. Malone, "The non-linear system experiment in participative management", *The Journal of Business*, January 1975, pp. 52-64.
12. Al-Qushayri, Translated by with an introduction by Hamid Algar, B.R. Von Schlegell, Principles of Sufism, Islamic book trust, Kualalumpur, Malaysia, 2004, p. 165.
13. Anderson, G., 'The Quality of Work life", Seminar on worker participation in Australia, South Australian Development, Department of Legal Studies and Industrial Relations Programme, University of Melbourne, Melbourne, Australia, 1975.

2

Methods of Research

ISLAMIC PRINCIPLES FOR RESEARCH WORK

"It is not for the Believers
To go forth together:
If a contingent
From every expedition
Go forth
To devote themselves
To studies in religion,
And admonish the people
When they return to them,
That thus they (may learn)
To guard themselves (against evil)"

(Q : 9:122)

In the above chapter, it is clearly advises the Muslims that not all of them should go to Jihad but some of them should stay behind and get insight Islam in order that they can help other people to understand Islam.

CRITIQUE OF EMPIRICAL RESEARCH

The empiricism is based on fact that apparent knowledge alone is the truth. The very fact that empirical investigation gives conflicting results from different samples shows that empirical investigation cannot be adopted as the only source of knowledge in social sciences. Even in organizational behaviour studies give conflicting results.

Social scientists study about human behaviour. Unlike natural sciences such as physics, chemistry, human behaviour cannot be studied like atoms, protons, etc. The whole research in social sciences is changed after natural science methodology, which is not justified. Human behaviour, be it in the realm of economics, sociology, psychology—cannot be reduced to the behaviour of atoms, protons, etc. There is a need to go to the divine guidance for understanding human behaviour. In the present day world there are religions, which claim to possess true knowledge in the form of divine guidance. One such religion is Islam. It claims that the word of God without any interpolation is to be found in the Holy Quran. The instructions of God, not the language of God is found in the Hadeeth, sayings and doings of Prophet Mohammed (SAW).

So far the social scientists, at least in the field of organizational behaviour, have not explored this knowledge. The researcher feels that this knowledge needs to be explored for understanding quality of work-life.

It is the creator of mankind who knows about the human nature. Therefore, human nature as described in Quran and Hadeeth should be the truth. Though empirical investigation does not subscribe to this view that there is a revealed knowledge, this researcher has relied on the Quran and Hadeeth.

IMPORTANCE OF ISLAMIC RESEARCH

Islamic research work cannot be restricted to any area because of Islam's nature as an all comprehensive way of life. Any aspect of our life is concerned with Islam and therefore any aspects of our life can and must be followed up by research for Islamic work.

In the field of social sciences and sciences, where Islam should be applied, there will be greatest need for research for knowledge. Because, in these fields of creation the law of natural sciences the man is simply discovering the laws of the creator of the universe.

In society on the other hand, the law of Allah, although applied in one way (since nothing happens in this world without the will of Allah) is today not specifically applied in human society at large. That is why we have to concentrate on putting into practice in society the revealed will of Allah and hence there is great need for research for Islamic work.

For example, in the field of economics, we have to research into the question of how to replace the prevalent system of economics, which is based on Riba (interest), because Riba (interest) is against the will of Allah. This replacement needs to be done by Muslims and in order to do it we have to know how it can be done we have to research into it, to find the methods of changing it.

Similarly in the field of biochemistry we need to find substitutes for alcohol which is used most medicines today, because even though in some schools, alcohol is perhaps allowed for medical purposes we would like to, if we can, avoid it altogether. The biochemist can find substitutes.

Similarly in the case of quality of work life, a researcher should callow knowledge from Islamic point of view. How for it is useful to working people and how he should be satisfied with the working life should be ascertained. When we clarify certain issues through research, our own conviction of the correct Islamic view on certain issues will grow and be measured. We do not simply believe that Islam is the right way we know it is, on the basis of our own research, and this makes our conviction grow.

Islamic research is for all fields of knowledge and all fields of application because Islam is for the entire world. To conclude let us look at a quotation from Ibn Khaldum, one of the well-known scholar, who lived in the fourteenth century.

He wrote an important book, the Muqadima in which he discussed a great variety of topics, one among them being education. He wrote:

The natural means for the perception of truth is ...... man's natural ability to think (This means: because we can think we can discover the truth. This is the natural way).

Which it is free from all misgivings and when the thinker entrusts himself to the mercy of God. (When we relate our thinking to Allah, then we can discover the truth that is the natural way).

Logic merely describes the process of thinking and mostly parallels it. Take that into consideration and ask for God's mercy when we have difficulty in understanding problems. (So realize that by logic we do not achieve the results because logic only describes the process, it does not bring the result, and when we have difficulty in understanding, then call to Allah, for he is the One who can give the knowledge).

Then (when we ask for Allah's mercy) the divine light will shine upon as and give us the right inspiration. God guides in his mercy. Knowledge comes only from God.

MEANING OF QURAN

The Glorious Quran is the Book of Allah, the Wise and Worthy of all Praise, Who has promised to safeguard it from any violations in its purity.

Praise to be Allah the Cherisher and Sustainer of the Worlds, who has said in His Noble Book.

"There has come to you from Allah.
Light and a perspicuous Book"

(Q : 5 : 15)

And may peace and blessings be upon the seal of the Prophet Mohammad, who has said that:

"The best among you is he who learned
The Quran and then taught it".

May the peace and blessings of Allah be upon him, his family and all his companions, it becomes incumbent upon each and every person who seeks the dignity of this world and the bliss of the hereafter to regulate his life according to it including the quality of work life, to implement its commandments and to pay homage to the magnificence of One who revealed it.

This is a unique book with a supreme author, an eternal message and a universal relevance. Its contents are not confirmed to a particular theme or style, but contain the foundations for an entire system of life, covering quality of work life as well as, spectrum of issues, which range from specific articles of faith and commandments to general moral teachings, rights and obligations, crime and punishment, personal and public law, and a host of other private and social concerns. These issues are discussed in a variety of ways, such as direct stipulations, reminders of Allah's favours as His creation, admonitions and rebukes. Stories of the past communities are narrated, followed by the lessons to be learned from their actions and subsequent fates.

The Quran enjoys a number of characteristics unique to it alone, some of which are as follows :

It is the actual word of Allah, Not created but revealed for the benefit of all mankind.

"Blessed is He who sent down the criterion
To His servant, that it may be
An admonition to all creatures"

(Q : 25 : 1)

It is complete and comprehensive
The Almighty says :
"Nothing have We omitted from the Book"

(Q : 4 : 38)

In another place we read
"And we have sent down to the
The Book explaining all things"

(Q : 16 : 89)

It is a theoretical and a practical book, not only moralizing but also defining specifically the permissible and the forbidden. The importance of understanding the message of the Quran is undeniable, but simply reciting it with the intention of seeking Allah's pleasure and reward is also an act of worship and meritorious in itself. Allah, Almighty says:

"So take what the Prophet gives you
And refrain from what he prohibits you"

(Q : 59 : 7)

Allah has perfected His religion for all mankind with the revelation of this Book. He says :

"This day have I perfected you religion for you,
Completed my favour upon you and have chosen
For you Islam as your religion".

(Q : 5 : 7)

It is Allah's eternal miracle revealed to the Prophet Mohammed (SAW) for all succeeding generations. In response to those who doubt the authorship of the Quran, Allah Almighty has challenged the most articulate Arabs to produce a whole book, ten chapters or even one solitary chapter, which can be remotely comparable to be Quran.

But to this day, no one has succeeded in meeting the challenge of the Almighty. The critics of the Quran have been struck dumb by it's ineffable eloquence and surprising beauty.

"Say, if the whole of mankind and jinn
Were together to produce the
Like of this Quran they could not
Produce the like thereof; even if they
Backed up each other with help and support"

(Q : 17 : 88)

The Almighty also says :

"Or they may say : he forged it
Say : Bring ye then ten chapters
Forged, like into it and call
(To your aid) whomsoever ye can
Other than Allah, if ye speak
The truth"

(Q : 11 : 13)

And again :

"Or do they say : he forged it?

Say; Bring then a chapter like
Unto it and call (to your aid)
Anyone ye can besides, Allah
If it be ye speak the truth "

(Q : 10 : 38)

It has been revealed to re-establish the sincere worship of Allah alone, without association of any partners with them.

"This is a Book with verses basic or
Fundamental (of established meanings)
Further explained in detail
From one Who are Wise and Well Aware
(It teaches) that you should worship
None but Allah"

(Q : 11 : 1-2)

"And they have been commanded no more
Than this : to worship Allah,
Offering Him sincere devotion, being true
In faith, to establish regular prayer
And to give Zakat, and that is
– The religion light and straight".

(Q : 98 : 5)

Allah Almighty has taken upon Himself the duty of preserving the Quran forever.

It contains a complete code, which provides for all areas of life, whether spiritual, intellectual, political, social or economic. It is a code, which has no boundaries of time, place and nations.

"Verily this Quran doth guide
To that which is most right"

(Q : 17 : 9)

In it's entirely, as He says:
"We have without doubt sent down
The message, and we will assuredly
Guard it (from corruption)"

(Q : 22 : 9)

It has been preserved, both in memory and in writing, that the Arabic text we have today is identified to the text as it was revealed to the Prophet. Not even a single letter has yielded to corruption during the passage of the centuries. And so it will remain forever, by the consent of Allah.

MEANING OF HADEETH

The Arabic word 'Hadeeth' literally means communication, story, conversation, religious or secular, historical or recent. According to Muhaddithin it stands for what was transmitted on the authority of the Prophet (SAW), his deeds, sayings, tacit, approval, or description of his sifat (features). However, physical appearance of the Prophet (SAW) is not included in the definition used by the jurist.

Hadeeth literature means the literature, which consists of the narrations of the life of the Prophet (SAW) and the things approved by him. It covers the narrations about the companions and successors as well. Sometimes other words were also used in the same sense such as chamber and attar. Most of the scholars use three terms : Hadeeth, Khabar and Athar as synonyms. There is another keyword 'Sunna' which also denotes Hadeeth. According to Arabic lexicographers sunna means 'a way, course, rule, mode of manner, of acting or conduct of life'.

The Arabic word hadeeth literally means communication, story, conversation, religious or secular, historical or recent. It has been used in the Quran 23 times. The following are the few examples :

(a) Religious communication, message of the Quran :
Almighty Allah says : ________________
"Allah has revealed (time after time) the most beautiful hadeeth (message) in the form of a book".
Muqadima III, 298
Almighty Allah says : ________________
"Then leave me alone with such as reject this hadeeth" (meaning the Quran).

(b) Story of a secular or general nature :
Almighty Allah says : ________________

"And whenever your meet such as indulge in (blasphemous) talk about our message, turn thy back upon them until they begin hadeeth (conversation) of same other things".

(c) Historical story :

Almighty Allah says : __________________

"Has the hadeeth (story) of Musa reached thee?"

This research is based on Quran and Hadeeth, because they are the basis of all Islamic principles, knowledge, behaviour and actions. Knowledge without application is useless in the Islamic perspective. This is one of the basic differences between Islam and other philosophies of sciences. Knowledge properly applied is the only knowledge Muslim employee will cherish.

Knowledge illuminates the mind and soul of every employee. It enables him to understand the reality and act accordingly. It is in this context, of utmost importance because it helps to operate in this world and makes working life meaningful and useful. This is the reason why knowledge is considered essential in every society as it gives man superiority over other living beings.

QURANIC METHOD OF REASONING

"Be ye worshippers
Of Him who is truly
The ye have taught
The Book and ye
Have studied it earnestly..."

(Q : 3 : 79)

The concept of reasoning in the Quran is different from reasoning in philosophy especially Greek philosophy. This is because European philosophers in general and Greek philosophers in particular, tend to use abstract reasoning, a kind of "rational" analysis of concepts, in order to build a philosophical system which "appears" (to them) to be "theoretically" convincing. The famous example for this process is Plato's Republic, wherein he tried to analyze the concept of justice. Aristotle did something similar, especially in his Metaphysics and his Ethics.

In the Quran, we find a very different situation: The Quran aims not just at theoretically convincing people of the truth, but also making them act according to the truth. A thoughtful action is very important in Islam. The Quran wants to build not only a theory, or a philosophical system of abstract ides, but also a good society in real life.

The first step in the Quranic reasoning is that the Quran asks man to remove any barrier that could stand between his reasoning and truth. There are many such barriers mentioned in the Quran, especially the following:

(1) Coercion (Ikrah)

Any kind of coercion should be removed from human thinking, so that Man can appreciate the truth in a free atmosphere. The principle of removing coercion in the Quran is expressed in a famous verse in (Q : 2:256): Which means "there should be no coercion in religion". (Religion here means a whole system of faith, worship, law, ethics, politics, society, education family life. As we know the word religion, in English, does not give the accurate meaning of the Quranic word Din, because the word Din in the Quran means a total way of life, a comprehensive system of ideas and action). So, "La ikrah Fi al Din" means there is no coercion in accepting Islam because truth is distinguished from falsehood. This means that the Quran relies on the fact that the Quran itself has made the difference between truth and falsehood clear. Once the difference between truth and falsehood has been made clear to the human mind there would be no need for any coercion. The first barrier, then, that should be removed according to the Quran, is compulsion of anything that would not allow freedom of thinking and reasoning.

(2) Imitation (Taqlid)

Imitation of any authority, e.g. ancestors, parents, customs, traditions is not permitted in Islam. All kinds of authorities, especially those of ancestors, should not be blindly obeyed. The Quran in several verses refers to the argument put forward by the unbelievers, who rejected Islam, because they wanted to follow the traditions of their fathers and ancestors. The Quran does not accept this as a valid argument, because the ultimate criterion according to the Quran is not because they are fathers or ancestors that they should be followed, but the ultimate criterion is whether they are right or wrong. The guidance which expresses this idea of rejecting blind imitation is given in various verses, e.g. (Q : 5:104) When it is said to them; "come to what Allah has revealed and to the Messenger, they say: enough for us that we found our fathers doing. Whatever if their fathers had no knowledge whatsoever, and no guidance".

(3) Whims (Hawa)

This is the third barrier from which human reasoning should be freed. The word, Hawa, in the Quran, means whims, irrational desires, passions or any kind of human prejudice; (racial, national, tribal, group or personal prejudice). This is because these whims tend to blind human reason from seeing the truth. There are verses in the Quran which condemned Hawa as a barrier between human reason and truth. It is enough to give the following examples:

(a) The advice given in the Quran to believers: "Follow not your passions lest you lapse from truth".

(Q : 4 : 135)

(b) The advice given to Dawud (A.S): "O Dawud We made you a viceroy in earth, so judge between people according to the truth and don't follow your own whims, lest they lead you astray from the way of Allah".

(Q : 38 : 26)

(4) Conjecture (Zann)

Zann means not to be sure of the truth, and to believe ideas, which you are not certain of their truth. The Quran recommends that man should be absolutely certain, especially about such a serious matter as faith. This is why the Quran rejects the idea of Zann as a substitute for truth.

This rejection expressed in many verses, e.g. "Most of them (the unbelievers) follow but conjecture, surely conjecture can, by no means, and take the place of truth".

(Q : 10 : 36)

(5) Magic (Sihr)

The Quran makes it very clear that magic should not be taken as a valid way of knowing the truth or acting according to the truth. It is regarded as a harmful superstition. Any kind of superstition, in fact, is rejected in the Quran, especially magic. It is referred to as something harmful, false and corruptive.

(Q : 2 : 102, 10 : 81, 20 : 69).

(6) Priesthood

There is no class of priesthood in Islam. The Christian priesthood, in Medieval Europe, had played a very notorious role against progress, especially scientific and social progress. They claimed a monopoly of guidance, monopoly of interpretation of the scriptures. They also claimed that they were infallible. This is why the Quran condemned the attitude of Christians and Jews, of glorifying their priests and treating them as Lords, beside Allah:

> "They take their priests
> And their anchorites to be
> Their lords beside Allah".

(Q : 9 : 31)

The Quran, therefore, removes all barriers coming under priesthood. Any Muslim employee, who is qualified, has the right and duty to understand, interpret and act according to the Quran.

Another group of phenomena, which the Quran emphasizes, are the human phenomena, phenomena of man, his creation, his relationship to other, the human family, working life, etc.

In the light of above it becomes clear that the commands of Allah as well as the proven commands of the Prophet (SAW) are binding on employees. The Prophet (SAW) total life is a good example, and ought to be followed by them.

Of all the divine attributes with which employee to endue himself for his task, knowledge commands precedence. Its acquisition is a duty on every man and every woman as laid by the Prophet (SAW) of Islam :

"Acquire knowledge, said he 'It enables the possessor to distinguish right from wrong: It lights the way to heaven'; it is our companion when friendless; it guides us to happiness, it sustains us in adversity; it is a weapon against enemies and an ornament among friends. By virtue of it, Allah exalted nations, and made them guides in good pursuits, and gives them leadership; so much so that their footsteps are followed, their deeds are imitated, and their opinions are accepted and held in respect".

—Ibn Abd al-Bar : Fadl al-Illam

The Ilul-Ilm (those who equip themselves with knowledge or the learned) naturally deserve our primary attention. For, knowledge is the means whereby the qualities, characteristic of the other types, are cultivated.

"God bears witness : There is no God save Him; and so bear witness the angels; and so, the men of learning with mental equipoise".

(Q : 3 : 16)

But one thing the Qur'an makes perfectly clear. Knowledge does not consist in the mere assemblage in one's memory of ideas or material on this or that subject. That does not constitute acquisition. The Qur'an desires correlation and synthesis helpful to a harmonious grasp of the varieties underlying them. The Book therefore insists on reflection as an indispensable aid to the proper acquisition of knowledge.

"We have not created the heavens and the earth and whatsoever is between them in sport; We have not created them expect to bear the truth; but most people know it not".

(Q : 44 : 38-39)

'But most employees know it not' is the regretful note that it strikes at every turn. Wherever attention is drawn to the manifestation of life calling for reflection and introspection, expressions such as 'herein are portents', 'herein are signs for folk who reflect', 'for men of knowledge', 'for folk who heed', and 'for folk who understand, echo and reverberate only to emphasize the importance which the Qur'an attaches to reflection as a means of obtaining insight. "Show us the nature of things as they really are' is a characteristic prayer of the Prophet. The first on the road to it is reflection".

—Hisin al Hisin

Knowledge, in the Quranic conception covers every field of life—the life of the vast universe working around employee in immediate contact as well as remote, and the life of employee himself moving onward with a knowledge of his past. An acquisition of knowledge therefore imposes on him the exercise of not merely his intellectual and physical faculties, but his spiritual : and nothing is prohibited to him in Islam except, probably, probing vainly the veil beyond which his reason or intuition has been found incapable of advance. And herein lays the fundamental distinction between the Quranic and the classic Greek culture which forms the essential basis of the modern European civilization. For, while the Greek mind reverted its attention on 'Mankind' alone or on the study of man as man, the Quranic mind has to take in its sweep the entire Universe, not merely the world of man, and of his spirit, but the worlds of plants, birds, animals, insects, planets, the worlds seen and the unseen—all interlinked in its consciousness, with each other, and understand and reflect on the purposes underlying each creation and grasp the supreme spiritual principle of their linkage operating for a unified existence :

> The Qur'an gives an employee full sanction to harness the forces at work both in him and in his external world, the forces of nature, through an appropriate study of them. But it makes one condition. It calls upon employee to bear in mind the balance set in his nature, and to exercise the power acquired through knowledge to help him display in his life such other attributes of God as will equip him to 'show affection to the family of God' for which he has been created with the privilege of representing Him on earth by "being a shepherd or keeper unto every other". If we may so express, the impersonal power of Nature that Science brings into play is to be given a personality and made

conscious of the balance set therein, as in the rest of creation. In other words, it is to be humanized, and "the spirit of God breathed" into it, to use a phrase of the Qur'an. This is the primary function of human activity and is to be kept in mind in order to appraise the full import of the injunction which sums up all that is required of man : "Believe and work for the pleasure of for God informed by knowledge. The wider and deeper this knowledge of one's own self and one's external world of relations to fulfil the role of the vicegerency of God on earth.

Those who aspire, in the language of the Prophet's (SAW) prayer, to the knowledge of the 'Nature of things as they really are'. This knowledge of Reality, the fountain-head of life is to be gained through what is termed 'sense of God' or 'attendance on God'. An acquisitive quality more freely developed in certain temperaments or minds spiritually inclined than in those particularly obsessed with the temporal aspects of life. Thus reality, however incommunicable, has in the context of the Quranic ideology to serve as a dynamic source of knowledge stimulating action worthy of the role employee has to play as the vicegerent of God on earth.

In the cultural process of Islam, the acquisition of knowledge, such as we have referred to above, is an indispensable condition of one's equipment for pleasure of God.

SOURCE MATERIAL-AL-QURAN

Knowledge-Significance

"And the blind and the seeing are not alike; neither darkness and light; nor the cool shade and the hot wind".

(Q : 35 : 20)

"And he who has been blind here, shall be blind hereafter, and stray further away from the road".

(Q : 20 : 114)

"Say: My Lord! Increase me in knowledge".

(Q : 20 : 114)

Sources of Knowledge

(I) The Book—Al-Quran : and the example of the Prophet

1. It is the Book wherein there is nothing doubtful—A guidance to the God fearing,
   Who believe in the Unseen, who observe prayer, and out of what we have bestowed on them, expend (in our way);
   And who believe in what hatch seen sent down to thee, and in what hath been sent down before thee, and have full faith in the life to come.
   These are guided by their Lord; and with these it shall be well. (Q : 2 : 1-4)
2. "Truly hath God been gracious to the believers by raising up from among their own people an apostle to rehearse unto them His revelations, and to purify them, and to give them knowledge of the Book and of Wisdom : for hitherto they were in manifest error". (Q : 3 : 164)
3. "God hath caused the Book and the wisdom to descend upon thee (Muhammad) : and what thou know not He hath caused thee to Know : and the grace of God toward thee hath been great". (Q : 4 : 113)
4. "Recite thou! For thy Lord is the most Beneficent, who hath taught the use of the pen; hath taught man that which the knew not". (Q : 96 : 3-5)
5. "Now hath a Light (Messenger) and a clear Book (Al-Qur'an) come to you from God, whereby God will guide him who shall follow his good pleasure to paths of peace, and will bring them out of darkness into light; and to the straight path will He guide them". (Q : 5 : 17)
6. "A noble pattern had ye in God's Apostle for all who hope in God and in the day hereafter, and often remember God". (Q : 33 : 31)
7. It is the Book wherein there is nothing doubtful—A guidance to the God fearing;
   Who believe in the Unseen, who observe prayer, and

out of what we have bestowed on them, expend (in our way);
And who believe in what hatch seen sent down to thee, and in what hath been sent down before thee, and have full faith in the life to come.
These are guided by their Lord; and with these it shall be well. (Q : 2 : 1-4)

8. "Truly hath God been gracious to the believers by raising up from among their own people an apostle to rehearse unto them His revelations, and to purify them, and to give them knowledge of the Book and of Wisdom : for hitherto they were in manifest error". (Q : 3 : 164)
9. "God hath caused the Book and the wisdom to descend upon thee (Muhammad) : and what thou know not He hath caused thee to Know : and the grace of God toward thee hath been great". (Q : 4 : 113)
10. "Recite thou! For thy Lord is the most Beneficent, who hath taught the use of the pen; hath taught man that which he knew not". (Q : 96 : 3-5)
11. "Now hath a Light (Messenger) and a clear Book (Al-Qur'an) come to you from God, whereby God will guide him who shall follow his good pleasure to paths of peace, and will bring them out of darkness into light; and to the straight path will He guide them". (Q : 5 : 17)
12. "A noble pattern had ye in God's Apostle for all who hope in God and in the day hereafter, and offer remembers God". (Q : 33 : 31)

(ii) Sunnath Allah : Nature and its Working

"Turn steadfastly to the way of devotion (Din)—the way of Allah (Fitrat Allah)—for which He hath fitted man. There is no altering in the way laid by Allah (Khalq Allah). That is the right way of devotion. But most people know it not". (Q : 30 : 29)

"Ye shall not find any change in the Sunnah Allah (way of God); ye shall not find any variableness in the Sunnah Allah". (Q : 35 : 43)

"The Sun and the Moon follow a system,
And the planets and the trees bend in adoration,

And the sky, He hath reared it on high,
And hath set the balance;
That in the balance ye should not transgress
But keep it poised and not scant the balance".

(Q : 55 : 5-9)

And (know) that this is My way, the right one; so follow it, and follow not (other) ways, for they will lead you away from His way. This He enjoins on you that you may keep your duty. (Q : 6 : 154)

"(Blessed is He) who hath created the seven heavens in layers. Thou canst see no disharmony in the handiwork of the Beneficent God. Then look again. Dost thou see any rifts?"

"Then look again, and yet again; Thy sight will return unto thee thwarted and tired". (Q : 67 : 3-4)

"Here are signs for men of understanding". (Q : 3 : 187)
"There are signs even in your own soul!" (Q : 51 : 21)

"And he hath subjected to you all that is in the Heavens and all that is on the Earth : All is from Him. Verily, herein are signs for those who reflect". (Q : 45 : 13)

And many are the signs in the Heavens and on the Earth; and in the succession of the night and of the day are signs for men of understanding.

Who standing, and sitting, and reclining, bear God in mind, and muse on the creation of the Heavens and of the Earth. "O Our Lord"! say they, "Thou hast not created all this in vain!" (Q : 3 : 190-191)

We have not created the Heavens and the Earth and what is between them for naught. (Q : 38 : 27)

It is He who hath appointed the Sun for brightness, and the Moon for a light, and hath ordained her stations that ye may learn the number of years and the reckoning of time. God hath not created all this but for a serious end. He makes his signs clear to those who understand.

Verily, in the alternations of night and of day, and in all that God hath created in the Heavens and in the Earth are signs to those who fear Him! (Q :10 : 5-6)

It is God who hath reared the Heavens without pillars thou canst behold; then mounted his throne, and imposed laws on the Sun and Moon : each travelled to its appointed goal. He ordered all things. He makes his sings clear that ye may have firm faith in a meeting with your Lord.

And He it is who hath outstretched the earth, and placed on it firm mountains, and rivers: and of every fruit He hath placed on it two kinds : He caused the night to enshroud the day. Verily in this are signs for those who reflect.

And on the Earth are tracts close to each other, gardens of grapes and ploughed fields of corn, and palm trees, single or clustered. Though watered by the same water, yet some make us more excellent as food than other : Verily in all this are signs for those who understand! (Q : 13 : 2-4)

SOURCE MATERIAL : AL HADITH

Importance

1. "Acquire knowledge", said the Prophet, "It enabled the possessor to distinguish right from wrong. It lights the way to heaven; it is our companion when friendless: it guides us to happiness; it sustains us in adversity; it is a weapon against enemies and an ornament among friends. By virtue of it, Allah exalted communities, and makes them guides in good pursuits, and gives them leadership; so much so, that their footsteps are followed, their deeds are imitated, and their opinions are accepted and held in respect".

   —Ibn Abd al-Bar : Fadl al-'Iim
2. Said the prophet : "God has inspired me to announce: For him who goes out in search of knowledge, I shall make easy his way to heaven; the benefits derived from knowledge are greater than the benefits derived from worship". —Baihaqi and Mishkat
3. It is the duty of the learned to spread knowledge. They should impart it to those who do not possess, for, knowledge unused is like a thing lost. —Bukhari
4. Narrates Abdullah bin Umar : The prophet once noticed two groups of his followers sitting in his

mosque, and observed : "Both are goodly groups, but one is better occupied than the other. One is invoking God for favours. It is for God to concede or not to concede the favours asked for. But the other group is engaged in acquiring knowledge and also in imparting it to those who are ignorant. This group is better occupied than the other. In fact, I am myself entrusted with the task of teaching". Saying this, he took a seat in the midst of this group. —Darimi and Mishkat

5. The best form of devotion to God is to seek knowledge. —Kunuzul Haqaiq

   The acquisition of knowledge is better than worship. —Awsat and Bazaar

6. To acquire knowledge is binding on all believers, both men and women. —Ibn Maja
7. A moment's contemplation is better than seventy years worship. —Kunuzul Haqaiq
8. It is narrated by Ali, the son-in-law of the Prophet: Said the Prophet : There is no goodness in that prayer in which one does not know that he prays, and there is no goodness in that knowledge which does not convey any sense; and there is no goodness in that reading over which one does not reflect. —Darimi
9. Said the Prophet : A learned man is like the stars in the firmament which in darkness light the way over land and sea. It is likely that the way-farer will miss his way when the stars disappear. —Ahmed : Musnad
10. Said the Prophet : The mind of the son of Adam is always young when engaged in search of knowledge. —Kunuzul Haqaiq
11. He who goes forth in search of knowledge, engages himself in the cause of God until he returns (home). —Tirmizi and Darimi
12. He who feels shy or is too proud to seek knowledge, will never gain knowledge. —Bukhari
13. Narrates Jabir : A person asked of the Prophet : Who among the learned is the greatest? Replied the Prophet: He who goes on gathering knowledge from others, for,

a truly learned man always hungers for further knowledge. —Muslim

14. Said the Prophet : Explain things to the common folk according to their understanding. —Bukhari
15. Said the Prophet : When you speak to others anything which is beyond their understanding, it is likely that such a thing might prove harmful to some of them. —Muslim
16. Said the Prophet : People will be called to account according to their sense of understanding. —Kunuzul Haqaiq
17. Said the Prophet : Do not talk foolishly before the wise; for they might get annoyed. Do not talk words of wisdom before people of weak understanding; for, they might talk lightly of you. Do not deny knowledge to these who are fit to receive it; for that will be committing a sin. Do not deliver a learned discourse before an ignorant person; for, he will regard you as an ignorant person. You have a right to your knowledge even as you have a right to your property. —Darimi
18. Said the Prophet : The religion of man is his sense of understanding, and he who has no sense of understanding has no religion. —Kunuzul Haqaiq
19. Said the Prophet : One will be ranked in this and in the life hereafter according to one's sense of understanding. —Kunuzul Haqaiq
20. Narrates Hafs : When the Prophet desired to appoint Ma'az as Judge of Yemen he asked him : "whenever a case comes up before you for decision, what procedure will you adopt to reach it? Ma'az replied : "I shall decide according to the Book of God". The Prophet then asked : "Suppose on any particular issue, the Book is silent?" Replied Ma'az : "I shall decide according to the example of the Prophet". The Prophet again asked : "Suppose you find no guidance either from the Book or from my practice?" Ma'az replied; "I shall then exercise my own personal judgment; but I

shall see to it that my judgment does not conflict with the Law". On hearing this, the Prophet gently tapped on the breast of Ma'az by way of approbation. Ma'az then expressed his thanks to God for having inspired the Prophet to express his satisfaction. —Abu Dawud

Reference

Ahmad Von Denffer, Research in Islam, Islamic foundation, 1996, p. 38.

3

Studies on Quality of Worklife

HISTORICAL BACKGROUND OF QWL

Many of the findings of earlier writers, particularly of scientific management, which focused attention on the mechanical and physiological variables of organizational functioning were tested in the field to increase the efficiency of the organizations. Surprisingly, positive aspects of these variables could not evoke positive response in work behaviour, and researchers tried to investigate the reasons for human behaviour at work. They discovered that the real cause of human behaviour was something more than mere physiological variables. Such findings generated a new phenomenon about the human behaviour and focused attention on the human beings in the organizations. As such, this new approach has been called 'human relations approach of management'.

Even in the writings of classical approach, notably, Taylor, Fayol, Henry Gantt, Follet, Urwick and others, the human element in the organization was recognized, but they emphasized it very little. The human relations approach was born out of a reaction to classical approach and during the last seven decades, a lot of literature on human relations has been developed. The essence of the human relations contributions is contained in two points: (i) organizational situation should be viewed in social terms as well as in economic and technical terms, and (ii) the social process of group behaviour can be understood in terms of clinical method analogous to the doctor's diagnosis of the human organism. Among human relations approach, there are many contributions and many more researchers are being carried on. For the first time, an intensive and systematic analysis of human factor in organizations was made in the form of Hawthorne experiments.[1] There will be relatively lengthy discussion of the results and implications of the Hawthorne studies because of their historical importance to the behavioural approach to the analysis of quality of work life problems.

The Hawthorne plant of the General Electric Company, Chicago, was manufacturing telephone system bell. It employed about 30,000 employees at the time of experiments. Although in respect of material benefits to the employees, this was the most progressive with pension and sickness benefits and other recreational facilities, there was great deal of dissatisfaction among the employees and productivity was not up to the mark. After the utter failure of an investigation conducted by efficiency experts, in 1924, the company asked for the assistance from the National Academy of Sciences to investigate the problems of low productivity.

In order to investigate the real causes behind this phenomenon, a team was constituted led by Elton Mayo (psychologist) Whitehead and Roethlisberger (sociologists), and company representative, William Dickson. The researchers originally set out to study the relationship between productivity and physical working conditions. They conducted various researchers in four phases with each phase attempting to answer the question raised at the previous phase. The four phases were as follows :

1. Experiments to determine the effects of changes in illumination on productivity, illumination experiments (1924-27);
2. Experiments to determine the effects of changes in

hours and other working conditions on productivity, relay assembly test room experiments, 1927-28;

3. Conducting plant-wide interviews to determine worker attitudes and sentiments, mass interviewing programme, 1928-30; and
4. Determination and analysis of social organization at work, bank wiring observation room experiments, 1931-32.

ILLUMINATION EXPERIMENTS

Illumination experiments were undertaken to find out how varying levels of illumination (amount of light at the workplace, a physical factor) affected the productivity. The hypothesis was that with higher illumination, productivity would increase. In the first series of experiments, a group of employees was chosen and placed in two separate groups. One group was exposed to varying intensities illumination. Since this group was subjected to experimental changes, it was termed as experimental group. Another group, called as control group, both groups increased production. When the intensity of illumination was decreased, the production continued to increase in both the groups. The production in the experimental group decreased only when the illumination was decreased to the level of moonlight. The decrease was due to light falling much below the normal level. Thus, it was concluded that illumination did not have any effect on productivity but something else was interfering with the productivity. At that time, it was concluded that human factor was important in determining productivity but which aspect was affecting, it was not sure. Therefore, another phase of experiments was undertaken.

RELAY ASSEMBLY TEST ROOM EXPERIMENT

Relay assembly test room experiments were designed to determine the effect of changes in various job conditions on group productivity as the illumination experiments could not establish relationship between intensity of illumination and production. For this purpose, the researchers set-up a relay assembly test room and two girls were chosen. These girls were asked to choose four more girls as co-employees. The work related to the assembly of telephone relays. Each relay consisted of a number of parts, which girls assembled into finished products. Output depended on the speed and continuity with which girls worked. The experiments started with introducing numerous changes in sequence with duration of each change ranging from four to twelve weeks. An observer was associated with girls to supervise their work. Before each change was introduced, the girls were consulted. They were given opportunity to express their viewpoints and concerns to the supervisor. In some cases, they were allowed to take decisions on matters concerning them. Following were the changes and resultant outcomes:

1. The incentive system was changed so that each girl's extra pay was based on the other five rather than output of larger group, say, 100 employees or so. The productivity increased as compared to before.
2. Two five-minute rests—one in morning session and other in evening session—were introduced which were increased to ten minutes. The productivity increased.
3. The rest period was reduced to five minutes but frequency was increased. The productivity decreased slightly and the girls complained that frequent rest intervals affected the rhythm of the work.
4. The number of rest was reduced to two of ten minutes each, but in morning, coffee or soup was served with sandwich and in the evening, snack was provided. The productivity increased.
5. Changes in working hours and workday were introduced, such as cutting an hour off the end of the day and eliminating Saturday work. The girls were allowed to leave at 4.30 p.m. instead of usual 5.00 p.m. and later at 4.00 p.m. productivity increased.

As each change was introduced, absenteeism decreased, morale increased and less supervision was required. It was assumed that these positive factors were there because of the various factors being adjusted and making them more positive.

At this time, the researchers decided to revert back to original position, that is, no rest and other benefits. Surprisingly, productivity increased not because of positive changes in physical factors but because of a change in the girl's attitudes towards work and their work group. They developed a feeling of stability and sense of belongingness. Since there was more freedom of work, they developed a sense of responsibility and self-discipline. The relationship between supervisor and employees became close and friendly.

MASS INTERVIEWING PROGRAMME

During the course of experiments, about 20,000 interviews were conducted between 1928 and 1930 to determine employee's attitudes towards company, supervision, insurance plans, promotion, and wages. Initially, these interviews were conducted by means of direct questioning such as 'do you like your supervisor? Or is he in your opinion fair or does he have favourites?' etc. since this method had disadvantage of either stimulating antagonism or the over-simplified 'yes' or 'no' responses which could not get to the root of the problem, the method was changed to non-directive interviewing where interview programme gave valuable insights about the human behaviour in the company. Some of the major findings of the programme were as follows :

1. A complaint is not necessarily an objective recital of facts; it is a symptom of personal disturbance the cause of which may be deep seated.
2. Objects, persons, and events are carries of social meanings. They become related to employee satisfaction or dissatisfaction only as the employee comes to view them from his personal situation.
3. The personal situation of the worker is a configuration, composed of a personal preference involving sentiments, desires and interests of the person and the social reference constituting the person's social past and his present interpersonal relations.
4. The position or status of a worker in the company is a reference from which the worker assigns meaning and

value to the events, objects and features of his environment such as hours of work, wages, etc.

5. The social organization of the company represents a system of values from which the employees derives satisfaction or dissatisfaction according to the perception of his social status and the expected social rewards.
6. The social demands of the worker are influenced by social experience in groups both inside and outside the work plant.[2]

During the course of interviews, it was discovered that employee's behaviour was being influenced by group behaviour. However, this conclusion was not very satisfactory and, therefore, researchers decided to conduct another series of experiments. As such, the detailed study of a shop situation was started to find out the behaviour of employees in small groups.

BANK WIRING OBSERVATION ROOM EXPERIMENTS

These experiments were carried on between November 1931 and May 1932 with a view to analyze the functioning of small group and its impact on individual behaviour. A group of fourteen male employees was employed in the bank wiring room: nine wiremen, three solder men and two inspectors. The work involved attaching wire to switches for certain equipment used in telephone exchange. Hourly wage rate for the personnel was based on average group output. The hypothesis was that in order to earn more, employees would produce more and in order to take the advantages of group bonus, they would help each other to produce more. However, this hypothesis did not hold valid. Employees decided the target for themselves, which was lower than the company's target, for example, group's target for a day was connecting 6600 terminals against 7300 terminals set by the company. The employees gave following reasons for the restricted output :

1. Fear of unemployment. The basic reasoning of employees was that if there would be more production

per head, some of the employees would be put out of employment.

2. Fear of raising the standards. Most employees were convinced that once they had reached the standard rate of production, management would raise the standard of production reasoning that it must be easy to attain.
3. Protection of slower employees. The employees were friendly on-the-job as well as off-the-job. They appreciated the fact that they had family responsibility that required them to remain in the job. Since slower employees were likely to be retrenched, the faster employees protected them by not overproducing.
4. Satisfaction on the part of management. According to employees, management seemed to accept the lower production rate as no one was being fired or even reprimanded for restricted output.

The employees in the group set certain norms of behaviour including personal conduct. The employee's behaviour was in conformity with both output norm and social norm were most preferred. This study suggested that informal relationships are an important factor in determining the human behaviour. During the course of experiments, employees were counselled for good human relations in the company's plant. The counselling was in regard to personal adjustment, supervision, employee relations, and management-employee relations. The supervisors tended to understand and accept the problems of employees and management tried to sense their feelings, which were helpful in formulating the action for resolving management employee conflicts.

IMPLICATIONS OF HAWTHORNE EXPERIMENTS

Hawthorne experiments have opened a new chapter in management by suggesting management through good human relations. A human relation involves motivating people in organization in order to develop teamwork, which effectively fulfils their needs and achieves organizational goals. Hawthorne experiments have tried to unearth those factors, which are important for motivating people at workplace. The major findings of experiments can be presented below.

1. Social factors in output. An organization is basically influenced by social factors. In fact, Elton Mayo, one of the researchers engaged in Hawthorne experiments, has described an organization as "a social system, a system of cliques, informal status system, rituals, and a mixture of logical, non-logical behaviour".[3] Thus, an organization is not merely a formal structure of functions in which production is determined by the official prescription but the production norm is set by social norms. Since people are social beings, their social characteristics determine the output and efficiency in the organization. Economic rewards and productivity do not necessarily go together. Many non-economic rewards and sanctions affect the behaviour of employees and modify the impact of economic rewards. While motivating employees, these factors should be taken into account.
2. *Group influence* : Employees being social beings, they create groups which may be different from their official group. In fact, groups are formed to overcome the shortcomings of formal relationships. The group determines the norm of behaviour of numbers. If a person resists a particular norm of group behaviour, he tries to change the group norm because any deviation from the group norm will make him unacceptable to the group. Thus, management cannot deal with employees as individuals but as members of work group subject to the influence of the group.
3. *Conflicts* : The informal relations of employees create groups, and there may be conflict between organization and groups so created. The conflict may be because of incompatible objectives of the two. However, groups may help to achieve organizational objectives by overcoming the restraining aspect of the formal relations, which produce hindrance in productivity. Conflict may also arise because of maladjustment of employees and organization. As the

individual moves through the time and space within the organization, there constantly arises the need for adjustment of the individual to the total structure. In the absence of such adjustment, either individual progresses upward at a rapid pace or the organization structure itself may change over the time while the individual remains standstill. In either event, the change takes place in the position of the individual with respect to organization structure, hence adjustment is required.

4. *Leadership* : Leadership is important for directing group behaviour, and this is one of the most important aspects of managerial functions. However, leadership cannot come only from a formally-appointed superior as held by earlier thinkers. There may be informal leader as shown by bank wiring experiments. In some areas, informal leader is more important in directing group behaviour because of his identity with group objective. However, a superior is more acceptable as a leader if his style is in accordance with human relations approach, that is, the superior should identify him with the employees.
5. *Supervision* : Supervisory climate is an important aspect in determining efficiency and output. Friendly to the employees, attentive, genuinely concerned supervision affects the productivity favourably. For example, in the bank wiring room experiment, an entirely different supervisory climate—more friendly to the employees and less use of authority in issuing orders—existed which helped in productivity, while in regular departments, supervisors were concerned with maintaining order and control which produced inhibiting atmosphere and resulted in lower productivity.
6. *Communication* : Through communication employees can be explained the rationality of a particular action, participation of employees can be sought in decision-making concerning the matter of their importance, problems faced by them can be identified and attempts can be made to remove these. A better understanding

between management and employees can be developed by identifying their attitudes, opinions and methods of working and taking suitable actions on these.

CRITICISMS OF HAWTHORNE EXPERIMENTS

Though Hawthorne experiments have opened a new chapter in management by emphasizing the importance of social factors in output, it is not without fault. The experiments have been widely criticized by some behavioural scientists because of lack of scientific objectivity used in arriving at various conclusions. Some critics feel that there was bias and preconception on the part of the Harvard researchers. One writer developed a detailed comparison between the conclusions drawn by the researchers and evidence presented, and found that their conclusions were almost entirely unsupported. He asked the question, "how it was possible for studies so nearly devoid of scientific merit, and conclusions so little supported by evidence, to gain so influential and respected a place within scientific disciplines and to hold this place for so long[4]. Following other criticisms have also been made against the Hawthorne experiments:

1. The Hawthorne researchers did not give sufficient attention to the attitudes that people bring with them to the workplace. They did not recognize such forces as class-consciousness, the role of unions, and other extra-plant forces on attitudes of employees.
2. The Hawthorne plant was not a typical plant because it was a thoroughly unpleasant place to work. Therefore, the results could not be valid for others.
3. The Hawthorne studies look upon the employee as a means to an end, and not an end himself. They assume acceptance of management's goals and look on the employee as someone to be manipulated by management.

In spite of these shortcomings, Hawthorne experiments

will be known for discovering the importance of human factor in managing an organization. The experiments have stimulated many researchers to study the human problems in management.

HUMAN BEHAVIOUR APPROACH

Human behaviour approach is the outcome of the thoughts developed by behavioural scientists who have looked at the organization as collection of people for certain specified objectives. Since management involves getting things done by people, the study of management must revolve around human behaviour. The approach, also known as 'leadership' 'behavioural science' or human resource approach, brings to bear the existing and newly developed theories and methods of relevant behavioural sciences upon the study of human behaviour. In contrast to human relations approach which assumes that happy employees are productive employees, human behaviour approach has been goal and efficiency-oriented and considers the understanding of human behaviour to be the major means to that end. The major differences between human behaviour to be the major means to that end. The human behaviour approach emphasizes human resources in an organization more as compared to physical and financial resources. Since this approach studies human behaviour ranging from personality dynamics of individuals at one extreme to the relations of culture at the other, this can be divided into two groups: interpersonal behaviour approach and group behaviour approach. Writers on interpersonal behaviour approach are heavily oriented towards individual psychology while writers on group behaviour approach rely on social psychology and emphasize on organizational behaviour.

Among the many individual and social psychologists who have contributed to management are Maslow (need hierarchy), Herzberg (motivation-hygiene theory and job enrichment), McGregor (theory X and Y), Liker (management systems and linking pin model), Argyrols (immaturity-maturity theory, integration of individual and organizational goals, and pattern of A B analysis), Blake and Mouton (managerial grid), Sayles (interpersonal behaviour), Bennis (organizational development),

Fiedler (contingency model of leadership styles), Tannenbaum and others (continuum approach of leadership). Besides, notable contributions have come from those who have expanded a particular concept formulated earlier to make it more practicable. They include Leavitt, Stogdill, Vroom, Reddin, etc.

Apart from psychologists who have concentrated more on individual behaviour in organization, significant, contributions have come from sociologists who have studied human behaviour in group and have emphasized on group behaviour. Notable among them are Homans (human group), Bakke (fusion process), Lewin (group dynamics), Katz and Kahn (social psychology of organizations). Some others have attempted to integrate the various views such as Dubin, Dalton, and Selznick, etc. Major conclusions of the contributions made by behavioural scientists can be presented as follows :

1. People do not dislike work. If they have helped to establish objectives, they will want to achieve them. In fact, job itself is a source of motivation and satisfaction to employees.
2. Most people can exercise a great deal of self-direction, self-control and creativity than are required in their current job. Therefore, there remains untapped potential among them.
3. The manager's basic job is to use the untapped human potential in the service of the organization.
4. The manager should create a healthy environment wherein all subordinates can contribute to the best of their capacity. The environment should provide a healthy, safe, comfortable and convenient place to work.
5. The manager should provide for self-direction by subordinates and they must be encouraged to participate fully in all important matters.
6. Operating efficiency can be improved by expanding subordinate influence, self-direction and self-control.
7. Work satisfaction may improve as a 'by-product' of subordinates making full use of their potential.

REVIEW OF THE EMPIRICAL STUDIES DONE IN THE WEST

Quality of Worklife—Beginning from Tarry Town

In the future, when we talk about quality of work life (QWL) we will refer to Topeka, Kalmar and Tarry town.

Volvo[5]

Volvo built a new car assembly plant in Kalmar, Sweden, in the early 1970s in which it attempted to incorporate technical, managerial, and social innovations that better served the needs of employees. The design cost about 10 percent more than a comparable conventional plant, but Volvo took the risk because it hoped to secure increased satisfaction and productivity as well as reduced turnover and absenteeism. The factory was designed to assemble 60,000 automobiles annually, using teams of fifteen to twenty-five employees for each major task. One team, for example, assembles electrical systems, while another assembles brakes. Each team has its own work area, and each is given substantial autonomy. The team is completely in charge of allocation of work among members and of setting the rhythm of its work.

There is no assembly line. Teams obtain a car from a buffer zone when they want one, moving it to their workplace on a trolley. When work is completed, the car is placed in the next buffer zone, a procedure that allows each team to work as its own pace as long as it can meet production requirements. Teams handle their own material procurement and manage their own inventory. The situation is much different from that of a traditional assembly line.

Volvo continued its efforts to increase efficiency and improve QWL through other experiments at its engine, bus assembly, cab, and truck plants throughout Sweden. Independent evaluations of Volvo's success Kalmar showed that both assembly and office employee's costs were the lowest in the company. Employees report that their jobs are better than those on a traditional assembly line, but still report a greater desire for initiative and personal growth on the job.

General Motors : Fremont[6]

A long history of labour-management conflict, poor

quality, and extremely high absenteeism characterized the General Motors and assembly plant in Fremont, California. Then Toyota and GM created a join venture that has since received international recognition for its quality, productivity, and labour climate. New United Motor Manufacturing, Inc. (NUMMI), now operates with virtually the same unionized labour force, but an entirely new socio-technical system.

The labour contact was reduced from over 400 pages to 15, a collaborative problem-solving system was established, and a strong job security provision was provided. As a result, absenteeism was reduced, eighty-two job classifications were reduced to four, and employees work as teams. The number of grievances field is almost negligible.

The reasons for this success appear to lie in the NUMMI philosophy, which has several elements. Employees are urged to search constantly for improvements, develop their full potential, and do their best to create a superior quality product. Team performance and mutual trust are emphasized. Every employee is expected to think and act likes a manager. In turn, NUMMI will attempt to provide its employees with a stable livelihood that has minimal risks of layoffs.

The emphasis at NUMMI is on creating a quality of work life that builds on pride of the employees in themselves, their group, and their work. Teamwork is heavily emphasized, as is full communication. Problems are solved through consensus approaches. Employees are urged to recognize and respect each other's rights. The impact of Toyota is especially clear in the insistence that there be harmony among the culture, structure, and operating systems.

Digital Equipment : Enfield

Unlike NUMMI, which ran the risk of inheriting previous labour-management problems, Digital Equipment Corporation's Enfield, Connecticut, plant is a Greenfield site—it started shipping products in 1983. The Enfield plant is small, with just 200 employees making printed-circuit-board modules for computer storage systems. The organizational hierarchy has just three levels, with employees reporting to group managers, who report to the plant manager.

There are two essential features of Enfield's socio-technical approach-participate team management and job enrichment.

Operating teams of twelve to eighteen members are encouraged to be self-managing. Operating teams of twelve to eighteen members are encouraged to be self-managing, and each employee is trained to have multiple skills and perform a wide range of tasks on the total product. Skill-based pay is used to reward employees for acquiring new skills and knowledge. Regular group meetings are held for goal setting, problem-solving, and communication. Teams of employees have the capacity to set their own work hours under flexitime system.

The results at Enfield are substantial. Compared with traditional facilities, the Enfield plant reduced the standard module-building time by 40 percent, using half the employees and half the space usually required. Overhead is also 40 percent less than normal, and scrap costs were reduced by 50 percent.

General Motors : Tarrytown[7]

Union-management relations in the auto industry have traditionally been adversarial. At the urging of the United Auto Employees, a National Committee on Quality of Work life was created in 1973. The Tarrytown assembly plant of General Motors was chosen as the pilot site because of a desire to solve the more difficult problems first. Tarrytown ranked seventeenth in quality (of eighteen plants); it had one of the highest grievance rates and experienced more strikes, and its absenteeism rate averaged 12 percent.

A steering committee was formed, a QWL philosophy statement was created and distributed, and actions were taken to build trust and respect between management and employees. A training program was initiated to provide employees with skills in problem-solving, cost analysis, team-building, and communications. Remarkably, all but 10 of the 3600 employees volunteered to participate.

The QWL program was comprehensive; was introduced slowly, and had a dual base of support from both management and the union. A profitable plant emerged : it rose to number one in quality and efficiency, absenteeism dropped to 3 percent, and grievances declined by 97 percent. Clearly, employees perceived a new environment in which their suggestions were sought and implemented, and the employees were valued for their skills and ideas.

Each plants experience with a quality of work life effort essentially a structured programme to involve employees in decisions affecting how they work. Each plant had a different problems and different reasons for beginning a quality of work life programme. Tarry town, a GM can assembly plant in New York State, is perhaps the plant with the greatest number of people ever to have undergone such a programme. The company was successful since it had a economic state when the programme began. Following is story of the developing and on going quality of work life programme at Tarry town, New York.

In 1970, the plant was known as having one of the poorest labour relations and production records in GM. Within seven years the plant turned around to become one of the best company.

A quality of work life (QWL) programme was developed at Tarrytown, due to frustration and desperation but with the mutual commitment by management and the union to change old ways of dealing with the employees on the ground floor.

What is special about the Tarry town story? First it earmarks the success. Second it illustrates the principles of successful organizational change that can be applied in a variety of environments. Third QWL programme involved more human beings and finally it was a new collective approach on the part of the management, union and employees to improve the quality of work life.

QWL is not an issue of compensations and benefits programme more and more it involves the human factors at work. It concerns what people require for their work environment so that their needs as human beings not just as employees are met. Restless and alienated blue collar and office employees want to alter the content of their jobs to give them challenge and more satisfying contact with others. Engineers and scientists are increasingly concerned about technical obsolescence. The term QWL is more than the needs satisfied by the 40-hour week, workman's compensation laws and job guarantees through collective bargaining. Richard E. Walton[8] has listed eight concepts of QWL.

1. Adequate and Fair Compensation

Does pay received meet socially determined standards of

sufficiency or the recipient's subjective standards? Does pay received for certain work bear an appropriate relationship to pay received for other work?

2. *Safe and Healthy Environment*

The employees should not be exposed to physical conditions or work arrangements that are unduly hazardous or unhealthy.

3. *Development of Human Capacities*

To varying degrees work has become fractionated, deskilled and tightly controlled. Planning the work is separated from implementing it. It enables the worker to use and develop his skills and knowledge, which affects his involvement, self-esteem and the challenge obtained from the work itself.

4. *Growth and Security*

Importance to be given to our extent to which the employee's assignments contribute to maintaining and expanding his capabilities, rather than leading to her obsolescence, knowledge and skills can be used utilized in future work assignments, to advances in organizational or career terms which peers, family members or associates recognize.

5. *Social Integration*

Employees achieved personal identify and self-esteem due to climate of their ware place, freedom, a sense of community.

6. *Constitutionalism*

What right does the employees have and how can be protect these rights? The organization culture respects personal privacy, tolerates dissert, high standards in distributing rewards, etc.

7. *The Total Life Space*

An employee's work should have a balanced role in his life. This role provides schedules, career demands, and travel that take a limited portion of the employee's leisure and family time.

8. *Social relevance*

Organizations acting in a socially irresponsible manner cause increase number of their employees to depreciate the value of their work and careers. For example, does the worker perceive the organizations to be socially responsible in its products, waste disposal, marketing techniques, employment practices and participation in political campaign?

Glasier[9] (1976) thinks the term QWL means more than job security, good working conditions, adequate and fair compensation more even than an equal employment opportunity. Seashore[10] (1975) has pointed out that much of the research and theorising in the quality of work life has been based on the assumption that it is the individuals own personal satisfaction or dissatisfaction that defines the quality of his or her work rather than any objective criterion.

But, due to individual differences in culture, social class, family norms, education and personality a wide range of human preferences exists and nay assessment of improvements in the quality of worklife would be subject to these differences in personal expectation. Among other things, the nature of different occupations can be responsible for differences in evaluating the quality of worklife situation. Other investigators look beyond these differences between individual perspectives and differences in-group membership to the study of these common expectations that determine the quality of work life.

Studies shows that a relatively few environmental variables account for about one half of the variability in job satisfaction, as broadly defined and as measured across all categories of employees (Seashore, 1975).

It can be concluded that there are in fact systematic and universal characteristics of the work environment, which yield high levels of satisfaction and well-being on the part of employees generally. There are sixteen critical dimensions of QWL, which measure the employee's perceptions of quality of worklife through a questionnaire survey that the general motors management administers annually to its employees. The dimensions are employee commitment, absence of apathy, personal development and utilization of ones abilities, employee involvement and influence, advancement based on merit, career goal progress, relations, with supervisors, work group relations, respect for the individual, confidence in the management, physical working environment, economic well being, employees state of mind, job stress, impact on personal life, and union management relation (Suri, 1984).[11]

Researchers viewed that employees often value factors such as job interest and good working condition above pay. They concluded that the pay becomes the most important factor in job satisfaction only when it is seen as compensation for dissatisfying and alienating job situation. Ganguli and Joseph[12] (1976) studied quality of working life among young employees in Air India with special reference to life and job satisfaction issues. Findings indicate that of the various physical and physiological working conditions, pride in organization, job earned community respect, reasonable working hours, etc. are more positively correlated with job satisfaction.

Based on improved working conditions in the organization, there is an evidence to highlight the implications of autonomy and participation in work. As Ritti (1970)[13] uses the result of research to support the argument that lack of opportunity to perform meaningful work is at the root of frustration among engineers and those who have more autonomy at workplace, feel more satisfied with their work life. Similar findings are found by other too (Andreatta and Rumbold, 1974, Brown, 1975).[14]

As technology advances, the idea of participate management will have more meaning and application for QWL. The same idea offered by Miles (1973)[15] defines the QWL movement as one which views employees in shop floor decision-making will increase their identification with their organization. Similar findings are reported by over (Anderson, 1975, Prideaus, 1975, Rosow, 1979, Harrison, 1985, Mohramam and Norelli, 1985, Schle Singer and Gshry, 1984)[16] who found that employee participation provides the operating manager with tools capable of enhancing both employee productivity and quality of working life.

Rosow[17] (1979) identified five aspects of quality of work life in public sector. They are pay benefits, job-security, training, development and participation. Thackeray (1981) found bore down and monotony produces an adverse effect on QWL. Sekaran and Wagner (1980)[18] worked on sense of competence for while collar employees of USA and India. Results indicate that experiencing meaningfulness in a job was the single-most important contributor to a sense of competence that has been correlated with QWL. Devis (1962)[19] describes the utility of social network for enhancing quality of work life.

Monotony in jobs brings boredom and hence promotes negative growth and dissatisfaction. When the job does not employ the whole person it does not provide him with an opportunity to develop and use his valued abilities, to exercise some selfdirection and control over the job and to feel part of a worthwhile productive community—the worker will feel dehumanized by the job and became either alienated from himself, becoming conditionally dead and passive and will become alienated from his society.[20]

Lawler and Hackman[21] identified five core dimensions, which provide job enrichment. They are motivation, satisfaction and quality of work, turnover and absenteeism.

Again, the Edward E. Lawler III[22] is that government should provide legislative measures for better quality of work life in the organization. Most of the organization does not motivate the employees and provide better working conditions, which leads to mental illness, alcoholism and drug-abuse. Bennett, S.N. *et. al.*,[23] expresses that pride and happiness in work leads to increase the quality of input and improve the quality of work also.

Yuves Delamotte and Shin-Inchi-Takezawa[24] in his study of quality of working life in international perspective, examined the main dimension of quality of working life movement, the issues are modern labour policies and interrelationship of policy position of concerned parties on the quality of working life.

Frank Blacker and Sylvia Shimmin[25] have observed that quality of work experience should be evaluated in terms of the achievement of specific objectives and development of self-managing process. In order to improve QWL they suggested job redesign should be objective. They also suggested the value of employee's participation in a change project would be an appropriate approach to evaluate quality of working life.

Rice, R.W. *et. al.*,[26] says that there is a relationship between work satisfaction and quality of employee's life. The work experience and outcomes can affect an employee's quality of life, both directly and indirectly through their efforts of family interactions, leisure activities, levels of health and energy.

Tenmings, Sandra Anu Ruff[27] in her investigation compared the data collected in 1963 and 1977 by the institute for social research to determine the changes that were important in the QWL issues during the period. Additionally various demographic categories of employees were examined to determine about QWL. The observation that was made from this study was that the findings of 1967 did not differ much from those of 1977. Textile cotton employers and union reported higher job satisfaction than the women and blacks and blue colour employers. Union employees were found to be more satisfied with extrinsic rewards from work than non-union employees.

Barry Wilkinson[28] outlines some theories regarding the relationship between technological change and work organizations, thereby drawing out the implications of QWL. He concludes that QWL developments depend on the emergence of new managerial ideology, where there is recognition of social and psychological importance of work organization and belief in the ability of employees to constructively participate in managerial decision.

A study conducted Martgomery, Lestile Lynn[29] of Harvard University, in the science decision of fortune 500 companies referred to as 'Infocorp' for evaluating the impact of the work redesign programme on Infocorp's employee's productivity and quality of work life. Data for the purpose of the study were collected through surveys, personal interviews and for measuring performances, from internal performance measurement documents. The study indicated that quantity and quality of work improve in relation to an internally established norm.

A study conducted by Stanley's Dennis[30] was to establish reliability, content, construct, concurrent, known group and predictive validity of two QWL indices. Richard T. Dc. George[31] asserts that quality of life has been carried over into the work place as concern for the quality of work life. He scales four compartments for analytical purposes. They are conditions of labour, the organization of the work performed. Relationship among employees and the tools or machines with which they work and attitude of the worker towards work.

While pronouncing the dynamics of team behaviour, and with actions among individuals working together, Eugene Randseep,[32] points out that teamwork is an important when employees consider their work environment to be safe and they regard themselves as competent and valuable.

Tommy, G. Thompson,[33] secretary in the United States Department of Human Health Services (HHS) says that "Through our my public service career, it has been clear to me that we can accomplish our mission and provide the level of service that public demands only if we can recruit and retain the best and the brightest and provide them with a work environment and supports them in getting their jobs done. Monitoring employee views about the quality of their work and the quality of their work life helps us get a sense of our strengths as an employer and identity areas where improvement can be made.

Donna, E. Shalaca[34] in her QWL survey concerns about employee commitment, morale and skill during a period of down sizing reorganization, and rapid technological change. She had a fact paying attention to QWL issues have become an integral part of Health Human Services (HHS) culture. HHS employers and the people they serve deserve no less.

A survey has been conducted in Finland by Duncam Callie (2003)[35] for the past 25 yeas. Many changes that have been taken place in the working environment. The survey reveals that certain physical work environment problems remains to be resolved, while many new, more social and psychological work environment problems are also seen. The survey covers 3000-6000 persons covering the entire population in Finland. The surveys carried were in 1977, 1984, 1990, 1997 and 2003, through personal, face-to-face interviews.

There have been marked differences between countries in the importance that governments and the social patterns of industry have attached employees perception of the quality of working tasks, the degree of involvement in decision-making, career opportunities and job-security to see whether the Scandinavian countries have a distinctive pattern from other European Union countries. Employees in Denmark and Sweden do appear to have higher quality of work tasks and better opportunities for participation.

As these were the aspects of working life that were most central to the reform programmes, the results are consistent with the view that there can be societal effects deriving from the policy orientation of the major economic interest groups.

Francis Green,[36] professor of Economics, University of Kent, UK in his book 'Demanding work' says that in most affluent countries average pay levels have risen along the economic growth (exception being USA), skill requirements have also be increased, potentially meaning a more fulfilling at work. However, set against these beneficial trends is increases in inequality, a strong intensification of work effort diminished job satisfaction, and less employee influence over daily work tasks.

In the affluent economics of the industrialized world, life at work in the early 21st century has evolved in a curious and intriguing way, employees have signification exception, being taken home increasing wages, exercising more acute mental skills, enjoying safe and more pleasant conditions at work and spending less time there yet they have also been working much more intensely, experiencing greater mental strain, sometimes to the point of exhaustion. In many cases work has come under increased and unwelcome control from above, leaving individual employees with less influence over their daily work lives and less fulfilling experience than before more demanding. Meanwhile a significant employees continue to endure great uncertainty regarding the future security of their employment. Overall, employees are getting no more satisfaction from their time at work than they used to even though the material wealth of nations has been increasing. Professor Grew shows how aspects of job quality are related, and how changes in their quality of work life stem from technological change and transformation in the political economic environment.

A study on quality circle and quality of work life done by Dov Elizuv (1990).[37] Quality circles have recently been suggested as a technique for enhancing employer quality of work life and.satisfaction with their work. This study attempts to analyze the relationship between employer participation in the quality circles, their sense of quality of work life perceived job reinforcement capacity and job-satisfaction. 143 employers of a large industrial corporation in Israel, half of them regularly participating in quality circles and half are not participating were surveyed. The results support the hypothesis of the study. A positive relationship was found the participation in quality circles and various aspects of quality of work life, perceived job reinforcement capacity and job-satisfaction. Results are discussed in the context of the arguments concerning the effects of participation in quality circles.

Women are largely underrepresented in the information technology[38] (IT) work force. The research examines the factors related to the work environment that may contribute to the high turnover of women in the IT work force. There is substantial research providing support for the relationship between job and organizational factors, on one hand and QWL (e.g. low job-satisfaction and high job strain) on the other hand. Results show that IT employees reported higher job-satisfaction and lower job strain than non-IT employees. Gender had no impact on QWL.

Feedback and autonomy were consistently related to job-satisfaction and work pressure was consistently related to job. Strain irrespective of the gender and the type of job. On the other hand, women IT worker job-satisfaction was affected by work-pressure, and women IT worker's job-strain was affected by task significance. Women IT employees job strain was not affected by autonomy, whereas job-strain experienced by non-IT employees was affected by autonomy.

In developing countries, the quality of working life becomes an important for their development. The experience of participation in decision-making at the workplace and progressive learning will help the employees to acquire the competences and skills. It would be tragic in industrializing the less developed countries they adopt the authorization management styles from which the advanced countries are beginning to break loose. Their best strategy would be to ignore nineteenth century models of industrial organizations and the dehumanizing value embodied in them and experiment in ways suitable to the condition of the third work with new forms of organization that give first importance to quality of life in the work place.[39]

QWL issues affect both the satisfaction of the employees and the productivity of large corporation. Corporate giants such as general motors and TRW Inc of USA have successfully conducted a study on it by Schilesinger[40] and Richard Walton have reported that at least one-third of fortune of 500 companies have QWL programmes underway.

A lot of thinking in the west has been going on with respect of 'Quality of working life'[41] by Davis L.E. and Cherns A.B.

Herrick and Maccoby[42] have observed that a central goal of our society, should be development of institutions of work that stimulates the creative abilities employees: activeness, cooperativeness interest in learning and self-development all of which will encourage positive attitudes of citizenship and spark the hope necessary to build a more just and human society.

Dyer and Hoffenberg[43] say that "..... it is now assumed that the quality of working life can be defined, in terms of the organization contribution to the economic and socio-psychological needs of those individuals actively engaged in furthering its goals".

REVIEW OF EMPIRICAL STUDIES IN INDIA

There are number of QWL studies in India. Some of them are discussed below : They were reviewed by Nitish De (1979)[44] starting the first experiment in BHEL (Tiruchy), a government post/office at Chaura Maidan, Simla, Income tax Department, New Delhi and Hindustan Machine Tools Ltd., Hyderabad. These experiments were carried out primarily from the National Labour Institute, New Delhi. The work has since been conducted by the public enterprises centre for continuing education, New Delhi. He says that these experiments remained static and did not become an occasion for containing changes.

The following areas of concern in QWL are listed by International Labour Office Directory of Institutions (1981). They are

- Hours of work and working time.
- Work organization and job content.
- Working conditions of women young employees, elder employees, and other special categories.
- Work-related welfare services and facilities.

- Shop floor participation in the improvement of the working condition.

Singh and Dewari[45] conducted a study on "Job-satisfaction among Bank employees". They concluded that job-satisfaction among bank employees was significantly related to their position in their hierarchy. Management followed by accountants reported the highest degree of job-satisfaction. Milkant and Tandon[46] pointed out the validity and relevance of socio-psychological factors in the India context. They suggest that management can initiate a number of changes in the work procedures, rationalize wage structures and improvements in employee's amenities and employees conditions, all these lead to improve QWL.

De points out that quality of work life is on indicator of how free the society is from exploitation, injustice, inequality, oppression and restriction on the continuity of growth of man, leading to his full development. Goel,[47] S.S. points out that for a QWL programme to work properly, it must be perceived as being a benefit to management and employees. But same management representative have expressed opposition to the concept of QWL because successful programmes might tend to evade managerial authority. Supervisor must understand that getting the work over worker and acting as constant over seems need not be the essential ingredients of supervisory work.

M.K. Varma[48] believes that quality work helps in achieving the desired results. Its aim is to provide a better quality of working life to workman at all levels in an organization, because better QWL is assured, the motivation among employees for actualizing better quality in their work, in their products, and in their productivity.

Asha Bhandarkar[49] in the literature survey concluded that several empirical surveys on QWL in the prevailing work environment conducted across companies in India have been found it to be poor. The following are some of the observations.

(a) Singh and Magger (1980) have surveyed 251 respondents who participated in a executive development programmes. The findings lead to conclude that QWL in Indian industry is poor. It is poor in the area of democratization of the decision-making process. The study revealed that managerial experience, hierarchy, and remuneration do not significantly influence their perception to QWL.

(b) Sayeed and Singh (1981) observed that QWL is related to job-satisfaction in the study conducted in a high QWL organization and a low QWL organization.

(c) Mongu and Magger (1981) conducted a study in eight public sector organization across textiles, fertilizers, engineering, electronics and leather goods industry. There was a significant gap between what the manager expect and what they have, indicating a poor QWL in public sector undertakings.

(d) The study conducted by Ghosh (1983) covered executives from industrial and service organization revealed that importance has been given to job-related factors such as employee commitment, involvement, influence, advancement based on merit and opportunities to use capabilities work environment, financial, personality and non-organizational factors.

(e) P. Singh (1984)'s conducted the study on QWL. QWL was measured in terms of opportunities for socio-psychological need fulfilment, work as an existing and creating place, and democratization of the work process.

Subash Ghosh[50] (1992) conducted a study on improvement of QWL in the micro-level in India. The concept of QWL covered all aspects of work related life including work-environment.

Sangeeta Jain[51] found that there were differences at various hierarchical level of the organization in perceiving their working life. Higher levels were found to have better perception regarding their working life than at worker level.

According to R.C. Monga,[52] the productivity concepts in a practical means providing products which meet reliability needs of consumers, waste and pollute less in use, qualitative, and easy to maintain and doing things rightly in a way to improve quality of working life.

Pradip, N. Khandwalla[53] discusses the important elements to organizational excellence. He says that team efforts are important than the individual efforts. Excellent teamwork is vital for human excellence.

Amarachand and Jayaraj[54] have emphasized on self-motivation as one of the values that contributed to growth of organizations. According to them one should not work in anticipation of a reward, but work like water, giving up all attachment to work. Working through freedom, working through love of such ideal should be cultivated. It will solve several problems like efficiency quality, perfection, accountability, etc.

Ahmed, N.[55] Observes that QWL is a generic phrase that covers person's feelings about every dimension of work, including economic rewards and benefits, security, safe and healthy working conditions, organizational and interpersonal relationship and intrinsic meaning to a personal life.

QWL EMPIRICAL STUDY BASED ON INDIAN PHILOSOPHY

S.K. Chakroborty[56] related the QWL to Hindu philosophy. According to him all the work life problems can be solved through the Ramayana and Mahabharata. Starting from the smallest ant to the biggest whale, lowest creeper to the tallest tree, every member in the organization, from peon to the manager including the entrepreneur all is employees. The entire Universe is working. All are working with one or more objectives like to live discharging family and social duties, to prevent ennui or boredom, to earn a reputation and win recognition, etc.

He says that a lot of thinking in the west has been going on for sometime with respect to 'quality of working life', which represent to his mind, an essentially normative thrust.

The Indian thought from the Rig-Veda through Bhagavad-Gita to Manusmriti, i.e. that the most super-ordinate character of work ethic is 'sacrifice'. Thus the Purusha Sukta or the Hymn of Man in the Rig-Veda is symbolic explanation of the process of the creation of the Universe. Here the primeval Purusha 'Sacrifices' Him self for the sake of bringing every aspect of cosmic existence into being.[57] The Manusmriti elaborates this concept.[58]

In Geetha there is a theory of sacrifice as base of all work. In sloka 4-31 Aurobindo remarks.

'Sacrifice is the law of the world and nothing can be gained without it, neither mastery here nor the possession of heavens beyond, nor the supreme possession of all'.[59]

He also explains an earlier sloka 4-26

'There is the psychological Sacrifice of self-control and self-discipline which leads to the higher self-possession and self-knowledge.[60] Aurobindo highlights the same idea in his interpretation of slokas 2.42, 43..... not only is sacrifice, yajna, the most important part of life, but all life, all works should be regarded as sacrifice as yajna. . . .[61]

Aurobindo once again deftly put across the same refined psychological principle as .... But we find here a sense entirely subtle, figurative and symbolic given to the word 'Sacrifice'... So entirely cosmic and philosophical that we can easily accept (it) as expressive of a practical fact of psychology and general law of nature and so apply them to the modern conception of inter-change between life and life.[62]

In the Geeta there is a concept Lokasamgraha in slokas 3.19 and 20.13. Radhakrishnan translates this work as "World-maintanance".[63] Without work being understood as sacrifice, with all its implications, there can be no Lokasamgraha either organizationally or nationally or internationally.

There is a sloka 3.14 in the same Geeta "From food creatures comes into being; from rain is the birth of food; from sacrifice rain comes into being, and sacrifice is born of work.[64]

From this he concludes that sacrifice is the basis of all the work. Without it nothing can be achieved. Through sacrifice all work are facilitated more wholesome and superior results. The same leitmotif contributes to better leadership and more teamwork. At last the forces of human response developments would tend to shift exclusively from external work to the internal mind.

WHY WORK

Why do we work? Why should work begin to be understood as a sacrifice? The following are the answers given by S.K. Chakraborthy.

1. The principal difference between human beings and other living entities is that former alone can ask for and pursue the quest to discover what they really are the immutable, all perfect, luminous consciousness or atman, which is a fragment of the Universal, supreme Brahman or Energy. Men like Vivekananda, Tagore, Tilak, Gandhi and Ramana have also proved this fundamental truth in contemporary times—if only we are ready to listen to them.[65] They were employees and achievers par excellence.
2. We are unable to live and act in the consciousness that we are the atman. This is because like a burning flame, concealed by a soot-smeared glass done our mind and nescience or avidya or wrong understanding, thus apparently sealing-off the radiant atman, sullies intellects. Avidya finds expression in acts of pettiness, deceit, anger, greed, pride, etc.
3. The super-ordinate reason why we human beings should work, is to gradually cleanse our sullied mind and intellect so that the perennial, luminous true self shines forth from our lower nature in its glory. This process of refinement is called chitta shuddhi in Geeta.[66]
4. It is only with the super-ordinate orientation of sacrifice that work can be converted to be a means of chitta shuddhi.

This kind of search for humanizing in work can clear our mind which have acrimony, back biting, anger, sycophancy, politicking, arrogance, jealousy, power-mongering, selfishness, egotism and the like in every organization. It is much more dehumanization of work than any machine. It is such a phenomena, which constitute the impurities of the mind.

He says that the great purpose of all work for all of us should, therefore be to combat and subdue these impurities, instead of intellectualize them under the delusive clock of organizational dynamics.

In the Geeta, slokas 5.11 and 6.12 specifically mention the role of work in effecting the purification of the mind and intellect.[67]

Singh rightly in his key note of atmashuddhi in the 'Geeta'; teaches about why should work say that 'self-purification is a highly subjective goal'.[68]

If purification through work means, in practice, overcoming pride, envy, selfishness, greed and similar tendencies of our mind. He says that within each one of us there is always an unfailing inner voice, which does invariably sound an initial warning against impure attitudes.

HOW TO WORK?

The main aim is to humanize the work. He says that in sloka 2.47 of the Geeta, 'Thou hast a right to action, but only to action never to its fruit, let net the fruits of thy works be thy motive; neither let there be in thee any attachment to inactivity.[69]

For man, work is impossible without the motive of results for himself. It is these motives for the self, which is amongst the biggest causes of dehumanization at the work place. The following are some of the suggestion:

(a) Reduction of concern about results or fruits is suggested as a psychological principle of conservation of energy.
(b) One should be apathetic to results for others, for the organization, for the nation, for humanity at large. A true worker-yogis is devoted to the good of all beings because he is free from his personal interest.
(c) The reason why attachment to results or fruits is warned against is sloka 2-62 and 63 in the Geeta.[70] The mind dwelling on sense objects becomes attached to them; attachment breeds; desires generates anger; anger leaders to confusion; confusion give rise to loss of memory; loss of memory breeds destruction of intelligence; and destruction of intelligence; and destruction of intelligence leads to man's annihilation (Figuratively).
(d) Another suggestion is to educate oneself too gradually from attachment of fruits or results.
(e) One of the reasons for dehumanization at work is not because of structure or system or machine but because

of ego. Sacrifice is the ego will improve the quality of work-life.

(f) He suggested that work is worship. Men like M.K. Gandhi, Tagore, Vivekananda, Ramana and Vinoba are some such examples of work are worship.

CONCLUSION

This chapter has attempted to sketch theoretical work in India and empirical work in western countries. According to Indian thought the man has a spiritual metaphysical dimension too to his personality, a dimension inherently superior to that of his economic, biological and social dimensions. It is from this point to view that some major clues have been provided to the key questions like what is work, why work and how to work? The aim is to improve the quality of work-life.

According to western empirical studies on QWL an employee has certain set of needs such as task autonomy, task significance, task variety, leisure, good working condition, rest and passes monitoring the benefits, etc. QWL movement emphasis an fulfilling these needs of the employees to make the work situation a pleasant one so that, employees can contribute their maximum potential for the organization. This idea is rooted in the philosophic thinking of western philosophers that human being is a bundle of needs, desires and wants, which must be constantly satisfied. This conceptualization of man has lead to ever increasing demand from the employees for satisfying their needs. The net result of QWL movements in the west is an employee who always looks at employer for need fulfilment. This is an un-ending process the conceptualization of human-being and therefore an employee atman (universal consciousness within) who always looks work as sacrifice and means of moksha (salvation) has lead to lethargic worker.

Moksha has a terminal value along with maya (illusion) and karma (cosmic causation) have made Indian employees other world and passive. If adopted in business organization this paradigm of QWL will lead to unproductive, lethargic and passive troop of employees. There is a need to search for the meaning of work and QWL, based on real human nature as enshrine in the Holy Quran and Sunnah.

NOTES AND REFERENCES

1. A detailed account of these experiments is available in several books: Elton Mayo, The human problems of an industrial civilization, New York: The Mac Milan Company 1933. T.N. Whitehead, The industrial Worker, Cambridge, Mass : Harvard University Press, 1938.
2. Delbert, C. Mill and William, H. Form, Industrial Psychology, New York, Harper and Row, 1951, p. 58.
3. Mayo, *op. cit.*
4. Alex Carey, "The Hawthorne Studies: A Radical Criticisms", *American Sociological Review*, June 1967, pp. 403-16.
5. Pehr, G. Gyllenhammar, People at Work, Reading, Mass : Addison—Wesley Publishing Company, 1977; and Pehr G. Gyllenhammar, "How Volvo Adapts Work to People", *Harvard Business Review*, July-August 1977, pp. 102-13. Recent results are reported in Berth Jonson and Alden G. Lank, "Volvo: A Report on the Workshop on Production Technology and Quality of Working Life", *Human Resource Management*, Winter 1985, pp. 455-65.
6. Robert, R. Rehder and Marta Medaris Smith, "Kzizen and the Art of Labor Relations", *Personnel Journal*, December 1986, pp. 83-93.
7. Robert Guest, "Quality of Worklife—Learning from Tarrytown", *Harvard Business Review*, July-August, 1979, pp. 76-87.
8. Richard, E. Walton, "Improving the Quality of Worklife", *Harvard Business Review on Management*, Vol. 1, New York, 1975, pp. 119-22.
9. Glassier, E.M. State 06 Art Questions about the Quality of Worklife, *Personnel*, Nov.-Dec. 20, 1976.
10. Seashore, S.E. Defining and Measuring the QWL in Davis, L.E. and Chen A.E., QWL, New York, 1975.
11. Suri, B.K., QWL Domain and its Components, Quality of Worklife, p. 108, Jan.-April 1984.
12. Ganguly, *op. cit.*
13. *Ibid.*
14. O.N. and Joseph, J.S. Quality of Working Life: Work Prospects and Aspirations of Young Employees in Air India, Central Labour Institute, Mumbai, 1976.
15. Ritti, R.R., Under Employment of Engineer Industrial Relations, 9(4), pp. 437-52, 1970.
16. Andrella, H. and Rumbold, B., Organizational Development in Action, Melbourne Producing Promotion Council of Australia, p. 64, 1974.
17. Miles, T., Quality of Work : An Emerging art and Science, Working Together Campaign, London, p. 18, 1973. .
18. Anderson, G., 'The Quality of Worklife', Seminar on Worker Participation in Australia, South Australian Development, Department of Legal Studies and Industrial Relations Programme, University of Melbourne, Melbourne, Australia, 1975.
19. Rosow, J.M., 'Human Dignity in the Public Sector Work Place', *Public Personnel Management*, Vol. 891), pp. 7-14, Jan.-Feb. 1975.
20. Sekaran, U., Perceived Quality of Working Life in, Banks in Major Cities in India, *Prajanan*, Vol. 14(3), pp. 273-84, 1981.

21. Davis, K., 'Human Relations at Work', Mc Grawhill, New York, 1962.
22. Maccoby M. Emotional Attitudes and Political Choices, *Politics and Society*, 2(2), 1972.
23. Edward, E. Lawler III and Richard Hackman, Corporate Projects and Employee's Satisfaction: Must they be in Conflict? *California Management Review*, Fall 1971, pp. 46-51.
24. Edward, E. Lawler III, Showed the Quality of Worklife be Legislated? *Personal Administration*, Jan. 1976, pp. 17-21.
25. Bennett, S.N. *et. al.*, Quality and Quality of Work in Rows and Classroom Group, *Educational Psychology*, 1963, Vol. 3(2), pp. 93-105.
26. Yuves Delamotte and Schi-Ichi-Takezawa. *Quality of Working Life in International Perspective*, Geneva, ICO, 1984, pp. 6-7.
27. Frank Blacker and Sylvia Shinemin, Applying Psychology in Organization, New York : Methods Inc. 1984, pp. 104-23.
28. Rice, R.N. *et. al.*, Organizational Work and the Perceived Quality of Life Towards a Conceptual Model, *Academy of Management Review*, April 1985, Vol. 10(2), pp. 296-310.
29. Tenmings Sandra Ann Ruff, An Investigation of Employee Responses to QWL Issue : A Demographic Analysis, the University of Oklawama, 1985.
30. Barry Wilkinson, Technology and Quality of Working Life, *Singapore Management Review*, Vol. 8, July 1986, pp. 21-30.
31. Martzomey, Leslive Lynn, Improving Productivity and Quality of Worklife: An Impact and Study on Work Design at Infocorp: Harvard University, 1986.
32. Stanley, Dennis, Quality of Worklife India: Its Development and Psychometric Validation, The University of Aaron, 1986.
33. Richard, T. De George, Business Ethics, New York : Mac Millon Publishing Company, 3rd Ed. 1990, p. 346.
34. Eugene Ramdseep, Team Work into Work Teams, Personal Today, Jan.-Man, 1990, pp. 33-35.
35. Thompson, G. Tommy, Secretary, United States Department of Health Human Services (HHS), dated 21.02.2005, Washington D.C., 20201.
36. Shalala, E. Donna, QWL—Issues United States Department of Health Human Services, Dec. 1996.
37. Gallie, Duncam (2003), The Quality of Working Life : Is Scandinavia Different? *European Sociological Review*, 19(1) : pp. 61-79.
38. Green, Francis, Demanding Work-Book, Professor of Economics, University of Kent, 2003.
39. Elizur, Dov, 'Quality Circle and Quality of Worklife'. *International Journal of Manpower*, Year 1990, Vol. II, No. 6, MCBUP Ltd., Israel.
40. Pascale Carayon, Peter Hoonakker, S. Marchand, Jen Schwarz, Job-Characteristics and Quality of Working Life in IT Work Force : The Role of Gender, *Personnel Research Annual Conference*, pp. 58-63, 2003.
41. Trist, E.L., Planning the First Step Towards QWL in a Developed Country. The QWL, New York, Vol. 1, Free Press, 1975.
42. Leonard Schlesinger and Richard Walton, Unpublished Background Committee, Harvard Graduate School of Business Administration.

43. Davis, L.E. and Cherns, A.B., The Quality of Working Life (Free Press, New York, 1975).
44. Herrick, N.Q. and Maccoby, M., Humanizing Work: A Priority Goal of the Seventies in the Quality of Working Life, *op. cit.*, p. 64.
45. Dyer, J.S. and Hoffenberg, M., "Evaluating the Quality of Working Life" in the Quality of Working Life, *op. cit.*, p. 138.
46. Nitish, R. De, New form of Work Organization in India, Conditions of Worklife, Branch Geneva, ICO, 1976.
47. Singh and Dewari, Job-satisfaction among Bank Employees, *Indian Psychological Review*, 24(2), 1983.
48. Milkant, V. and R. Tandon, An Alternative Approach for Improving QWL in India, PECEE, New Delhi, 1982.
49. Goel, S.S., Quality of Worklife Programmes, *Personnel Today*, Oct.-Nov. 1988, pp. 3-6.
50. Varma, M.K., Quality Circle a Catalyst for Motivation, *Personal Today*, Oct.-Nov. 1988, pp. 27-38.
51. Asha Bhandarkar, Motivational Research in India. *A Literature Review*, unpublished paper prepared for ICPE, Yugoslavia, 1988, pp. 40 and 88-89.
52. Ghosh, Subash, Quality of Working Life in two Indian Organizations, Implications of Case Studies, *Decision*, Vol. 19, No. 2, April-June, 1992, pp. 89-99.
53. Sangeeta Jain, Quality of Worklife (QWL), New Delhi, Deep and Deep Publications, 1998.
54. Monga, R.C. Dynamics of Productivity Management, *Productivity*, Vol. 33, No. 1, April-January, 1992.
55. Pradip, N. Khandwalla, Organizational Designs for Excellence, New Delhi, Tata McGraw-Hill, 1993, p. 43.
56. Amarchand, D. and Jayaraj, B.J. Corporate Culture and Organizational Effectiveness, New Delhi, Global Business Press, 1992.
57. Ahmed, N. Quality of Worklife: A Need for Understanding Indian Management, 1981, 20(1), pp. 29-33.
58. Chakraborty, S.K. "Managerial Effectiveness and Quality of Worklife"—Indian Insights, Tata-McGraw Hill Publishing Company Ltd., New Delhi, 1977.
59. Low, A. Zen and the Art of Creative Management, Play Boy paper backs, New York, 1970, p. 37.
60. O' Plahery, W.D., 'The Rig Veda', Penguin, Harmondsworth, 1981, pp. 29-32.
61. Buhler, G., 'The laws of Manu, Clarendon Press, Oxford, 1886, pp. 87-88.
62. Aurobindo, Sri, The Message of the Gita, Sri Aurobindo Ashram, Pondicherry, 1977, p. 81.
63. *Ibid.*, p. 80.
64. *Ibid.*, p. 34.
65. *Ibid.*, p. 52.
66. Radhakrishna, S., The Bhagavad Gita, Blacke, Bombay 1976, pp. 139-40.
67. *Ibid.*, p. 136.
68. *Ibid.*, p. 124.

69. Osborne, A., Ramana Maharishi and The Path of Knowledge, B.I. Publications, New Delhi, 1979. pp. 81-84.
70. Bhave, Vinoba, Talks on the Geetha, Sarva Seva Sangh Prakashan, Varanasi, 1974, pp. 34-35. Vikarma or mind and heart applied to external action are Necessary to Convert Karma into Akarma or pure, unsullied action.
71. Aurobindo, *op. cit.*, pp. 88, 99.
72. Singh, I.P., The Gita—A Workshop on the Expansion of Self, Somaiya, Bombay 1977, p. 85.

4

Tawheed and Quality of Worklife

IMPACT OF TAWHEED ON QWL

The researcher is influenced by Ismail Raja Farooqui's[1] work while writing this part of the thesis. Al-Tawheed is the belief and witnessing, "there is no god but God". This statement has the highest value in the whole of Islam, the entire culture, entire civilization and entire history is absolute in this sentence. All the diversity, wealth and history, culture and learning, wisdom and civilization of Islam are compressed in this shortest of sentences—LA ILAHA ILLALAH (There is no god but God). Islam comprises of all the diversity, culture and learning, wealth and history, wisdom and civilization.

Al-Tawheed is the only reality, of truth, of the world, of space and time, of human history and destiny. It stands on the following foundation.

A. Duality

God and non-God are the ultimate realities in the universe. Creator and creation are two separate entities. The creator is one, Allah (SWT). Godhood is enjoyed on Him alone; the Eternal, the Creator, the Transcendent. Nothing is like unto

Him.[2] He is absolutely unique and has no of partners and associates.[3] The second is the order of space-time, of experience, of creation. It includes all creatures, the world of things, plants and animal's humans, jinn and angels, heaven and earth, paradise and hell, and all their becoming since they came into being. They are created out of nothing. The two orders of creator and creation are utterly and absolutely different as far as their being or ontology, as well as their experience and careers, are concerned. It is never possible that the one be united with, infused and, confused with or diffused into the other. Neither can the creator be ontologically transformed so as to become the creature, nor can the creature transcend and transfigure itself so as to become, in any way or sense, the creator[4]. This is called Wahadatul Shuhud.

B. Ideationality

The relation between God and non-God is that of master and servant in nature. Its points of reference in man are the faculty of understanding. As organ and repository of knowledge, the understanding includes all the cognitive functions, such as memory, imagination, reasoning, observation, intuition, apprehension, etc.

They ascribed the jinn as associates to Allah. (though Allah did create the jinn). They ever ascribed to him sons and daughters. All this they did with no knowledge. —(Q : 6 :100)

A human being is endowed with comprehension. The endowment is strong enough to understand the will of God in either or both of the following ways: when that will is expressed in words, directly by God to man, or 'the laws of nature', the divine will is deductible through observation of creation.[5]

C. Teleology

The nature of the cosmos is purposive, serving a purpose of its creator, and doing so out of design. In the creation of the world, God is neither playing nor has he done in vain.[6] It is not the work of chance. It is created in perfect condition. Everything that exists does so in a measure proper to it and fulfils a certain universal purpose.[7] The world is indeed a "cosmos", an orderly creation, not a "chaos". In it, the will of the creator is always realized. His patterns are fulfilled with the necessity of natural law, for they are innate in the way other that what the creator has ordained for it.[8] This is true of all creatures expect man. Human action is the only instance where the will of God is actualized not necessarily, but deliberately, freely and voluntarily. The physical and psychic functions of man are integral to nature and as such they obey the laws pertinent to them with the same necessity as all other creatures. But the spiritual function viz. the understanding and moral action fall outside the realm of determined nature. They depend upon their subject and follow his determination; actualization of the divine will by them is of a qualitatively different value than necessary actualization by other creatures. Necessary fulfilment applies only to elemental or utilization value for fulfilment to the moral. However, the moral purposes of God, His commandments to man, do have a base in the physical world, and hence there is a utilization aspect to them. But this is not what gives them their distinctive quality, namely, that of being moral. It is precisely their aspect of being fulfil able in freedom, that is, the possibility of being fulfilled or violated remaining always open that gives them the special dignity we ascribe to things "moral".[9]

D. Capacity of Man and Malleability of Nature

Since everything was created for a purpose—the realization of that purpose must be possible in this mundane life or worldly life.[10] Otherwise there is no escape from cynicism. Creation itself, the processes of space and time, would lose their meaning and significance. Without this possibility *takkleef* (charge, moral obligation, and responsibility), falls to the ground: and with its fall, either God's purposiveness or His might is destroyed. Realization of the absolute, namely, the divine *raison d'être* of creation, must be possible in history, that is within the process of time between creation and the Day of Judgment. As subject of moral action, man must therefore be capable of changing himself, his fellows or society, nature and his environment, so as to actualize the divine pattern or commandment, in him as well as in them.[11] This capacity is the converse of man's moral capacity for moral action as subject. Without it man's capacity for moral action would be impossible and the purposive nature of the universe would collapse. Again, there would be no recourse from cynicism. For creation to have a purpose and this is a necessary assumption its God is God and His work is not a meaningless travel de single—creation must be malleable or transformable. The malleability of creation implies changing its substance, structure, condition, and relations so as to embody or concretize the human pattern or purpose. This is at once true of all creation, including man's physical, psychic, and spiritual natures. All creation is capable of realization of the ought to be of the will or pattern of God or the absolute[12] in this space and in this time.

An employee in Islamic culture gets a purpose of life; he is not created in vain. Nay, he is the vicegerent of the creator. This very purpose of life gives him a sense of direction in his job life as well. The modern man and modern employee are still on the lookout for meaning of worklife. He is not able to get a proper answer. This makes him cynical, alienated and frustrated. On the contrary, Tawheed gives an employee a purposive life: Life well defines, well articulated with details and sense of clear direction. Boredom, cynicism associated with the loss of meaning of life will not be experience when one internalizes Tawheed. It gives full meaning of work.

E. Responsibility and Judgment

We have seen that man stands under the obligation to change him, society and environment so as to conform to the divine pattern. We have also seen that creation is malleable and capable of receiving his action and embodying its purpose. It follows from these facts that man is responsible.[13] Moral obligation is impossible without responsibility or reckoning. Unless man is responsible and somehow and somewhere he will be reckoned with as far as his deeds are concerned, cynicism becomes once more inevitable. Judgment or the consummation of responsibility is the necessary condition of moral obligation or moral imperativeness. It flows from the very nature of normalitiveness.[14] It is immaterial whether reckoning takes place in space-time or at end or it may be both, but it must take place. To obey God, i.e. to realize his commandments and actualize his pattern is to incur falah. Not to do so, i.e. to disobey Him, is to incur punishment, sufferings, unhappiness and the agonies of failure.[15]

The above five principles are self-evident truths. They constitute the core of al-Tawheed and quintessence of Islam. All the revelations came from heaven. All the prophets have taught these principles and built their movements upon them, these principles are built by God in the very fabric of human nature, constituting the natural religion or natural conscience upon which human acquired knowledge. Naturally all Islamic culture is built up on them and together them from the core of al-Tawheed knowledge, personal and social ethics, aesthetics and Muslim life and action throughout history.

THE EFFECTS OF TAWHEED ON QUALITY OF WORKING LIFE

The works of Sayyid Qutb[16] in this part of articulation influences the researcher. Let us study the effects, which the belief in 'LA ILAHA ILLALAH' brings forth upon the life of an employee, and see why he should always be a success in life.

1. An employee who believes in this kalima can never be narrow minded in outlook. He believes in a God who is the creator of the heavens and the earth, the master of the East and the West and sustainer of the entire universe. After this belief he does not regard anything in the world as a stranger to himself. He looks upon everything in the universe as belonging to the same lord whom he himself belongs to. He is not biased in his thinking and behaviour. His sympathy, love and service do not remain confined to any particular sphere or group. His vision is enlarged, his intellectual horizon widens, and His outlook becomes liberal and as boundless as is the kingdom of God.
2. This belief produces in an employee highest degree of self-respect and self-esteem. The believer knows that Allah alone is the possessor of all power, and that none besides him can benefit or harm a person or provide for his needs or give and take away life or wield authority or influence. This conviction makes him in different to and independent and fearless of all powers other than those of God. He never bows his head in

homage to any of God's creatures, nor does he stretch his hand before anyone else. He is not overawed by anybody's greatness. This quality or attitude of mind cannot be produced by any other belief.

3. Along with self-respect this belief also generates in an employee a sense of modesty and humbleness. It makes him unostentatious and unpretending. Such an employee never becomes proud, haughty or arrogant. The boisterous pride of power, wealth and worth can have no room in his heart, because he knows that whatever he possesses has been given to him by God, and that God can take away just as He can give.
4. This belief makes an employee virtuous and upright. He has the conviction that there is no other means of success and salvation for him except purity of soul and righteousness of behaviour. This belief creates in him the consciousness that, unless he lives rightly and acts justly he cannot succeed.
5. Such an employee become dependent and broken-heart under any circumstances. He has firm faith in God who is the master of all treasures of the earth and heavens. Whose grace and bounty have no limit and whose powers are infinite. This faith imparts to his heart extraordinary consolation, fills it with satisfaction and keeps it filled with hope. In this world he might meet with rejection from all doors, nothing herein might serve his ends, all means might one after another, desert him, but faith in and dependence on God never leave him. Such a profound confidence can result from no other belief than belief in one God.
6. This belief produces in an employee a very strong degree of determination, patient perseverance and trust in God. When he makes up his mind and devotes his resources to fulfil the divine commands in order to serve God's pleasure, he is sure that he has the support and backing of the Lord of the universe. This certainty makes him firm and strong like a mountain, and no amount of difficulties, impediments, and hostile opposition can make him give up his resolution.

7. The declaration inspires bravery in an employee. There are two things which makes an employee cowardly (i) fear of death and love of safety, and (ii) the idea that there is some one else besides God who can take away life and that an employee, by adopting certain devices can ward-off death. The first idea goes out of his mind because he knows that his life and his property and everything else really belong to God, and he becomes ready to sacrifice his all for His pleasure. He gets rid of the second idea because he knows that no weapon, no man or animal has the power of taking away his life. God alone has the power to do so.
8. The belief in LA-ILAHA-ILLALAH creates an attitude of peace and contentment, purges the mind of the subtle passions of jealousy, envy and greed, and keeps away the ideas of resorting to base and unfair means for achieving success. The employee understands that wealth is in God's hands, and He does it out more as He likes that honour, power, reputation and authority—everything is subjected to His will, and He bestows them as He wills, and that an employee's duty is only to endeavour and struggle fairly. He knows that success and failure depend upon God's grace. If He wills to give, no power in the world can prevent Him from doing so and if He does not will it, no power can force Him to give.
9. The most important effect of belief is that it makes an employee obey and observe God's law. One who has belief in it is sure that God knows everything hidden or open and is nearer to him than his own jugular vein. If he commits a sin in a secluded corner and in the darkness of night, He knows it He even knows our thoughts and intentions, bad or good. We can hide from everyone, but we cannot hide anything from God, we can evade everyone, but it is impossible to evade God's grip.

Surah (Al-Asr 103) the declining day says that throughout the history of man there has been one worthwhile and trust-worthy path. All other paths lead only to loss and ruin. That path is first the adoption of faith, followed up with good deeds and exhortation to follow the truth and to stead fastness.

Faith is the characteristics by which the minute, transient human being attains closeness to the absolute and ever blasting originator of the Universe, and all that exist in it. He thus establishes a link with the whole world, which springs from that one origin, with the laws governing it and with the powers and potentialities created in it. This proximity grants an employee a certain power, limitless scope and freedom. It endows him with great enjoyment of life, its beauty and its constituents with whose "souls" he lives in mutual friendship. From this everlasting happiness, delightful joy and live intimate understanding of life and all creation are derived.[8]

1. The qualities of faith such as the worship of one God which elevates an employee above servitude to others and establishes within him the truth of the equality of all employees. So that he neither yields nor bows down his head to any but to one the absolute. The result is that an employee will enjoy true liberty, which radiates from within his conscience following his realization of the fact that there is only one power and one Lord in this world.
2. Godliness is the second quality of dignified humanity. This quality determines for an employee the source from which he derives his concepts, values, criteria, considerations, doctrines, laws and whatever brings him into relation with Allah. Thus equity and justice replace personal desires and self-interest. This strengthens the believer's realization of value of his life and above all strictly mundane values. He derives directly from Allah and which therefore rank highest in value and the most sound and the most deserving of devotion and esteem.
3. A third quality of faith and dignified humanity is the clarity of the relationship between creator and the created; the restricted creature is connected with the ever lasting Truth without any mediator. It supplies an employee's heart with light, his soul, with contentment and gives him confidence and purpose. It estimates

from his mind perplexity fear, anxiety and agitation as well as lawful haughtiness on earth and unjustifiable tyranny over people.

4. Steadfastness along the path ordained by Allah is the next quality of such employees. This must be maintained so that good does not occur casually, incidentally or without deliberations but springs from definite motives and heads towards certain aims.
5. Another quality is belief in the dignity of an employee in the sight of Allah. This heightens an employee's regard for himself and restrains him from aspiring for a position higher than that which the creator has defined for him. For an employee to feel that he is dignified in Allah's sight is the loftiest conception he may attain of himself.
6. Purity of motivation is yet another quality of the dignified humanity established by faith. This directly follows the realization of an employee's dignity in Allah's sight. His supervision over men's conscience and His knowledge of their innermost undertakings. The moral human being whom the theories of Freud, Karl Marx and their type are not deformed is bashful that another human being may come to know what coincidental unhealthy feelings the awesome presence of Allah in his innermost consciousness and his awareness makes him tremble. He therefore attends to self-purification and spiritual cleansing. He feels that Allah's supervision over him. It stimulates within him healthy awareness, sensitivity, and foresight. It is a responsibility towards all humanity in relation to goodness, pure and simple. The worker feels all these in every action. He achieves a higher degree of self-respect and calculates the results before taking any steps. He is of value in the world and the whole realm of existence and has a role in its smooth running.
7. The final quality is an employee's elevation above greed for worldly gains and the choice of Allah's richer, ever lasting reward for which all employees should strive as the Quran directs them to do and which results in elevation, purification, and cleaning of

their souls. The believer has to move between this life and the next and between the heavens and the earth. The elevation of an employee lessens his anxiety about the results and fruits of his deed. He does well only because it is good and Allah requires it. It is never his concern whether it leads to further goodness in his own short lifetime. Allah, for whom he performs the good, never dies nor does He forget nor ignore any of employee's deeds. The reward is not to be received here for this life is not the last. Thus the believer acquires the power to continue to perform good deeds sustaining by their over whelming belief. This is that guarantees that doing well becomes a deliberate way of life and not a casual incident or motiveless event.

8. When this belief is entrenched in human being, who offers full explanation of human existence, the heart is purged of all impurities. An employee's heart is released from all the bondages or ties except those of the one and unique being.
9. When the human heart releases itself all shackles, false ideas, evil desires, and fear of earthly powers, it is cleared of all confusions.
10. When the reality of Allah is established in the human mind, the heart feels nothing but Allah in the whole universe.
11. When this stage is reached an employee attributes every movement of his life to the first cause event, i.e. Allah, Apparent causes do not disturb him. The mind is released of all anxieties and tensions associated with the apparent causes. The Quran establishes this truth in the Muslim concept of faith. It has put side apparent causes and associated events directly with the will of Allah.
12. He says, "When you threw (a handful of dust) it was not your act, but Allah's" (Q : 8: 17). "There is no triumph except that given by Allah" (Q : 8: 10 and Q : 3: 126). "You have no will except as Allah will's" (Q : 76: 30).
13. From this concept of the unity of Allah a perfect path of life based on the explanation of human existence

and whatever outlooks, feelings and traits it stimulates. Such a path is based on the worship of Allah alone, who is the real and permanent being and whose will is the only effective power in the world. From Him human beings receive their beliefs, outlook, values, criteria, legislation, institutions, systems, ethics and traditions. Such qualities must be obtained from the one and permanent being and one truth.

14. It is a path for performing activities, doing work and making scarifies absolutely and only for Allah, and for wishing to be nearer the truth. This path also strengthens the links of love, brotherhood, mutual sympathy and responsiveness between all beings and individual hearts.
15. The liberation of the human soul by priesthood and extreme spiritualism is available and easy to achieve but Islam does not approve of it because according to it, man's vicegerency on earth and the leadership of mankind are a part of its divine path of liberation. This is a harder way that guarantees and secures the humanity of man and achieves the victory of the divine will within his being. This is the real liberation.
16. It is life in its entirety and religion in its totality and whatever results follow after it are no more than the natural fruits of its establishment in the hearts and minds of mankind. It is being considered as a foundation for the realistic and practical system of human life with its effects clearly appearing in legislation as well as in belief.

CONCLUSIONS

1. The present day civilization faces the problem of meaning of life and meaning of quality of worklife. Employees become cynical, feel bore because they have lost the meaning of life. Tawheed gives them the meaning of life and enriches them their experience about working life.
2. It provides them a motivational basis in their job life. The concept of Tawheed makes them do the work not

for external motivators like money, fear of supervision, working condition, fringe benefits, recognition, autonomy and host of other motivators. They do the work to satisfy, nay to please his creator, seeking the pleasure of the creator, because summom bonum of their work lives is to seek the pleasure of God.

3. An employee to be qualitative employee will have to get rid of anxiety, and fear. By internalizing Tawheed in worker's mind is freed of all apparent reasons and tensions associated with these reasons. It is a mind, which experiences decision of God in all aspects of working life. Such mind alone can be totally productive and creative. Creativity in production demands that mind should be free of all shackles of superstitious, unproductive thoughts, false ideas, etc. He is always contact with God which gives him a feeling of strength, denied to non-believer.
4. An employee who is influenced by Tawheed is not worried about task autonomy, task significance, task variety, which are luxuries given by western thought. He works whatever be the type of work, for him work is ordained by God.

Notes and References

1. Al Tawheed: Its implications for thought and life by Ismail Raja al Baroque, International Institute of Islamic Thought Herndon, Virginia, U.S.A., 1995.
2. All is the creator of the heavens and earth. Nothing is like unto him. He is All Hearing. Allah seeing (Q : 42:11). Transcendent is He beyond all their descriptions of Him (Q : 6: 100). Sight can never reach him. His sight reaches all things (Q : 6: 103).
3. Proclaim: Allah is one, Eternal. He neither begets nor is begotten. Nothing is ever comparable to him (Q : 112: 60). They ascribed the Jinn as associates to Allah, (though Allah did create the Jinn). They even ascribed to Him sons and daughters. All this they did with no knowledge (Q : 6: 100).
4. O, have they chosen a deity from the earth who raises the dead? If there were them gods besides Allah, then verily both (the heaven and the earth) would have been disordered. Glorified by Allah, the Lord of the throne from all that they ascribed (to Him). He will not be questioned as to that which He does but they will be questioned. Or have they chosen other deities besides Him? Say: Bring your proof (60 their deity) .... (Q : 21: 21-4).

5. As to the patterns of Allah is creation, you will never find exception. The patterns of Allah are immutable (Q : 35: 43).
6. (Righteous are) those who ponder the creation of heaven and earth and affirm. "I Allah you have not created this creation in vain" (Q : 3: 191) certainly, we have not created heaven and earth and what is in between in sport (Q : 21: 16).
7. [Allah] who created everything and did so perfectly (Q : 32: 7). . . . [Allah] who created and perfected His creature (Q : 87: 2). . . . [Allah] who made for you the earth a place of settlement, to firemen a protective canopy and who formed you in the best of forms (Q : 40: 64). . . . To everything Allah has prescribed its nature and fixed its place in the eternal orders (Q : 36: 12).
8. Allah is the Lord of heaven and earth. He created all things. To each and everything He prescribed its measure (its character, course or destiny) (Q : 25: 2) say: Nothing will happen to us except what Allah has decreed for us (Q : 9: 51)
9. This is the lesson of the dramatic account given in the Quran of the Amana-Allah offered to nature, but which nature could not bear, and which man voluntarily accepted and carried. In essence, it is the moral principle that taklif (Obligation) necessarily implies qudrah (capability to act) and ikhtiyar (freedom to choose) (Q : 33: 72).
10. I (Allah) have not created jinn and humans but to serve me (Q : 51: 56).... [Allah] who created life and death you may prove yourselves worthy in your deeds (Q : 67: 2).
11. *Ibid.*
12. The seven heavens and the earth, and all that are in those, praise (obey), Allah nothing exists but it praises (obeys) Allah (Q : 17: 44).
13. And they [all humans] shall be reckoned with (Q : 21 : 23) (There are numerous other passages in the Quran whose main support is the affirmation of man's responsibility)
14. This is what Islam understands by the idea of hisab. Yawn al Hisab is the Day of Judgment. The idea that Allah (SWT) is going to reckon (to do hisab) with human is ubiquitous in the Quran and it may be said to be the very foundation of the whole moral/religious system.
15. Any casual reading of the Quranic surah(s) revealed in Makah will confirm this understanding of Allah's relation to man as covenantal. It is equally the understanding of all previous prophets and their followers. The same covenantal spirit provides the religious and moral foundation of the ancients. It is evident in Mesopotamia's Enema Elisha and the code of law of hip pit Ishtar and Hamunvabi. See James B. Pritchard, Ancient near Eastern Texts (Princeton: Princeton University Press, 1955).
16. In the shade of the Quran by Sayyid Qutb, Vol. 30, Crescent Publishing Company, Aligarh-20200.

5

Motivational Basis in Islamic Paradigm

After the chapter Tawheed, the next one is motivational basis in Islamic paradigm. Many organizations incorrectly view motivation as a personal trait, i.e. some have it and others not. Some managers label employees who lack motivation as lazy. Such a label assumes that an employee is always lazy or is lacking in motivation. Motivation is the result of the interactions of the individual and the situation. But employees differ in their basic motivational drive.

Motivation is the willingness to exert oneself towards organizational goals, conditioned by the ability to satisfy some individual needs. But general motivation is concerned with effort towards a goal.

If an employee who has such a need will exert himself utmost to achieve the organization goals. The above definition has three elements such as need, effort and organizational goal. The effort element is a measure of intensity. When an employee is motivated, he or she tries hard. Therefore motivation is a need satisfying process.

THEORIES OF MOTIVATION

The motivation concepts were developed in the year 1950s. Three specific theories were formulated during this period. They are best-known explanation for employee's motivation. They are the hierarchy of needs theory.

Hierarchy of Needs Theory

The most well known theory of motivation is Abraham Maslow's hierarchy of needs.[1] He hypothesized that within every human being there exists a hierarchy of five needs. These needs are:

1. *Physiological*: It includes food, shelter, thirst, clothing, sex and other bodily needs.
2. *Safety*: It includes security and protection from physical and emotional harm.
3. *Social*: It includes affection, belongingness, acceptance and friendship.
4. *Esteem*: It includes internal esteem factors such as self-respect.
5. *Self-actualization*: The drive to become what one is capable of becoming: includes growth, achieving one's potential and self-fulfilment.

As each of these becomes substantially satisfied, the next need becomes dominant. From the motivation point, the theory would say that although no need is even fully gratified, a substantially satisfied need no longer motivates. If an employer wants to motivate an employee according to Maslow, employer has to understand what level of the hierarchy that employee had and focusing as satisfying those needs at or above that level.

Maslow separated the five needs into higher order needs and lower-order needs. Physiological and safety needs were described as lower order needs and social, esteem and self-actualization as higher order needs. The difference between the two orders was made on the promise that higher order needs are satisfied internally (within the person), whereas the lower order needs are satisfied externally (as pay, union contracts, etc.). The natural conclusion drawn from Maslow's classification is that in times of economic plenty, almost all permanent employees have their lower-order needs substantially met.

CRITICISM OF MASLOW THEORY

The research does not validate the theory. Maslow provided no empirical substantiation and several studies that sought to validate the theory found no support for it.[2] One researcher reviewed the evidence and concluded that 'although of great societal popularity, need hierarchy as a theory continues to receive little empirical support'.[3]

Furthermore, the researcher stated that the available research should certainly generate a reluctance to accept unconditionally the implication of Maslow's hierarchy.[4]

THEORY X AND THEORY Y

Douglas McGregor proposed two different views of human beings: one basically negative labelled theory X and the other basically positive, labelled theory Y.[5] McGregor concluded that an employer's view of human beings is based on a certain grouping of assumptions and that he or she tends to hold his or her behaviour towards employees according to these assumptions.

Under theory X, the four assumptions held by an employer are :

1. Employees inherently dislike work and whenever possible, will attempt to avoid it.
2. Since employees dislike work, they must be coerced, controlled or threatened with punishment to achieve goals.
3. Employees will avoid responsibilities and seek formal direction whenever possible.
4. Most workers place security above all other factors associated with work and will display little attention.

In contrast to these negative views about the nature of employees, McGregor listed the four positive assumptions that he called theory Y.

1. Employees can view work as being as natural as rest or play.
2. Employees will exercise self-direction and self-control if they are committed to the objectives.
3. The average employee can learn to accept, even seek, responsibility.
4. The ability to make innovative decisions is widely accepted.

From the above, theory X assumes that lower order needs dominate individuals. Theory Y assumes that higher-order needs dominate individuals. McGregor himself held to the belief that theory Y assumptions were more valid than theory X. Therefore; he proposed such ideas as participative decision-making, responsible and challenging jobs and good group relations as approaches that would maximize an employee's motivation.

CRITICISM OF X AND Y THEORY

There is no evidence to confirm that either set of assumptions is valid or that accepting theory Y assumptions and altering one's actions accordingly will lead to more motivated employees.

MOTIVATION—HYGIENE THEORY

The motivation—psychologist Frederick Herzberg[6] proposed hygiene theory. In the belief that an individual's relation to his or her work is a basic one and that his or her attitude towards his work can determine the individual's success or failure. Herzberg investigated the question, "what do people want from their jobs?" He asked people to describe, in detail, situations when they felt exceptionally good and bad about their jobs. These responses were tabulated and categorized. From the categorized responses, Herzberg concluded that the replies people gave when they felt good about their jobs were significantly different from the responses given when they felt bad.

The intrinsic aspects of work such as achievement, advancement, recognition, the work itself and growth are related to job-satisfaction. They are called motivators. The extrinsic factors such as working conditions, salary, job-security, company policy, supervisors and interpersonal relations are called hygiene factors. When they are adequate, employees will not be dissatisfied. Herzberg suggests emphasizing on the motivators.

CRITICISMS OF HERZBERG THEORY

1. The procedure that Herzberg used is limited by its methodology. When things are going well, employees tend to take credit themselves, contrarily; they blame failure on the external environment.
2. Herzberg assumes that there is a relationship between satisfaction and productivity. But the research methodology he used looked only at satisfaction, not at productivity. To make such research relevant, one must assume a high relationship between satisfaction and productivity.[7]

Contemporary Theories of Motivation

These theories represent the current state of the art in explaining employee motivation.

(a) ERG Theory

Clayton Alderfer of Yale University has reworked Maslow's need hierarchy with the empirical research. His revised need hierarchy is labelled as ERG theory.[8] Alderfer argues that there are three groups of core needs, existence, relatedness and growth. Hence it is called ERG theory. The existence group is concerned with basic material existence requirements. It includes basic physiological and safety needs. The second groups of needs are those of relatedness—the desire for maintaining interpersonal relationship. It includes social and status needs, and the last growth needs—an intrinsic desire for personal development. It includes self-actualization.

Criticism: There is also evidence that it doesn't work in some organizations.[9]

(b) McClelland's Theory of Needs

David McClelland and his associates[10] developed McClelland's theory of needs. The theory focuses on three needs: achievement, power and affiliation. They are defined as follows:

> *Need for achievement*: The drive to excel, to achieve in relation to a set of standards, to strive to succeed.
> *Need for affiliation*: The desire for friendly and close interpersonal relationships.

Some employees have a compelling drive to succeed. They are striving for personal achievement rather than the rewards of success *per se*. They have a desire to do something better or more efficiently than it has been done before. This drive is the achievement need. McClelland found that high achievers differentiate themselves from others by their desire to do things better.[11]

Need for power is the desire to have impact, to be influential, and to control others. Employees, who have a high need for power enjoy being 'in-charge', strive to influence over others, prefer to be placed into competitive and status-oriented situation, and tend to be more concerned with prestige and giving influence over others than with effective performance.

Those employees who have a need for affiliation will strive for friendship, prefer-co-operative situations rather than the competitive ones, and desire relationships, involving a high degree of mutual understanding.

(c) Cognitive Evaluation Theory

In the late 1960's one researcher proposed that the introduction of extrinsic rewards, such as pay of work effort that had been previously intrinsically rewarding due to the pleasure associated with the context of the work itself would tend to decrease the overall level of motivation.[12] This proposal is called the cognitive evaluation theory.

This theory suggests that when extrinsic rewards are used by organization as payoff for superior performance, the intrinsic rewards, which are derived from employees doing what they like, are reduced. In other words, when extrinsic rewards are given to someone for performing an interesting task, it causes intrinsic interest in the task itself to decline.

The explanation is that the employee experiences a loss of control over his own behaviour so that the previous intrinsic motivation diminishes. Furthermore the elimination of extrinsic rewards can produce a shift from an external to an internal explanation.

CRITICISM OF THE THEORY

In reality of the extrinsic rewards stopped, the employee will not be part of the organization. The evidence indicates that very high intrinsic motivation levels are strongly resistant to the detrimental impacts of extrinsic rewards.[13] Even when a job is inherently interesting, there still exists a powerful norm for extrinsic payment.[14] At the other extreme, the extrinsic rewards appear to increase intrinsic motivation.[15] Therefore, the theory may have limited application to work organizations.

(d) *Goal Setting Theory*

In the late 1960's, Edwin Locke proposed that intentions to work toward a goal are a major source of work motiavation.[16] Goals tell an employee what needs to be done and how much effort will need to be expanded.[17] The evidence strongly supports the value of goals. The specific goals increase performance that difficult goals when accepted result in higher performance than do easy goals; and that feedback leads to higher performance than doe's non-feedback.[18]

If factors like ability and acceptance of the goals are held constant, we can say that employee can accept the more difficult the goal, the higher the level of performance. But once an employee accepts a hard task, he or she will exert a high level of effort until it is achieved, lowered or abandoned.

(e) *Equity Theory*

Equity theory[19] says that the employees compare their job inputs and outcomes with those of others and then respond so as to eliminate any inequities. There are four referent comparisons that an employee can use :

1. *Self-inside*: An employee's experiences in a different position inside his or her current organization.
2. *Self-outside*: An employees experience in a situation or position outside his or her current organization.
3. *Other-inside*: Another individual or group of individuals inside the employee's organization.
4. *Other-outside*: Another individual or group of individuals outside the employee's organization.

Employees will compare themselves to friends, neighbours, co-workers, colleagues in other organization, or past jobs they themselves have had. Equity theory recognizes that individuals are concerned not only with the absolute amount of rewards for their efforts but also with the relationship of this amount to what others receive.

(f) Expectancy Theory

One of the most widely accepted explanation of motivation is Victor Vroom's expectancy theory.[20] Expectancy theory argues that the strength of a tendency to act in a certain way depends on the strength of an expectation that the act will be followed by a given outcome and on the attractiveness of that outcome to the individual. Expectancy theory says that an employee will be motivated to exert a high level of effort when he or she believes that effort will lead to a good performance appraisal, that a good appraisal will lead to organizational rewards like a bonus, a salary increase, or a promotion, and that the rewards satisfy the employee's personal goals. The theory focuses on three relationships—

1. *Effort-performance relationship*: The probability perceived by the individual that exerting a given amount of effort would lead to performance.
2. *Performance reward relationship*: The degree to which the individual believes that performing at a participation level will lead to performance.
3. *Rewards personal goals relationship*: The degree of which organizational rewards satisfy individual's personal goals or needs and the attractiveness of those potential rewards for the individual.

ISLAMIC CRITIQUE OF QUALITY OF WORKLIFE AND MOTIVATION THEORIES

The quality of worklife movement started by western thinkers basically relates to motivational and working milieu of an organization. QWL concept was known as job-satisfaction previously. The new terminology used for humanizing the work situation is quality of worklife. With major component of QWL concept is creating an environment in which the motivational levels of the employees reach to their peak points. Therefore, it is pertinent to offer Islamic criticism of the above theories of motivation and the QWL concept itself.

All the above theories postulated that an employee has certain set of needs. These needs are his goals. Motivation is goal directed behaviour. Therefore, to increase motivational levels of employees an organization should provide need fulfilment.

Maslow[21] believes that there are five needs of human-being, i.e. physiological, safety, social, esteem and self-actualization. Maslow described a human-being as a bundle of needs which must be satisfied. He pointed out that only ten percent of the population in western countries satisfies self-actualization need.

The ontological assumption is that human-being is self-actualizing. Is he really self-actualizing? Nobody has an answer. Similarly, Theory X and Y offer certain assumption above human nature. Theory X manager makes certain assumption about indolence, lethargic, work shirking, nature of employees. Theory Y managers are suppose to make positive assumptions of nature of their subordinates. Again this theory relies on unproved assumption about human nature. This human nature really an evil as made out by Douglas McGregor? Is it really an angelic as pointed by McGregor? Though not stated expressly, he advocated in his theory as well as in his personal life. McGregor advocated Theory Y assumption. This is over simplification of human nature. This leads us to question? What exactly is human nature? To get answer to this question we should turn divine guidance.

Herzberg[22] postulated that the job satisfaction is different from job-dissatisfaction. According to this theory job-satisfaction is caused by what is called by a set of motivator's recognition, growth, advancements, work itself and achievement. According to him provision of motivators provides job-satisfaction to an employee and job-satisfaction will leads to better performance. The theory postulated that hygiene factors such as company policy, salary, supervision, inter-personal relations are context factors and provision of these will not lead to job-satisfaction and consequently motivation. But non-availability of these context factors will lead to job-dissatisfaction, and will have no impact on motivation. This according to Herzberg is due to two parts of human nature postulated by western philosophical thought.

According to this thinking human being is partly animal and partly human. The animal nature of human being avoids those situations, which cause pain. Therefore, non-provisions of context or hygiene factors will lead to job dissatisfaction. But there is human being in an employee and satisfaction of motivational needs of an employee will appear to his higher self and leads to better performance. Here again human beings viewed as a bundle of needs, which must be satisfied. The basic assumption is that an employee has two natures—animal and human is questionable?

McClelland's[23] conceptualization of human needs such as need for achievement, need for power, need for affiliation, again reflects the western thinking about their preoccupation with human being as a set of needs. It is a piety that the western thinkers have reduced employees to needs satisfying machines. What a baser description of human nature! On the contrary divine guidance informs us that human nature is the best of creation. The book of the Creator of the universe describes human beings as "Ashraful Maqluqat" (The best of creations).

Ironically for the fifty years, many organizations in the western countries and some organizations Muslim countries believed these theories and designed work situation on the basis of the prescription offered by western psycho-philosophical thought. The results can be seen by one and all: A new theory replaces the older one.

ISLAMIC THEORY OF MOTIVATION

In Islamic framework, general motivation stems from the

need of the man to seek pleasure of Allah. It is an internal state which makes an employee to seek 'raza' (pleasure) of Allah.

Islamic theory of motivation postulates that:

1. Human needs are to be satisfied by human beings; Islam does not advocate complete asceticism according to the Holy Quran.
2. However, human needs should be controlled, according to the requirement of sharia: unbridled human needs will lead to misery in this world.
3. Man has got inherent tendency to seek the pleasure of God. This is rooted in the psyche nature of man. This is ultimate need of a man. This need has to be realized in this life, in his/her mundane life.
4. The inner urge to seek the pleasure of God is ingrained in human mind before his birth. Every human being is born with innate capacity to know Allah and his unity. He is equipped with potentiality to get full knowledge of his creator.

According to Islamic theology, yhere are four-lives of human beings, viz.

I. Alame-arwah (Spiritual Life Before Birth)

All the souls of human beings were created from soul of Adam to last surviving human being. The purpose of creation of human souls without physical body is beautifully explained in the following verse:

> "He created man from a clot. Read and your.
> Lord is most Honourable who taught (to write)
> With the pen, Taught man what he knew not"
>
> —(Q : 96 : 25)
>
> "He created man: taught him the mole of expression".
>
> —(Q : 55: 3-4)
>
> "We have indeed created man in the best of moulds. Then do we abase him (to be) the lowest of the low except such as believe and do righteous deeds, for they shall have a reward unfailing". —(Q : 95: 5-6)

> "By the soul and the proportion and order given to it, and its enlightenment as to its wrong and its rights".
>
> —(Q : 91 : 7-8)
>
> "Glorify the name of your Lord, the most high that creates them makes complete. And who makes things according to a measure, then guides".
>
> —(Q : 37 : 1-3)

Therefore, every human being at the time of birth has an innate capacity to identify is creator. That is the reason why in Muslim theology postulates that every child is every Muslin. Every child—be it Hindu, Christian, Jew—is a Muslim. This innate urge of identifying himself with his creator is carried over to Alame-e-Duniya, i.e. this present world. Even in Alame-e-Duniya, i.e. mundane life when faced with extreme situation in which human being gives us hope of getting any source has innate urge to look to this creator for help. This urge is to be found not only among Muslims but among all human beings including Christians, Jews and Hindus. All polytheist, when they are in dangerous situation call for help from their creator. This beautifully explained in the Holy Quran.

> Say "Who is it
> That delivers you
> From the dark recesses
> Of land and sea,
> When ye call upon Him
> In humility
> And in secrete:
> If he only delivers us
> From these (dangers)
> (We vow) we shall truly
> Show our gratitude?" —(Q : 6 : 63)
>
> "Or, who listen to the
> Distressed when he calls
> On Him, and who relieves
> His suffering, and makes you

(Mankind) inheritors of the earth
(Can there be another) god
Besides Allah? Little it is
That he heed! —(Q : 27 : 62)

II. Alame-Duniya (Earthy Life)

In Alame-Duniya every human-being carries the impression he has ingrained of his creator in Alame-Arwah. Moreover, every human being has a soul in which Allah had breath. Therefore, the Holy breath of Allah is to be found. The Quran an this point explains this :

"He it is who created from clay" —(Q : 6 : 2)

"Surely I am going to create to mortal of the essence of black mud fashioned in shape. So when I have made him complete and breathed into him of my spirit, fall down making obeisance to him". —(Q : 25 : 28-29)

"O people: if you are in doubt about the raising then surely we created you from dust, then from a small life germ, then from a clot, then from a lump of flesh complete in make and incomplete, that We may make clear to you, and We cause what We please to stay in the wombs till an appointed time, them We bring you forth as babies, then that you may attain your maturity; and of you is he Who is caused to die, and of you is He Who is brought back to the worst part of life, so after that having knowledge he does not know anything". —(Q : 22 : 5)

"This is the knower of the unseen and the seen, the Mighty, the Merciful, Who made good everything that He has created and He began the created of man from dust. Then he made his progeny of an extract of water held in light estimation, and then He made him complete and breathed into him of His spirit". —(Q : 32 : 6-9)

This soul of human being is an about in which the Holy breath of Allah exist. Evidently every human being has innate desire to go back to his creator and to work exclusively for seeking His pleasure. The relationship between soul and the creator is the relationship of love between two lovers. A soul, which has face separation from the creator, wants to see and get back to the creator. In this world the human soul has a burning desire to do think which please his love. Its lover—its creator, its sustainer, its nourisher. The mission of Prophet (SAW) is not to convey something a new to human-beings, but it is just remaining what human soul forgotten due to lapse of time. Pointing out the role of Prophets in conveying the message of Allah. The Holy Quran says :

"O ye children of Adam!
Whenever there come to you
Messengers from amongst you
Rehearsing my signs into you,
Those who are righteous
And mend (their lives),
On them shall be no fear
Nor shall they grave". —(Q : 7 : 35)

Say; "O men! I am sent—
Unto you all, as the messenger
Of Allah, to whom belonged
The dominion of the heavens
And the earth; there is no god
But He: it is He that gives
Both life and death. So believe
In Allah and His Messenger,
The unlettered Prophet,
Who believeth in Allah?
And His words: Follow him
That (so) ye may be guided". —(Q : 7 : 158)

"We have truly sent thee
As a witness, as a
Bringer of Glad Tidings,
And as a Warner;
In order that ye
(O men) may believe
In Allah and His Messenger,
That ye may assist
And honour Him,

And celebrate His praises
Morning and Evening". —(Q : 48 : 8-9)

This shows that the job of a Prophet (SAW) is to re-established the relationship of servitude between the creator and human being. The innate desire to do those acts which please His creator is called RAZA-YE-ILAHI. Islamic theology postulates that the summom bonum of human life is to seek pleasure of God. Even prophets including last Prophet (SAW) has been asked by the creator to seek and to do things exclusively to get God's pleasure. The Holy Quran says :

"We sent not a messenger
Except (to teach) in the language
Of his (own) people, in order
To make (things) clear to them
So Allah leads astray
Those whom He pleases
And guides whom He pleases
And He is exalted in power,
Full of Wisdom". —(Q : 14 : 4)

III. Alame-Barzakh (Spiritual Life After Death)

"It is Allah that takes
The souls (of man) at death
And those that die not
(He takes) during their sleep
Those on whom He
Has passed the decree
Of death, He keeps back
(From returning to life)
But the rest He sends
(To their bodies)
For a term appointed
Verily in this are signs
For those who reflect". —(Q : 39 : 42)

The mystery of life and death, sleep and dreams, is a fascinating enigma, of which the solution is perhaps beyond the ken of man. In death we surrender our physical life, but our soul does not die; it goes back to a plane of existence in which it is more conscious of the realities of the spiritual world: "Allah takes the soul".

IV. Alame-akhirath (Life After Death)

"Everyone shall taste the death". —(Q : 3 : 185)

"Whoever you are, death will overtake you
Through you remain in lofty towers
Death is inevitable". —(Q : 4 : 78)

Everyman is a mortal whether he is rich or poor; high or low, scientist or philosopher, saint or sinner. No one can avoid death. Death snatches away affectionate children from loving breasts of weeping mothers, husbands from the consoling bosom of their wives, a rich man from the heap of his fortune, a king from his subject. It spares no mortal on the face of the earth.

Man is composed of body, life and soul. Life infuses vigour and vitality into the body of man. Body ceases to function when life departs, and this stage is called death. Life pertains to this ephemeral world. Soul, which is of greater importance than life, gathers impression in this life and its real functions commence in the life after death. It is a turning point of man's life from the physical world to the eternal one.

It is only the prophet's who can describe it because they see all such happenings by the "Divine light" which has been given to them by the creator. The object of the body is to carry the soul to the required stage from where the soul is to begin to attain the love of Allah. The prophet (SAW) has said,

"Value five things before five things;
Your youth before your old age;
Your healths before you fall ill;
Your riches before you become poor;
Your leisure before your occupation; and
Your life before your death"
"Soul is from the order of Allah". —(Q : 17 : 85)

"Verily I created man from clay; so I fashioned
Him and instilled in him from my own spirit"—(Q : 32 : 9)

Therefore, the soul is a special diving thing. The object of soul is to attain to its original source, i.e. Allah. It must return to its source as body returns to earth. Allah is love soul strives to attain love.

"Nothing will avail of on that Day,
Property, sons, etc. except whom
Comes to Allah with a sound soul". —(Q : 26 : 88-89)

"It is only the soul that attains
Peace and perfection. It was the
Trust of this soul which was
Offered to the entire creation and
None except man accepts it". —(Q : 33 : 72)

Though, mundane life is important, mundane needs such as sex, wealth-seeking behaviour, need for accumulation of money/wealth are necessarily only to the extent they do not come in the way of the ultimate need of human being, i.e. seeking pleasure of God.

The following are the motivators for human being. The Holy Quran says,

"Fair in the eyes of men
Is the love of things they covet?
Women and sons;
Heaped up hoards
Of gold and silver; horses
Branded (for blood and excellence);
And (wealth of) cattle
And well-tilled land,
Such are the possessions
Of his world's life;
But with Allah
Is the best of the goals?
(To return to)". —(Q : 3 : 14)

From the above verse it is clear that sex is the dominating motive of human-being. Islam does not discourage sexual part of a human life, it is controlled. This control is also not unnatural, within certain limit prescribed by sharia, a human being gratify his/her sexual urge. Islamic literature has copious literature on regulating human sexual behaviour. The second motivator emphasize in the above verse is wealth-seeking. Desire for wealth and provision for future are not discouraged. The creator of mankind tells us that wealth-seeking behaviour is normal behaviour of a human being. This motive is recognized the second order of importance in the above verse. However, Islamic law imposes limitations within which this need is to be fulfilled. For example, desire for wealth alone as the end of life is not approved. A human being is required to shun all those economic activities such as interest dealings, selling of prohibited products, such as alcohol, drugs, etc. within the limits imposed by sharia, a human being can gratify this need. However, at the end the verse emphasize on the terminal value of a human, i.e. Falah (success) in the life hereafter. We should not be construed as seekers of Falah should give up the above mentioned. Sexual and monitory behaviour of life. The whole burden of the above verse that a human being should not sight of Falah in gratifying mundane needs.

ISLAMIC THEORY OF WORK MOTIVATION

A Muslim employee who has internalized this absolute and ultimate value of seeking pleasure of God always strives towards this goal in all aspects of his/her behaviour, be it in relationship with his subordinates, colleagues, company policies, and work itself. He has acquired meaning of work; work is a way of seeking the pleasure of God. This galvanizes him/her to extent his utmost. In fact, this is called Jihad-e-Akbar. Jihad which has been translated as Holy war in English does not convey the true shade of meaning. Jihad means exerting one's utmost in his/her endeavour.

This conceptualization of RAZA-YE-ILAHI (pleasure of God) is superior to self-actualization of western theories. Self-actualization for what? The Islamic theory of work motivation answers the question that self-actualization is for RAZA-YE-

ILAHI, (pleasure of God) for it is an inborn urge of human being.

From the above it is clear that an employee is always RAZA-YE-ILAHI's (pleasure of God) seeker and falah-seeker. Does it mean that he has no motives other than RAZA-YE-LLAHI (pleasure of God) in his job life? Yes, he has and should have other motives as a non-Muslim employee. He has need for power, need for affiliation, need for achievement, task autonomy, task variety, task significance, needs: He has desire for achievement, growth, advancement, work it, as postulated in western thought. These needs are totally sub-servant to RAZA-YE-ILAHI (pleasure of God) need. The basic difference between Islamic theory of motivation and western theory of motivation is that western behavioural scientist has over emphasized these needs. They have reduced human being to a need-seeking animal. This is totally one sided view of human nature. Human being is sublime; human being is sermon; human being has Holy Spirit of God in him. To reduce such a human being to autonomy-seeker, achievement-seeker, recognition-seeker, advancement-seeker, power-seeker, wealth-seeker, is totally product of the creative mind of the western thinker. This is not reality; this is not phenomena. The very fact that empirical research gives conflicting results which do not validate the theories shows that human thinking cannot be relied as exclusive source of knowledge. In an Islamic organization an employer should provide a minimum level of opportunities for the baser need fulfilment of the employees. The organization should provide and build up a culture of RAZA-YE-ILAHI (pleasure of God). It is that organization which provides this need satisfaction will be successful. The entire organization culture should provide falah as the motivational basis. This will galvanize the productivity, improve the results and workers put in the best performance.

An employee whenever he finds RAZA-YE-ILAHI (pleasure of God) need deficiency should stand before God and offer two rakahs nafil prayer. Whenever an employee wants to fulfil a need, he should stand before Allah and offer two rakahs of supererogatory prayer (Salat al-Hajrat). Afterwards, offer thanks giving and praise to Allah and invoke peace and blessings upon the Holy prophet (SAW). The Holy prophet (SAW) observed:

> "When someone seeks fulfilment of a need from Allah, he should first carefully perform ablution, say two rakahs of supererogatory prayer and then offer thanks giving and praise to the Lord; afterwards, he should invoke peace and blessings of Allah as the Holy prophet (SAW) and finally utter this prayer to Allah.

There is no duty save Allah the element the bountiful. Glory is to Allah, Lord of the magnificent Throne! Praise is to Allah, Lord of the Worlds! I beg of thee the means of (obtaining). They mercy and securing they pardon; participation in every righteousness and protection from every sin. Leave no sin or none unforgiving no anxiety unrelieved and let no need of nine unfulfilled wherewith thou art pleased. O thou the most merciful of those who show mercy!

—Tirmidhi, Ibn Majah

AL-JANNAH

Allah knows more about man and his nature.

> "Did we not assign into him two eyes and a tongue and two lips and guide him to the two highways (good and bad)". —(Q : 90 : 8-10)

> "Lo! We have shown him the way whether he be grateful or disbelieving". —(Q : 76: 3)

> "When the Lord said into the angels: Lo! I am about to create a mortal out of more". —(Q : 38: 71)

Since Allah created us, He is the one who knows us the best, we understand ourselves from the Quran.

The word AL-JANNAH refers to Heaven or Paradise. The main aim of any Muslim employee is to enter Heaven. This factor motivates him to get the pleasure of God. It is a reward given by God for his life including worklife. Heaven is a place where a rewarded employee can see the sight of reality and divine beauty, which is more pleasant than the all the pleasures.

> "The rewarded employee will be the one who will enjoy the sight God every morning and evening, and then he recites the following verse of the Quran Some faces on that will been (in brightness and beauty) looking towards their Lord". —(Q : 80: 22-23)

The following verses are quoted in the Quran about Heaven:

> "To those who believe and work righteousness, that their portion is Gardens, Beneath which rivers flow, every time they are fed with fruits therefrom, they say; "Why, this is what we were fed with before" for they are given things in similitude; And they have therein spouses purified and they abide there in (for ever)". —(Q : 2 : 25)

Heaven is Garden, which has beautiful landscape around rivers is flowing with crystal water and fruit trees of which the choicest fruit is before him. The employee can select and eat, as he likes:

> "Say: Shall I give you
> Glad tidings of things
> For better than those?
> For the righteous are Gardens
> In nearness to their Lord
> With rivers flowing beneath;
> Therein is their eternal home;
> With spouses purified
> And the good pleasure of Allah
> For in Allah's sight
> Are (all) his servants? —(Q : 3 : 15)

> "On the other hand, for those
> Who fear their Lord?
> Are Gardens, with rivers?
> Flowing beneath; therein

Are they to dwell (for ever?)
An entertainment from Allah;
Is the best (bliss?)
For the righteous" —(Q : 3-198)

"But those who believe
And do deeds of righteousness,
We shall soon admit to Gardens,
With rivers flowing beneath,—
Their eternal home:
Therein shall they have?
Spouses purified
We shall admit them
To shades, cool and ever deepening —(Q : 4 : 57)

"It any do deeds
Of righteousness,—
Be they male or female
And have faith,
They will enter Heaven,
And not the least injustice
Will be done to them". —(Q : 4 : 124)

"Allah will say: This is
A day on which
The truthful will profit
From their truth; theirs
Flowing beneath, there eternal
Home: Allah well-pleased
With them, and they with Allah;
That is the mighty Triumph
(The fulfilment of all desires)" —(Q : 5 : 189)

"Be holding the Garden before you!
Ye have been made
Its inheritors, for your
Deeds (of righteousness)" —(Q : 7 : 43)

"Their Lord doth give them
Glad tidings of a Mercy

From Himself, of His good pleasure.
And of Gardens for them,
Wherein are delights
That endure" —(Q : 9 : 21)

"They will dwell therein
For ever. Verily with Allah
Is a reward, the greatest (of all)" —(Q : 9 : 22)

"Allah hath promised to Believers,
Men and Women, Gardens
Under which rivers flow,
To dwell therein,
And beautiful mansions
In Gardens of everlasting stay
But the greatest bliss
Is the Good pleasure of Allah?
That is the supreme triumph" —(Q : 9 : 72)

"The righteous (will be)
Amid Gardens
And fountains
(Of clear-flowing water)" —(Q : 15 : 45)

"For them will be Gardens
Of Eternity; beneath them
Rivers will flow; they will
Be adored therein
With bracelets of gold,
Green garments of fine silk
And heavy brocade" —(Q : 18 : 31)

"Gardens of Eternity, those
Which (Allah) most Gracious
Has promised to His Servants
Is the unseen: for His promise
Must (Necessarily) come to pass"

"They will not there hear
Any vain discourse, but
Only salutations of peace
And they will have therein
Their sustenance, morning
And evening
Such is the Garden which
We give as an inheritance
To those of our servants
Who guard against evil" —(Q : 19 : 61-63)

"For those who believe
And do righteous deeds,
Are gardens as hospitable?
Homes, for their (good) deeds" —(Q : 32 : 19)

"Gardens of eternity will them
Enter: therein will they
Be adorned with bracelets
Of gold and pearls:
And their garments there
Will be of silk"
"And they will say:
Praise be to Allah,
Who has removed from us?
(All) sorrow: for our Lord
Is indeed oft-forgiving
Read to appreciate (service)" —(Q : 35 : 33-34)

"Fruits and they
(Shall enjoy) honour and dignity
In garden of delight
Facing each other
On raised couches
Round will be passed
To them a cup
From a clear flowing fountain
Crystal-white of a taste
Delicious to those
Who drink (thereof)" (Q : 37 : 41-49)

"This is a message
(Of admonition): and verily,
For the righteous
Is a beautiful place
Of (ferial) return
Gardens of eternity
Whose doors will (ever?)
Be open to them" —(Q : 38 : 49-50)

"Have been built:
Beneath them flow
Rivers: (such is) —(Q : 39 : 20)

"And those who feared
Their lord will be led
To the garden in groups
Until behold, they arrive there:
Its gates will be opened;
And its keepers will if say;

"Peace is upon you!
Well have ye done?
Enter ye here
To dwell therein
They will say: praise is
To Allah who has
Truly fulfilled his promise
To us, and has given us
(This) land in heritage
We can dwell in the Garden
As we will: how excellent
A reward for those
Who work (righteousness?)

"But those who believe and work
Righteous deeds will be
In the meadows
Of the gardens: they shall
Have, before their lord,
All that they wish for,

That will indeed be
The magnificent bounty
(Of Allah)
That is (the bounty) where of
Allah gives Glad Tidings
To his servants who
Believe and do righteous deeds" —(Q : 42 : 22-23)

"Those who have believed
In our signs and submitted (to us)
Enter ye the Garden,
Ye and your wives,
In (beauty and) rejoicing
To them will be passed
Round, dishes and goblets
Of gold, there will be" —(Q : 43 : 69-72)

"As to the righteous
(They will be) in
A position of security,
Among gardens and springs;
Dressed in fine silk
And in rich brocade
They will face each other
So: and we shall
Wed them to maidens
With beautiful, big
And lustrous eyes" —(Q : 44 : 51-54)

"(Here is) the description
Of the gardens which
The righteous are promised
In it are rivers
Of water installing
Rivers of milk
Of which the taste
Never changes: rivers
Of wine, a joy
To those who drink;
And rivers of honey

Pure and clear, in it
There are for them
All kinds of fruits
And forgiveness from their lord" —(Q : 47 : 15)

"And the garden
Will be brought nigh
To the righteous: no more
A thing, distant
(A voice will say)
This is what was
Promised for you
For every penitent
Heedful one
Who feared?
The most gracious unseen
And brought a heart
Turned in devotion (to him):"

"Enter ye therein
In peace and security
This is a day
Of eternal life!
There will be for them
There in all that they wish
And there is more
With us" —(Q : 50 : 31-35)

"As to the Righteous
They will be in Gardens
And in Happiness
Enjoying the (Bliss) which
Their Lord hath bestowed
On them, and their Lord
Shall deliver them from
The chastisement of the Fire
(To them will be said)
Eat and drink you,
With profit and health
Because of your (god) deeds" —(Q : 52 : 17-19)

"As to the Righteous
They will be in the midst
Of Gardens and Rivers
In a Sure abode with
A sovereign Omnipotent" —(Q : 54 : 54-55)

"There will be two Gardens-
Then which of the favours
Of your Lord will ye ḍeny?
Abounding in Branches
In them (each) will be
Two springs flowing (free)
In them will be fruits
Of every kind, two and two
They will recline on carpets
Whose inner livings will be?
Of rich brocade: the fruit
Of the Gardens will be
Near (and easy of reach)
In then will be (maidens)
Caste, restraining their glances
Whom no man or Jin
Before them has touched;
Like into zombies and Loral
Is the any reward?
For good other than good
Dark green in colour
(From plentiful watering
In them (each) will be
Two springs pouring for the water
In continuous abundance:
In them will be fruits
And dates and pomegranates
In them will be
Fair (Maidens) good, beautiful;
Maidens restrained (as to
Their glances) in (goodly) pavilions
Whom no man or join
Before them has touched
Reclining on green cushions

And rich carpets of beauty
Blessed be the name
Of thy lord
Full of majesty
Bounty and honour" —(Q : 55 : 46-78)

"These will be
Those nearest to Allah
In gardens of Bliss:
(They will be) on couches
Encrusted (with gold and precious stones)
Round about them will (serve)
Youths of perpetual (freshness)
With goblets, (shining) beakers,
And cups (filled) out of
Clear flowing fountains
And with fruits,
And that they may select,
And the flesh of fouls
And that they may desire
And (there will be) companions
With beautiful big,
And lustrous eyes,
Like unto pearls
Well guarded
A reward for the deeds
Of their past (life)" —(Q : 56 : 16-26)

"Be of those nearest to Allah
(There is for him) rest
And satisfaction and
A Garden of delights" —(Q : 56 : 88-89)

"Good news for you this day!
Gardens beneath which flow rivers!
To dwell therein for aye!
This is indeed
The highest Triumph" —(Q : 57 : 12)

"And he will be
In a life of bliss
In a garden on high
The fruits whereof
(Will hang in bunches)
Low and near
Eat ye and drink ye,
With full satisfaction
Because of the (good)
That ye sent before you,
In the days that are gone!" —(Q : 69 : 21-24)

"As to the righteous
They shall drink
Of a cup
Mixed with kafur
A fountain where
The devotees of Allah
Do drink, making it
Flow in unstinted abundance" —(Q : 76 : 5-6)

"A mixture of Tashim
To spring, from (the waters)
Where of drink
Those nearest to Allah" —(Q : 83 : 21-20)

"(Other) faces that day
Will be joyful
Pleased with their striving
In a garden on high
Where they shall hear
No (word) of vanity
Therein will be
A bubbling spring
Therein will be couches
(Of dignity) raised or high,
Goblets placed (ready)
And cushions set in Rous
And rich carpets
(All) spread out" —(Q : 88 : 8-16)

"Yea enter thou
My heaven" —(Q : 89: 30)

From the above verses, it is clear that the Allah's reward for his pleasure will motivate a Muslim employee to do the work. My heaven means Allah's own heaven. It is a reality and final bliss for all it is an inward state of joy and satisfaction. The good pleasure of Allah is the final bliss of salvation. The good pleasure is mutual. The truly saved is one whose will has been become completely identified with Allah's universal will.

The reward is felicity, happiness, achievement, salvation, the attainment or full filament of desires for Allah's good pleasure. Those who strive and work in Allah's cause are promised.

a. A mercy specially from himself
b. His own good pleasure
c. The garden of perpetual delights
d. The supreme reward

I. Garden

"The Garden" signifies their environment all they see about them. It will give comfort, rest, and satisfaction and a feeling of beauty and dignity. It is a beautiful landscape. The rivers are flowing with crystal waters and fruit trees of which the choicest fruit. The fruit of goodness is goodness.

II. Water

There are four kinds of drinking water:

1. The delicious, cool and pure water.
2. Milk, which never turns sour, whose taste is like that of fresh warm milk.
3. Wine, no like any wine an earth there is no intoxication. It is a joy to drink.
4. Honey, which is pure and clear with no admixture of ware or any foreign substance.

The above drinks will cool the spirit, feed the heart, warm the affections and sweeten the life.

III. Wine

The wine will be of the utmost purity and flavour, so precious that it will be protected with seal. The seal itself will be of costly material of musk, which is most highly esteemed in the east for its perfume. It will heighten the enjoyment and helping for digestion.

IV. Hur (Opposite Sex)

Heaven will have a society of companions of the opposite sex. They are very beautiful women in heaven. Their eyes are big wonder and beauty, prefiguring grace, and innocence. These beautiful women are like rubies and coral! They have a pink or red of a beautiful complexion. There are finest and most costly ornaments to wear and beautiful clothes to wear. The clothes will be green colour and most refreshing to eyes.

V. Fountains

The garden of heaven consists of fountain. There are three fountains namely tasnim, kafur and zanjabil.

Tasnim

It literally indicates height fullness and openness. It is the name of a heavenly fountain, whose drink is superior to that of the purest wine. It is the nectar drink by those nearest to Allah, but a flavour of it will be given to all.

Kafur

It is fountain in the realms of bliss. It is a seasoning added to the cup of pure, beautiful wine which causes no intoxication but stands for all that is agreeable, wholesome and refreshing. It is a cool and refreshing. It is a given as soothing tonic in eastern medicine.

Salsabil (Zanjabil)

The cup of kafur (camphor) was mentioned for coolness and refreshment to the righteous that had first passed to great event of judgment. The second stage is described when they enter the garden in garments of silk, and found that their former humility in the probationary life is rewarded with high honour in the new world that have entered. The third stage is where they settle down in bliss, with garments of silk and heavenly brocades, with ornaments and jewels, wit an ordered feast of set service, and the cup of zanjabil. This word literally means ginger. In eastern medicine ginger is administered to give warmth to the body and zest to the taste; that is appropriate for the royal feast.

The reward of heaven is said to be Allah's own nearness. It is Allah's good pleasure which raises the soul above itself. It is the state of permanent assurance and final bliss. The motivated Muslim employee will try for true and lasting values; this is the kind of pure bliss to aspire for, and not the fleeting enjoyment of this word, which is always leave a string behind.

In Muslim theology, there are three stages, which pass the human soul. First is Ammara, this soul seeks it satisfaction in the lower earthly desires. The second is the lawwama which self-reproaching soul feels conscious of sin and resist it and third and final is muthmainaa this is the final stage of bliss (i.e.) pleasure of God. For this the reward in heaven. This motivates the Muslim employee to do the work.

Hazrat Abu Huraira says that the Prophet had said, "God says that he has ready for his pious servants such boons that no eyes have seen or ears heard or which could even be guessed. You may read the following verse of the Quran if you like.

Now no one knows what delights of the eye are kept hidden (in reserve) for them—as a reward for their (good) deeds".

—Bukhari, Muslim

The Prophet had said, "Even a place (just enough) to hold a whip in paradise is better than all the paraphernalia of worldly life".

The Prophet had said, "The most prosperous man of this world will be brought before God and ordered to be thrown into hell and when the fire of the hell has had its full effect on his body he will be asked if he had ever seen good and ever lived in luxury? His reply will be in the negative, 'By God, never!' Then a man will be brought before God who had suffered much and lived under strained circumstances in the world and ordered to be sent to paradise and when the joys of paradise would have full effect on him he will be asked if he had ever met with difficulties and seen hardships and his reply will be: 'Never, Oh! God', have I suffered from want or seen hard times".

—Muslim

PUNISHMENT

The word punishment refers to Hell. A Muslim employee will never like to go to Hell on the Day of Judgment. He will seek the pleasure of God and prefer the reward Heaven. This fear of punishment motivates the Muslim employee to get the pleasure of God. There are large numbers of verses in the Quran regarding the Hell.

"Those who reject
Our signs. We shall soon
Cast into the fire:
As often as their skins
Are roasted through
We shall change them for fresh skins,
That they may taste
The chastisement: for Allah
Is Exalted in Power, Wise" —(Q : 4 : 56)

"When their eyes shall be turned
Towards the companions
Of the fire, they will say:
Our Lord! Send us not
To the company
Of the wrong-doers" —(Q : 7 : 46)

"The companions of the Fire
Will call to the companions
Of the Garden: Pour down
To us water or anything
That Allah doth provide
For your sustenance" —(Q : 7 : 50)

"I will fill Hell with Jinns
And men all to getter" —(Q : 11 : 119)

"In front of such a one
Is Hell, and he is given,
For drink, soiling fetid water" —(Q : 14 : 16)

"And thou wilt see
The sinners that day
Bound together in fetters:
Then garments of liquid pitch,
And their faces covered with Fire" —(Q : 14 : 49-50)

"But those who deny (their Lord)
For them will be cut-out
A garment of Fire
Over their heads will be
Poured out boiling water with it will be melted
What is within their bodies?
As well as (their) skins
In addition there will be
Maces of iron (to punish) them.
Every time they wish
To get away there from,
From anguish, they will be
Forced back therein, and
(It will be said) Taste ye
The chastisement of Burning!" —(Q : 22 : 19-22)

"Nay, they deny the Hour
(Of the judgment to come)
But Blazing Fire for such
As deny the Hour
When it sees them
From a place for off,
They will hear its fury
And its raging sighs" —(Q : 25 : 11-12)

"As to those who are
Rebellious and wicked, their abode
Will be the Fire: every time" —(Q : 32 : 20)

"This is the Hell
Of which ye were promised" —(Q : 56-63)

"Is that the better entertainment
Or the Tree of Zaqqum?
For we have truly
Made it (as) a trial
For the wrong-doers
For it is a tree
That springs out
Of the bottom of Hell-fire" —(Q : 37: 62-64)

"Verily the trees
Of Zaqqum
Will be the food
Of the sin feel
Like molten grass
It will boil
In their insides,
Like the boiling
Of scalding water
(A voice will cry)
Seize ye him
Into the midst
Of the Blazing Fire" —(Q : 44 : 42-47)

"Yea, such! But
For the wrong-doers
Will be an evil place
Of (Ferial) Return!
Hell—they will burn
Therein—an evil bed
(Indeed, to lie on)!" —(Q : 38 : 55-56)

"The sinners will be
In the punishment of Hell
To dwell therein (for aye)" —(Q : 43 : 74)

"The Day we will
Ask Hell, "Art thou
Filled to the full
It will say Are there
Any more (to come)" —(Q : 50 : 30)

"This is the Hell which
The sinners deny
In its midst
And in the midst
Of boiling hot water
Will they wonder round" —(Q : 55 : 43-44)

"(They will be) in the midst
Of a fierce Blast of Fire
And in Boiling water
And in the shades
Of Black smoke" —(Q : 56 : 42-44)

"Is the chastisement of Hell:
And evil is (such) destination
When they are cast therein,
They will hear
The (tenable) drawing in
Of its breath
Even as it blazes forth" —(Q : 67 : 6-7)

"Truly Hell is
As a place of ambush" —(Q : 78 : 21)

"And Hell Fire shall be
Placed in full view
For him who sees" —(Q : 79 : 36)

"Verily from (the height of)
Their Lord, that Day,
Will they be veiled
Further, they will enter
The Fire of Hell
Further, it will be said
To them: This is
The (reality) which ye
Rejected as false!" —(Q : 83 : 15-17)

"Some faces, that Day,
Will be humiliated,

Labouring (hard), weary
The while they enter
The Blazing Fire,
The while they are giving,
To drink, of a boiling
No food will there be
For them but a bitter Dhari
Which will neither nourish?
Not satisfy hunger" —(Q : 88 : 2-7)

"And Hell, that Day,
Is brought (face to face)
On that Day will man
Remember, but how will
That remembrance profit him?
He will say: Ah!
Would that I had
Sent forth (Good Deeds)
For (this) my (Future) life!"

"For that Day,
His chastisement will be
Such as none (else)
Can inflict, And His bonds
Will be such as none (other)
Can bind" —(Q : 89 : 23-26)

From the above verses it is clear that the reward of Hell on every Muslim employees for their work. This fear motivates the Muslim employee to get the pleasure of God. It is from Hazrat Adi bin Hatim that the Prophet had said, "On the Day of Judgment, every one of you will be face to face with his God".

The man at that time will be looking around (in wonder and helplessness) and his right he will see nothing but a record of his actions, while on the left also he will see the same and in from of him will be the raging fire. So "O people! Save yourself from the fire of Hell even it you can do it by just giving a piece of dry date". —Bukhari Muslim

Hell camouflaged with the pleasures of the world and paradise with hardships. The Prophet had said that hell was surrounded by pleasures and worldly desires while paradise was surrounded by labour and troubles.

The Prophet had said that he had seen nothing more fearful that hell but those wishing to avoid it were sleeping and he had not seen anything more pleasant than paradise but those wishing to gain it were sleeping. —Trimizi

Hazrat Abu Saeed and Abu Huraira say that the Prophet had said, "A Crier will address men of paradise and say, 'Here you will always remain healthy and never be sick, ever live and never die, always be young and never face old age, ever live in luxury and never face pain and trouble". —Muslim

Hazrat Noman bin Basheer says that the Prophet had said, "The person undergoing the lightest punishment in hell will be one whose sandals and their straps will be of fire which will make his brain boil as a kettle on the fire and he will think that no one is in greater pain that he although he will be the least suffering among the people of the hell". —Muslim

Hazrat Suhaib Roomi reports that the Prophet had said, "When men of paradise will be settle in their abodes God will ask them if they liked that He should give them something more. Men of paradise will reply, 'Hast not Thou brightened our faces, saved us from hell and given us paradise? (What else is there we shall desire now?)". The Prophet said, "Then the curtain will be lifted and they will see God face to face and nothing would be more pleasant to them than the sight of their Creator. The Prophet then recited this verse of the Quran: 'To those who do right there is a goodly (reward)—yea, more than in measure". —(Q : 10-26)

Hazrat Abu Musa says that the Prophet had said that whosoever loved this world caused loss to the next world and whosoever loved the nest world caused a loss to his present world. "So you should prefer the abiding thing over the transitory one". —Ahmad, Al-Baihiqi

NOTES AND REFERENCES

1. A. Maslow, Motivation and Personality, Harper & Ro, New York, 1954.
2. E.E. Lawler III and J.L. Suttle, "A Casual Correlation Test of the Need Hierarchy Concept, *Organizational Behaviour and Human Performance,*

April 1972, pp. 265-87; D.T. Hall and K.E. Nougaim, "An Examination of Maslow's Need Hierarchy in an Organization Setting", *Organizational Behaviour and Human Performance,* February 1968, pp. 12-35. And J. Rausehenberger, N. Schmitt and J.E. Hunter, "A Test of the Need Hierarchy concept by a Markor Model of change in Need Strength", *Administrative Science Quarterly,* December 1980, pp. 654-70.

3. A.K. Korman, J.K. Greenhaus, and I.J. Badin, "Personnel Attitudes and Motivation" in M.R. Rose and L.W. Porter (des), *Annual Review of Psychology* (Palo Alto, CA: Annual Reviews, 1977), p. 178.
4. M.A. Wahba and L.G. Bridwell, "Maslow Reconsidered; A Review of Research on the Need Hierarchy Theory, "*Organizational Behaviour and Human Performance,* April 1976, pp. 212-40.
5. D. McGregor, the Human side of Enterprise McGraw-Hill, New York, 1960. For an updated analysis of Theory X and Theory Y constructs, see R.J. Summbers and S.F. Cronshaw, "A study of McGregor's Theory X, Theory Y and Influence of Theory X, Theory Y Assumptions on casual Attributions, for Instances of Worker Poor performance", in S.C. McShare (ed), *Organizational Behaviour,* ASAC 1988 Conference Proceedings, Vol. 9, part 5, Halifax, Mova Scotia, 1988, pp. 115-23.
6. F. Herzberg, B. Mausher, and B. Synderman, The Motivation to work, John Wiley, New York: 1959.
7. R.J. House and L.A. Wigdor, "Herzberg's Dual Factor Theory of Job-Satisfaction and Motivation: A Review of the Evidence and Criticism", *Personnel Psychology,* Winter 1967, pp. 365-89; D.P. Schwab and L.L. Cummings. "Theories of Performance and Satisfaction : A Review, "Industrial Relations", October R. Braito, "A specification Issue in Job-Satisfaction Research", *Sociological Perspectives,* April 1988, pp. 175-97.
8. C.P. Alderfer, "An Empirical Test of a New Theory of Human Needs", *Organizational Behaviour and Human Performance,* May 1969, pp. 142-75.
9. J.P. Wanous and A. Zwany, "A Cross Sectional Test of Need Hierarchy Theory", *Organizational Behaviour and Human Performance,* May 1977, pp. 78-97.
10. David McClelland, The Achieving Society, van Nostrand Reinhold, New York, 1961. J.W. Atkinson and J.O. Raynor, Motivation and Achievement (Washington, D.C. Winstow, 1974); D.C McClelland, Power: The Inner Experience (New York: Irvington, 1975); and M.J. Stahl, Managerial and Technical Motivation: Assessing Needs for Achievement, Power and Affiliation, Praeger, New York, 1986.
11. McClelland, The Achieving Society.
12. R. De. Charms, Personal causation; The Internal Affective Determinants of Behaviour Academic Press, New York, 1968.
13. H.J. Arnold, "Effects of Performance Feedback and Extrinsic Reward upon High Intrinsic Motivation", *Organizational Behaviour and Human Performance,* Dec. 1976, pp. 275-88.
14. B.M. Staw, "Motivation in Organizations: Toward Synthesis and Redirections" in B.H. Staw and G.R. Salancik (Eds) *New Directions in Organizational Behaviour* (Chicago: St. Clain, 1977) p. 76.
15. B.J. Calder and B.M. Staw, "Self-perception of Intrinsic and Extrinsic Motivation", *Journal of Personality and Social Psychology,* April 1975, pp. 599-605.

16. E.A. Locke, "Toward a Theory of Task Motivation and Incentives", *Organization Behaviour and Human Performance*, May 1968, pp. 157-89.
17. P.C. Earley, P. Wojnaroski and W. Prest, "Task Planning and Energy Expended: Exploration of How Goals Influence Performance", *Journal of Applied Psychology*, February 1987 pp. 107-14.
18. G.P. Latham and G.A. Yukl, "A Review of Research on the Application of Goal Setting in Organizations", *Academy of Management Journal*, December 1975, pp. 824-45.
19. P.S. Goodman, "An Examination of Referents used in the Evaluation of Pay", *Organizational Behaviour and Human Performance*, October 1974, pp. 170-95.
20. V.H. Vroom, Work and Motivation, John Wiley, New York, 1964.
21. *Ibid.*
22. *Ibid.*
23. *Ibid.*

6

Stress Inoculation in Islam

Dear worker

"When you panic
You do things in Fear
The Moment you
Think of God (Allah)
Who is the creator of entire world, all praises to Him (Allah)
Speaks the word
Commit the acts
You know you are
In balance and control
You do good, feel happy
It is important to
Believe and have a faith in God
At the panic stage
When you sense the
Fear, panic, desperation
Belief and faith will fill-up
In your heart and
Mind and say

I will not panic
I will not be scared
Dear worker
Have a faith
Do prayer (Salah) five times a day
Stead fast,
Give zakat and
Do Haj
Do it, Do it,
You will be successful in this world
And on the Day of Judgement" —S. Shamsuddin

CONCEPT OF STRESS IN THE WESTERN THOUGHT

Introduction

The western scientific thought on the concept of stress is related to physics. Scientist had been using to denote the effect of overload on machines. Over worked machines, over loaded pieces of equipment tend to show lower productivity are said to be under strain. Such strain it allowed to build up over period of time finally causes the machine to break down. The excessive load is normally called stress.

The word 'Stress" is derived from the Latin word 'Stringere' mean to draw tight. Most of us are aware of tightness in the throat, increased breathlessness the rush of blood to the face, butterflies in the stomach and other symptoms, which are associated with most forms of stress.

'Stress' is the general term applied to the pressures people feel in life. The presence of stress at work is almost inevitable in many jobs. For examples, a survey by the National Association of Working Women reported that one-third of the respondents perceived their jobs as very stressful and another 62 percent saw their work as somewhat stressful.[1] When pressure begins to build up, it can cause adverse strain on one's emotions, thought processes, and physical condition. When stress becomes excessive, employees develop various symptoms of stress that can harm their job performance and health and even threaten their ability to cope with the environment. Stress is a major cause of low productivity, misallocation of resources, and poor morale.[2]

People who are stressed may became nervous and develop chronic worry. They are easily provoked to anger and are unable to relax. They may be uncooperative or use alcohol or drugs excessively. These are common symptoms of stress. Stress also leads to physical disorders, because of the internal body system changes to try to cope with stress. Some physical disorders are short-range such as an upset of stomach. Others are long-range, such as a stomach ulcer. Stress affects the heart, kidneys, blood vessels, and other parts of the body.

There is emerging evidence that in some situations an organization can be held legally liable for the emotional and physical impact of job stress on employees.

"Peter Randall[3] was transferred from a small city to very large city where his commuting time to work was nearly one hour. He disliked city noises, heavy traffic and crowds and he felt he was wasting his time while commuting. His new job also had more responsibilities. Within a few months, he developed intestinal problems. When a medical examinership showed no medical cause of his difficulties; he was sent to a counsel. There was only slide improvement, so finally his counsellor in cooperation with his physician recommended that he should be transfer to a smaller city. His firm arranged his transfer, and within a short time his problems disappeared".

Poor working conditions, sustained conflicts with supervisors, traumatic events or intentional harassment of employees sometimes results in anguish, neurosis, or even suicide. If liability is established, employees could claim benefits under workers' compensation laws, as well as sue for financial damages.[4]

IF METALS BREAK DOWN UNDER CONSTANT OVERLOAD HOW ABOUT INDIVIDUALS?

A particular situation may be stress for an employee or not, it depends on the perception of the worker. Stress therefore lays in the eyes of beholder, like redness of the apple, the blueness of the sky or the greenness of the grass.

The most influence concept of stress came from Sely, H. (1936).[5] He observed an identical biochemical changes in a number of organisms adapting to a variety of environmental condition. He termed this series of changes of general adaptation syndrome. During the initial phase, termed the stage of alarm, the organism orients to the demand the environment is making on it and begins to experience it as threatening. This state cannot be maintained for very long. In the stimulus, which has elicited the alarm response, is too powerful (ex: a poison) the organism dies.

If survival is possible the organism enters the stage of resistance in which the organism musters the resources to cope with the demand. If the demand continues for too long these adaptive resources are work out and the organism reaches the stage of exhaustion in which serious damage can occur. Selye was not sure what it was that an organism lost in the stage of resistance that cause it to pass into the stage of exhaustion, although he was convinced it was more than simple calorific energy.

According to the theory developed by Hans Sely, the human body cannot instantly rebuild its ability to cope with stress. As a result, employees become physically and psychologically weakened from trying to combat it. This condition is called burnout. It is a situation in which employees are emotionally exhausted, become detached from their work, and feel unable to accomplish their goals. Some jobs like those in the helping professions (such as counsellors, health care professionals and social workers) and those with continuous high stress (such as air-traffic controllers and stock brokers) are more likely than others to result in burnout.

COPING WITH STRESS

Walton B. Cannon[6] (1935) studied the effects of stress on human beings and animals in terms of the well-known fight or flight syndrome. Under duress human beings tend to choose between two alternatives. The first is to make all attempts to resist (i.e. fight) the environment pressures and through that process emerge victorious. The second is to avoid the pressure (flight) through the use of variety of defence mechanisms. This is their way of reducing the pressure. It was cannon who first elaborated as the psychological basis of stress.

INDIVIDUAL FACTORS IN STRESS

Lazarus and others[7] have found the events in the environment are not of themselves stressful, but the individual, as a threat perceives them before the stress arises. The stress experience according them is determined by the appraisal of what is at state. The notion of appraisal broaden the concept of stress to include psychological factors particularly personality variables such as the need for power.

In other words, what one employee sees as a threat. These different appraisals seem to produce specific physiological changes, which in turn have employees. Some evidence has supported the view that appraisal plays a crucial role in determining the impact of a stressor on an individual health. Jemmot *et. al.*,[8] (1983) for example found the secretion rate of the immune systems of a group of students under academic pressure was not uniform. The relationship between exam pressure systems was moderated by certain personality variables.

Similarly, Arsenault and Dolan[9] (1983) found the relationship between Job stress and work outcomes such as absenteeism and performance.

TYPES OF STRESS AT WORK

I. Role Stress

Almost any job condition can cause stress, depending upon an employee's reaction to it, i.e. one employee will accept a new work procedure while other rejects it. Work overload and time deadlines in the case of software industries put employees under pressure. Some of these pressures arise from supervision, so a poor quality of supervision can cause stress. Examples are autocratic supervisor, an insecure political climate, and inadequate authority to match one's responsibility.

Some jobs provide more stress than others.[10] Those that involve rotating shift work, machine-paced tasks, or hazardous environments are associated with greater stress. Executive stress may arise from the pressure for short-term financial results or the fear of a hostile takeover attempt. A general and widely recognized cause of stress is change of any type, because it requires adaptation by employees. It tends to be especially stressful when it is major or unusual, such as temporary layoff or transfer. A related source of stress that affects many employees is worry over their financial well-being.[11] This can arise when cost-saving technology is introduced, contract negotiations begin, or the firm's financial performance suffers. The following are different types of stress at work.

Each worker from the time of birth plays a variety of roles such as son/daughter, brother/sister, student/teacher, husband/wife, father/mother, boss/subordinate/peer mate.

Each of these positions or role occupied by an employee is connected by set of norms guidelines for appropriate behaviour, these guidelines are devised by society from religions values.

Each of these roles called for different types of behaviour, often causing problem. Thus ensuring stress. Role stress is when an employee plays multiple roles.

Pareek[12] (1993) outlines the component of role stress. According to him 'a role is a position that is occupies in a social system, as defined by the functions'. One performs in response to the expectations of the significant members of the social system, and one's own expectation from that position. There are two-role systems: role space and role set and each has a built in potential for conflict and stress.

I. Role-Space Conflict

It refers to conflict between the self, an employee's role and other role occupied by him. Role stress may take various forms:

(a) Self-role Distance

It refers to conflict between the self-concept and the expectations from the role. Roles, which call for behaviour, which is not in accordance with the value system of an employee result in self-role distance.

(b) Role-Stagnation

As an employee occupies a role over a period of time, he grows into that role and many behaviour patterns become habitual. When he has to assume a new supervisor he has to leave old role. The type of stress is called role stagnation.

(c) Inter-role Distance

This type of conflict arises due to multiple roles. Life, which becomes fast due to increase in demand for time, energy and other resources. Ex. Manager may have a role of an executive, father, son, etc.,

II. Role-Set Conflicts

Role conflicts and ambiguity are also related to stress[13]. The role-set conflicts refers to incompatibilities among the varying expectations that significant others have from role incumbent. The following are role-set conflicts.

(a) Role-Ambiguity

This result when an employee is not clear about the expectations of the organization from him. When a new work or job is offered without sufficient orientation provided to him.

(b) Role-expectation Conflict

This is due to the conflicting expectations of different role senders, e.g. boss, colleagues and customers.

(c) Role-Overload

This type of stress is rapidly on the increase as more and more work is being demanded from employees. Example software industry when an employee is pressed for time as he is unable to handle the total quantum of work.

(d) Role-Erosion

Instead of feeling overloaded, an employee may feel that some of his duties or work is being taken away from him or he is given demotion. This type of stress result is known as role erosion.

(e) Role-Inadequacy

It refers to stress experienced when an employee is not supplied with enough resources, e.g. Information, manpower, facilities and finance.

(f) Personal Inadequacy

It occurs when an employee feels that be lacks the expertise or skills necessary for different role performance.

(g) Role-Isolation

In a role set, an employee may feel that some roles are closer to him, others are at a relatively distance. Distance is measured by case of interaction between linkages. If linkages are strong, feelings of role isolation will low. Its linkages are weak, role isolation feelings will be high, with alienation at the end.

BURNOUT

It is a state of physical, emotional and mental exhaustion, caused by emotion in work situation. When employees have become burnout, they are more likely to complain, attribute their errors to others, and be highly irritable. The alienation they feel drives many of them to think about leaving their jobs, to seek out opportunities to become trained for new careers and actually to quit.[14] Organizations need to identify both the jobs that lead to early burnout and the employees who exhibit some of the burnout symptoms. Sometimes it may be possible to change the parts of a job that contribute to burnout. In other cases the firm can help employees learn how to cope better with stressful work situations.

Employees in service-oriented organizations such as teaching, health care, police, and military service are more likely to have burnout than people in manufacturing organizations. The effect of burnout is labour turnover, intention to leave the job, poor physical health, sleep problems, alcohol intake, loss of appetite, nervousness, backache, and stomach-ache, etc.

I. Decision-making Stress

One of the important types of stress in organization occurs as a result of having to make difficult decisions. Janis (1982)[15] suggested two reasons why this maybe so: People's awareness of their limited knowledge and problem-solving capacities and their awareness of the various losses which may result from choosing any of the options available.

Janis argued that decisional stress significantly reduces the quality of an individual's decision. At extreme, this can cause people simply to withdraw from a situation and make decision without seeking out or considering relevant information.

Cameron and Meichenlaum (1982)[16] developed a programme based as the appraisal concept of stress, that stress is a function of an individual's perception of a situation and his or her resources to cope with it.

II. Relationship At Work

The work life in an organization consists of Interpersonal relationship. They are:

(a) Relationship with employer
(b) Relationship with subordinates
(c) Relationship with colleagues

These relationships may cause friction and leads to stressful work life. Stress may arise due to the interpersonal relationship at work. Through inoculation of Islam the stress can be relieved at work. The human life according to the Quran is to express itself a system of activity promoting peace and harmony in work life. Every employee has every freedom is will and act. There is the assurance to every individual:

In Islamic theology an employee is not suppose to give up his mundane life. He should not become recluse. He should live in this world and in this organization with all the problems, turbulences and troubles. He has to cope with stress while fighting out the situation. The fighting does not result in burn out phenomena for the employees. He is always in commune with his creator. This proximity reduces the stress. A transient, the weak employee gets the strength of a mighty force by his closeness to the al-mighty.

CREATION OF MAN

As already stated the leading idea of the Quran 'Laillaha Illallah' there is none worthy of worship except God, determines employees place in the scheme of creation. The Quran points out that an employee is made of the goodliest fabric[1] he whom mala'ik were made to offer obeisance and for whom what so ever is in the heavens and what so ever is in the earth are made to do service. Thus raised in the scale of creation and placed immediately next to God, an employee's importance is further emphasized by investing him with the privilege of living an earth as the vicegerent of God Himself. The employee should play a good role and get in it the pleasure of God.

"O ye mankind! surely we have created you a male and female, and made you tribes and families that you may recognize each other; surely the noblest of you in the sight of God is the one among you most mindful of his duty. God knows fully awake". —(Q : 49-13)

The God has created Human being as male employees and female employees. They are all belongs to one organization. They should recognize each other. They should perform their work or duty as a role given to them. The good employee is one who works for the pleasure of God. God knows everything.

"O Man, Be mindful of your Lord, who hath created you of one man and of him created his wife, and from the twain hath spread abroad so many men and women. Verily is God watching over you". —(Q : 4 : 1)

Again it was given in the Quran that God created an employee and from the same he created his wife also, for performing their roles in this world and He is watching over them. Their work is to satisfy Him.

PURPOSE OF CREATION

The purpose of creating the organization, work and other creatures are only for the benefit of human being. Therefore, an employee should realise this and get the pleasure of God. The following are the verses from the Quran:

> "Allah it is who hath revealed the work with truth and the Balance". —(Q : 42 : 16)

> "By the soul and Him who balanced it and infused in the same the sense of discrimination and the power of choosing between the wrong and the right, happy is he who kept it pure and unhappy is he who corrupted it". —(Q : 91 : 7-10)

The truth has been given to an employee to perform his work. Since Allah's soul is in him, he will realize the right and wrong, if he keep it in pure he feels very happy, otherwise he feels unhappy.

> "Surely we created man of the goodliest fabric, then we rendered him the vilest of the vile". —(Q : 95 : 4-5)

> "Then we rendered him the vilest of the vile save those who believe and work righteously". —(Q : 95 : 5-6)

Faith alone is not enough for the pleasure of God, but also the role-played by an employee. This is the way of fulfilling employee's responsibility as the vicegerent of God on earth. The quality of work is to assume in the context of role to be discharged by the organization.

Mankind is a fold every member of which shall be a keeper or shepherd unto every other and be accountable for the welfare of the entire fold. —Bukhari : Kitabal iman

O Lord: Lord of my life and of everything in the Universe! I affirm that all human beings are brothers unto one another.

—Ahmed : Mushad in Abu Dawud

An organization consists of different roles of person like an employee, supervisor, subordinate, manager, co-worker, each employee have a different role, and they are accountable for their work, and all should work for the welfare of the organization for the pleasure of God. All the employees should treat others as brothers and sisters.

The responsibility of employees is extended further states the prophet.

> "All creatures of God form the family of God and he is the best loved of God who loves best His creatures."
>
> —Baihaqui-Kitabul Iman, Shuab-ul Iman

The role of an employer is that he should think the entire organization is a family of God. He should perform his role that should satisfy all including the God. Respect the ways of God, and be affectionate to the family of God.

The role of employee is that should respect all the employees in the organization. He should show affection to all.

Those employees who respect the ways of God and follow them in their work life alone are to be truly regarded as the vicegerents of God on earth. They have to satisfy not only to themselves but also their subordinates of an organization. Their aim of work-life is to satisfy God.

> "There is not an animal in the earth or creatures flying as two wings, but they are people like into you. We have neglected nothing in the book (of our degrees). Then into their Lord will they be gathered?" —(Q : 6 : 38).

God (Allah) has created the entire universe and all the creatures for the benefit of human beings. His aim is to shape both an employee's life as well as organization as a whole in ways that His kingdom may really be established and that peace, contentment and well-being of workers may fill in the organization. The Islamic way of the work-life is based on Tawheed a unique concept of in the organization that is why it is necessary to discuss the system of Islam.

God who is the creator and Ruler and Lord of the universe has created man (employee) and provided him all facilities. He has endowed employee with the faculties of thinking and understanding and has given him the power to distinguish right from wrong. Employees are also been invested free will and the power to use the resources of the world, however he likes. An employee should not think himself totally free and realize that the earth is not his permanent. He has been created to live on it only for a probationary period and in due course, he will return to the Lord, to be judged according to the way he has spent that period. The only right way for employee is to acknowledge God and to follow His guidance and His commands in all his work. His sole objective is to satisfy Him and get the pleasure.

If an employee follows a Tawheed and righteousness, which he is free to choose, he will be rewarded in this world and the next. In this world he will live a peaceful and contentment and in the Hereafter he will qualify for the heaven or eternal bliss, al-Jannah.

CONCEPT OF STRESS IN ISLAM

Islamic theology does not subscribe to the theory of evolution. Man was created by Allah. Man was totally regulated by nature in initial stages of his creation. His instinct, desires, will, and was regulated by nature. He was in paradise and he was not aware of his life. Allah decided to give him a limited freedom and sent Adam to earth. The life, which was totally regulated by nature, was given freedom. By sending Adam to earth, Allah created a life, which is aware of itself. A life which knows that it has freedom, a life which knows that it can create, a life which knows that it can produce, a life which has been given the faculty of reasoning. This life is also aware that it is not completely free from nature. In spite of separation from the nature it is dominated and regulated by nature to a limited extent. This life is aware that there is an end to itself in the form of death. Man knows that there are natural calamities such as floods, typhoons, Tsunami's, earthquake and diseases over which he has no control. He is not totally part of nature nor can he transcend or dominate nature. This dualism is the root cause of stress in Islamic thought. Man knows that he has the productive capacity to build two hundred story building. But at the same time he knows that this building may fall down due to earthquake. He has invented medicines for thousands of diseases, he can reduce pain, he can control diseases but also aware that diseases called death for which there is not medicine. This dualism is the root cause of anxiety.

This anxiety produces loneliness. When he was in paradise there was no loneliness. When Allah sent Adam to earth he felt lonely. Therefore, man must relate himself to this society to the nature and to his creator to get rid off his loneliness, anxiety and stress. During loneliness, employees used to take alcohol for relieving loneliness.

The Quran forbids the drinking of alcohol by employees, which leads to problem.

> "O ye true believers come not to prayer when ye are drunk, but wait till ye can understand what ye utter" —(Q : 4 : 46)

O ye who believe! Forbid not the good things which God

has made lawful for you go not beyond this limit. God loves not those who out step it.

And eat of what God hath given you for food, that which is lawful and whole some, and fear God, in whom ye believe.

—(Q : 5 : 87-88)

O believers! Surely wine and games of chance, and statues, and the diving arrows, are an abomination of Satan's work! Avoid them that ye may prosper.

Only would Satan sow hatred and strife among you by wise and games of chance, and turn you aside from the remembrance of God, and from prayer, will ye not, therefore, abstain from them? Obey God and obey the Apostle, and be on your guard: but it ye turn back, know that our Apostle is only bound to deliver a plain announcement. —(Q : 5 : 92-93)

From the above it has been clearly stated that if an employee takes alcohol for relieving stress it leads to problem. Instead of that having faith and pray to God, will relieve stress.

The above are stress related problems, and their effect as work life. Now-a-days the software technology also increasing the stress-related problems.

The important thing lost in the stage of resistance of stress is faith. Faith as God (Allah) Faith as God is the real basis of faith. Faith in God does not mean nearly in His existence but also in all His attributes and accepting all that is due to Him. The successful employee is who have faith as God and believes in Him to be the creator and sustainer and firmly stands upon it, not flinching from it by any threat or force or lust. The Quran says about such people.

Those who declare that the sustainer is God and stand firer as it they will have no fear or sorrow. They will enter paradise and remain there forever. This will be the reward of their Good conduct. —(Q : 22 : 13-16)

At another place the Quran says, "Those who declare that their sustainer is God and stand firer as it, angels descend as them and say, have no fear or sorrow but take the good tidings of paradise which is promised to you. We are your comrades in this world and also in the next. —(Q : 41 : 30-31)

God is the creator, sustainer and master of the universe and of all that exists, in it including organic and in organic. Life in all its forms including work-life, our physical organs and faculties, the apparent control, which we have in our life all, are under Him. They have been bestowed on us entirely by God. The Quran says about it.

> "Then, Exalted be God, the sovereign king, the true. There is no god but Him, the Lord of the noble Throne".
> —(Q : 23 : 116)
>
> "To Him belongs the sovereignty over the heavens and the earth He gives life, and He makes to die, and He has power over everything". —(Q : 57 : 2)
>
> "Say who is it that provides you our of heaven and earth, or who is it that has full power over hearing and sight, and who is it that brings forth the living out of the dead brings forth the living out of the dead and brings forth the dead out of the living? And who is it that governs in all matters? They will surely say: God" —(Q : 10 : 31)
>
> "Verily, to Him belong all creation and all authority, blessed be God, the Lord of all the worlds".—(Q : 57 : 54)

The current research is based on the Islamic philosophy. Adopting Islamic values and beliefs can relieve the stress of an employee. The basic Islamic value is Tawheed, i.e. only one God, He is Allah and others values are Prayer, fasting, giving zakat, performing Haj, controlling anger, patience, visiting graveyards, reciting Quran and sleeping.

STRESS INOCULATION IN ISLAM

The best way of relieving role stress of an employee is to trust in Allah who is the only One Who will deliver the outcomes. Putting the trust in Allah is called tawakkul, making tawakkul is a sign of belief in Allah. It is a sign of belief in the unseen that is controlled by Allah Tawakkul is the reliance of the heart on, and its confidence in Allah. An employee should make tawakkul in performing their roles believing that Allah is the most merciful the most graceful, the Exalted in might, the one with absolute knowledge wisdom and justice. Tawakkul gives an employee a sense of optimism that can encourage them to avoid excessive risk.

Tawakkul does not mean that an employee does not do what is necessary to achieve in his role but expects Allah to grant him success. Tawakkul comes after one does his role. A manager is doing his work sincerely. He goes to office on time and leaves his office. He does all his assignments, projects in the office and at the same time he is performing his role as a father in home. He is discharging all the obligations of home. He does best of his ability and then he has tawakkul on Allah. For all the outcomes rest on Allah. This is called tawakkul. Tawakkul gives the sense of satisfaction to an employee.

Tawakkul comes from belief in Allah and His attributes. It is evident from the following verses:

"And put your trust on the Exalted in might, the merciful"
—(Q : 26 : 217)

"You say: Indeed this affair is wholly Allah's"
—(Q : 3 : 154)

And the sun, the moon and the stars (all) governed by laws under His command. Is it not His to create and to govern? "Nor shall they compass ought of His knowledge except as He wills" —(Q : 2 : 255)

"It any trust in Allah, behold! Allah is exalted in might, wise" —(Q : 8 : 49)

Tawakkul provides a reward:

Allah promised a reward for Tawakkul.
"........... And when you are resolved, them put your trust in Allah. Ho! Allah loves those who put their trust in Him"
—(Q : 3 : 159)

From the above verses tawakkul comes after and not before one perform his role. It is the duty of every employee to perform his work or role first and put their trust in Allah, for which they receive reward.

"But that which is with Allah is better and more lasting: (It is) for those who believe and put their trust in their Lord"
—(Q : 42 : 36)

The reward that Allah has in store for mankind in for those who trust Him.

"To dwell therein forever: Excellent reward for those who do well. Those who persevere and put their trust in their Lord". —(Q : 29 : 58-59)

I. Prayer

Besides tawakkul, the other ways of relieving role stress of an employee is through prayer (Salah). If an employee feels stress, he can pray two rakat 'Nafil' by which his stress will be relieved. Through prayer his heart and mind will get purified. He realizes the Allah's will thereby, he plays his role as ordained by Allah's. This gives him a feeling of relief that the outcomes is in the hands of Allah. By prayer an employee attaches himself to the almighty. This attachment gives him the feeling of sufficiency. An employee, being finite human being, by attaching himself with almighty, finite being becomes infinite or at least comes closer to it. This feeling of infinite gives in a strong courage.. An employee with all this limitations as a human being, gets rid-of the burden of being man by attaching himself with the supreme being. That is the reason why the Prophet (SAW) has asked a Muslim to offer salah as if he is seeing God. If he cannot do that at least he should feel that he is being watched by Allah. Stress is burden of being man. Proximity to the Supreme Being reduces the stress. A gentle feeling of peace and tranquillity descends on him.

"When you threw (a handful of dust) it was not your act, but Allah's". —(Q : 8 : 17)

"There is no triumph except that given by Allah"
—(Q : 8 : 10 and Q : 3 : 126)

"You have no will except as Allah wills" —(Q : 76 : 30)

The other method of relieving stress at work is prayer. Prayer gives insight into the working of worker's mind, these thoughts and feelings and the very object of his life. An employee stands face to face with the creator before Him his heart, and gives an account of his nun dance struggles, his achievements, and disappointments, and to ask of him the things that matter. His prayer at such a moment is an expression of pressure feelings. Through which is stress will be relieved.

II. Fasting

The other way of preventing role stress is fasting. Fasting gives the purification of self and self-restraint. The Quran says:

> "Oh ye who believe! Fasting is prescribed to you as it was prescribed to those before you that ye may (learn) self-restraint". —(Q : 2 : 183)

Fasting is the best exercise for self-restraint without which the realization of omnipresence of Allah. In fasting employee's tongue, eyes and thoughts are controlled. This will reduce the role stress.

Fasting not only develops angelic qualities in an employee but even the quality of restraints of animal nature and devotion to Allah in common with angles. Fasting provides a sense of thankfulness and remained an employee very great pleasures that with His unbounded Grace and Benevolence. By performing different roles, an employee works for the pleasure of Allah. This pleasure will relieve stress.

III. Consultation

One of the methods of decision-making in Islam is through consultation, which by consensus and concludes by voting it a consensus is not reached. The following are some of the verses from Quran:

> "Say: O people of the Book! Come to common terms as between us and you: that we worship none but Allah! That we erect not from among ourselves, Lords and patrons other than Allah. It then they turn back, say ye. Bear witness that we are Muslims (submitting to the will of God)". —(Q : 3 : 64)

The culture of the companions of the prophet can also be described as a culture of dialogue or consultation. The value of dialogue was shared by all members of the society of all companions irrespective of their age, gender, race or ethnic origin. Any decision taken by a manager in an organization is for the benefit of workers and pleasure of Allah. Before it, he should consult with all the workers. This type of decision-making will not experience any type of stress.

> "Oh no soul do we lay a responsibility greater than it can bear". —(Q : 2 : 286)

IV. Socialization of Employees

The better way of maintaining relationship in the organization is to attend the functions like marriage, festival etc. of the employees and presenting the gifts to them.

When an employee visits his employer or supervisor or co-worker, he should take some gifts for them. Exchange of presents and gifts arguments sentiments of love and promotes intimate relationship. This promotes intimate relationship. The gift creates a soft corner in the heart of the receiver for the donor.

When an employee attends a feast, says a prayer at the end of the meal invoking Allah to bless the host with extensive means, grace favour, salvation and His Mercy. This feels promote personal relationship among organizational members. Hazrat Abu Athhim b. Talah (R.A.A) once invited the Holy prophet (S.A.W) and his illustrious companions (R.A.A) to a feast. When the meal was over, the Holy prophet (S.A.W) observed : "Reward your brother". The illustrious companions (R.A.A) submitted : "How can we reward him, O prophet of Allah (S.A.W)?", The Holy prophet (S.A.W) observed:

> "When a man pays a visit to his brother and eat, and drinks there, he can reward his brother by praying for Allah's favour and blessings upon his brother".
>
> —Abu Dawud

The Holy prophet (S.A.W) once visited the house of Hazrat sa'ad. "Udabah (R.A.A). Udabah said (R.A.A) presented to the

Holy prophet (S.A.W) bread and olive oil. The prophet of Allah (S.A.W) took the meal and then prayed for him:

> "May the fasting people break their fasts with your provisions! May the pious partake of your meals and may the angels pray for Allah's mercy and forgiveness for you".
>
> —Abu Dawud

V. Visiting a Sick Employee

If an employee of an organization becomes sick, it is the duty of other employees to visit him. This will create a better relationship among themselves and relieving of stress. An employee should enquire about the health of a sick employee. Visiting a sick employee is not a social requirement or mutual co-operation and sympathy, but it is also right of an employee over another and an essential pre-requisite to devotion to Allah. He who is devoted to Allah cannot remain unconcerned with the creation of Allah. The offering of sympathy, consolation and assistance to the sick is for the remembrance and pleasure of Allah. The following are some of Hadeeth related to visiting of a sick employee.

THE HOLY PROPHET (S.A.W.) HAS SAID

'On the day of Judgment Allah said : 'O son of Adam! you did not visit me when I was ailing? The man will submit : 'O creator! You are Lord of the whole universe. How could I dare enquire after your welfare? Allah shall ordain : such and such person from among my creatures fell ill and you did not enquire after his health. If you had gone to enquire after his welfare, you would have found me there. (In other words, you would have earned my favour and blessing). —Muslim

> "He who enquiries after the health of an ailing Muslim brother will find a dwelling place on the highest level of paradise". —Ai-Adab-ul Mufrad

Hazrat Abu Huraira (R.A.A) has reported that the Holy prophet (S.A.W) observed :

> "When a person goes to enquire after the health of a Muslim brother or just pays a call on him, a caller from the heaven pronounces, "you have done well; your walking is propitious; you have earned a dwelling place in paradise".
>
> —Tirmidhi

When an employee visits a sick employee, he should sit by the side of sick employee, he should pass his hand over his head or body and utter words of sympathy and consolation, so that the sick may start thinking about the reward and recompense awaiting him in the eternal world.

Hazrat Ayesha bin saad (R.A.A) reports that her father related "Once while in Mecca I fell gravely ill. The holy Prophet (S.A.W) came to enquire after my health. I enquired about my daughter's health. The Holy prophet of Allah (S.A.W) placed his hand on my fore head and passed it over my face and belly then said the following prayer :

> "O" Allah, bless Sa'ad with health and complete his Hijrat. Since then whenever I recall to mind that moment I feel the soothing sensation of the holy hand of the Holy prophet (S.A.W) to the depth of my inner-self".
>
> —Al-Adab-ul-Mufrad

Hazrat Zaid B. Arqam (R.A.A) relates : "Once my eyes become sore. The holy prophet (S.A.W) visited me to enquire after my health and said : "Zaid, what do you do when you are suffering from sore eyes". I submitted : "I endure this illness with patience". The Holy prophet (S.A.W) observed : If you observe patience and endurance while you are afflicted with sore eyes, Allah shall admit you into paradise as a reward for this".

Hazrat Ibn Abbas (R.A.A) states : "Whenever the holy prophet (S.A.W) visited a patient to enquire after his health, the prophet (S.A.W) used to sit at the head of the ailing person and repeated the following prayer at seven times :

> "I beseech Allah almighty Who is the Lord of exalted heavens to grant you health"!

The holy prophet (S.A.W) observed : "The patient will certainly to restored to health if this prayer is offered seven times, except in case the hour of his death has come".

—Mishkat

Hazrat Jabir (R.A.A) reports that the holy Prophet (S.A.W) paid a visit to an old lady Umma salma (R.A.A) to require after her health. Umma salma (R.A.A) was shivering with intense fever. The holy Prophet (S.A.W) enquired : "How are you feeling?". The lady submitted "May Allah curse this fever.

When an employee visits a sick, he should enquires about his condition and prays for his brother's recovery. Whenever the Holy Prophet (S.A.W) visited a patient he first enquired about his health and then used to observe. "There is no need to worry. By the Will of Allah, this illness will disappear and will prove a means of purging you of all sins". Afterwards, the Holy Prophet (S.A.W) used to pass his right hand over the region of pain and discomfort and say this prayer :

> "Allah! Remove this pain. O Lord of mankind, grant health to this person. You are the Healer. There is none from whom we expect recovery from illness save you. You alone can grant such recovery that this disease may be completely uprooted".

Do not sit besides the ill person for long, nor make noise near him. However, if the sick person is you intimate friend or a near relation and himself insists on your sitting beside him for a longer time, you should comply with his wishes.

Hazrat' Abdullah b. 'Abbas (R.A.A) states : "It is part of the Sunnah not to sit for long beside a patient, nor to make noise near him".

Do ask the relations of the patient about his condition and express your sympathy. Offer them all possible assistance or cooperation. For example, fetch the doctor, or convey a message about the condition of the patient, or fetch medicines, etc. or if required, extend financial help also.

Hazrat Ibrahim b. Abi Habla (R.A.A) relates : "Once my wife fell ill. In those days I used to pay frequent visits to Hazrat Umm al-Darda (R.A.A). Whenever I called on her, she used to enquire : "Say, how is your wife?" I answered : "She is still indisposed". Thereafter, she used to send for food. I sat down and dined at her home and then came back. One day, when I called on her and she enquired about my wife's health, I replied : "By the grace and favour of Allah, she has nearly recovered from her illness. "Hazrat Umm al-Darda (R.A.A) thereupon observed : "When you used to say that your wife was unwell I used to arrange a meal for you. Now that she has gained her health, I need not arrange a meal for you".

When you visit the house of a patient to enquire after his health, avoid looking about in the house. Sit in a manner that the inmates of the house, particularly the women are not within your sight.

Once Hazrat "Abdullah bin Mas'ud (R.A.A) went to the house of an ailing person to enquire after his health. He was accompanied by some others also. One of his companions started gazing a lady of the house. When Hazrat "Abdullah (R.A.A) perceived it, he observed to his companion, "It would have been better if you to gouge out your eyes".

When you go to enquire after the health of a sick employee request him to pray for you also. It is recorded in Ibn Majah : "When you visit a patient to enquire after his health, request him to pray for you. The prayer of a patient is as much effective as the prayer offered by angels". (The implication is that the angels offer prayers only at the command of Allah and hence their prayers are always granted).

STRESS COPING MECHANISM IN ISLAMIC PERSPECTIVE

The best way of reducing the stress is depend upon the supreme (Allah). It makes human independent of all the other entities in this Universe.

The following are the 'Islamic' methods by which the stress can be relieved:

I. Prayer (Salah)

The word Salah refers to "Remembrance" in the Quran, i.e. remembrance of God. Whatever we do in this world including the work life should be in accordance with the law of God. Our work, our relationship with superiors, subordinates and co-workers, our acts of eating and drinking in work. Each of our action should be strictly in obedience to the law of God. It is necessary to make our self earnestly feel that we are a slave of God and we have to maintain sub-servience to Him every moment of our life and in every work we do.

This continuous remaining is necessitated by the fact that concealed in man's nafs is a Satan who continuously instigates him by saying: "You are my slave" employee reminds himself several times in a day that he is not slave of Satan but of God. This work of admonition is performed by salah. Soon after we get up in the morning, salah reminds us of this very fact before we start our daily work. While we are doing our work during the day, it reminds us five times. And when we are about to go to bed, this admonition is repeated for the last time. If we remember God in our every action, our stress will be reduced.

Quran has made a reference to this remembrance thus:

> "And when the salah is ended then disperse in the land and seek of Allah's bounty (i.e. exert yourself in search of lawful means of sustenance), and remember Allah profusely, so that ye may gain success and well-being".
>
> —(Q : 62 : 10)

> Salah makes us the practice of obedience : salah has been made compulsory five times in a day, so that they are tested in obeying the commandments of God in their work life. It is said in the Quran: "And truly it (salah) is hard save for the humble minded". —(Q : 2 : 45)

Salah makes the fear of God, which is necessary to be kept alive in the heart uninterruptedly. If an employee believes that God is aware of every of his action, even in the darkness and when he is alone, all the time at every place. He will not commit any mistake and he will try to satisfy the God. This leads to free of tensions.

It is possible to hide oneself from the whole world but it is impossible to hide from God. An employee can escape from the punishments of the whole world but it is impossible to escape from the punishment of God. It is this belief, which restrains employee from violating the injections of God. Faith on God and following salah leads to stress free life.

"Salah prevents man from evil and lewdness"—(Q : 24 : 45)

Salah is offered when we are clean and have done Wudu'. From this we can judge that salah evokes and revives in to belief in His being Omnipresent seer and knower. This creates on that the God provides everything. We have to leave our feelings, worries, etc to the God, and we should follow salah. This leads to free of stress.

Divine law is fulfilled through salah. The Quran that is recited in the salah is intended to keep Muslims informed of the commandments and law of God. salah makes Muslims the understanding life and its meaning. If Muslim follows it, they will be free from stress.

One of reason for the stress is loneliness. This loneliness can be relieved by salah. All the people are united and standing in front of God and all are equal in front of God. This type of prayer, i.e. Salah removes the loneliness. Salah is the greatest instrument to build up their collective strength.

Salah prepares a man for Allah's Ibadat, i.e. servitude and obedience. If one offers salah regularly considering it his duty according to the Divine injunction, it keeps alive in his mind the fear of God, the belief in His Omniscience and Omnipresence and the conviction that he is accountable before Him. This continuous practice that the belief that he is slave of none but God, and that God alone is his real sovereign and ready to carryout God's commandment is developed in him are necessary to transform the entire life of an employee into one of servitude and worship of God. This leads to relief from stress.

Imagine a person who hears the voice of Adhan five times in a day and feels that some big thing is being testified and we are being summoned to the presence of a highly powerful sovereign: who every time on hearing this call, leaves all his work and runs to that sublime being whom he considers Master of himself as also of the entire universe. Who before every salah purifies his body and soul with 'Wudu' and who performs with again in the salah. With the cleaning and purifying of body and soul through salah, stress will be eliminated.

Salah creates a purposeful Assembly. During to the salah Muslim gather in a mosque and gathering itself provides innumerable advantages. They meet each other, recognize each other and come to know each other. It is in this capacity they are all slaves of God, followers of one Prophet, believes in one book, and only one aim of life for all. They all have gathered in mosque to fulfil only one aim and have to carry on fulfilling it even after going back from mosque. This kind of attachment and this type of acquaintance automatically creates on the feeling that the Muslims are all one community, they are all soldiers of the same army, their aims, their interest, their profit and losses are all common, and their lives are integrated with each other. This type of attachment, feelings creates a relaxed to mind and reducing the stress. Even the loneliness also is relieved.

When Muslims look at each other it will be a friendly feeling and is like a brother looking at a brother. When Muslims notice that their brother is in tattered clothes, another with sorrowful looks, some other come with a stained face, while yet another is disabled, applied or blind, than inequitably sympathy will arise from their heart. They take pity on the poor and them helpless each other. The stress of the person will be relieved by our visit and if the news of anybody's death, all will join to perform his funeral salah and share the grief of the bereaved family. Thereby through salah they share their feelings. This will reduce the stress of the concerned family members.

The most important pillar of religion is prayer, which is a continuing symbol of an employee's firm pledge of obedience and conformity to His Will which his repeatedly renews by presenting himself and prostrating before his Creator, Sustainer and Lord. Its frequency and regularity strengthens the bond between an employee and God, reminds him again and again that he is not free but a slave tied to the pillar of God's orders and within the limited sphere is authorized to live in and profit by this world.

Hazrat Abu Huraïra says that he heard the Prophet (SAW) ask whether any dirt would be left on his body if any of them took a bath five times a day in a stream flowing by his house. (The companions) replied in the negative, saying that nothing of dirt would be left. The Prophet (SAW) then said that five times of prayers were just like that and, that God removes the filth of sins by them.

—Buhari, Muslim, Tirmizi, Nasai, Ibn Maja

Just as no dirt or filth will be left on the body by five times of daily bath, in the same way no uncleanliness of sins will be left after offering five times of daily prayers and God will forgive the sins restoring the purity of soul. However, there is one condition that the prayer is real prayer and not merely for show and devoid of its soul, like a lifeless body and a burden from which one wished to be relieved as soon as possible. It is performed with careful regard of all its constituents and with sincerity of purpose, which is its due. In prayer the servant is at the feet of his Master. How can disrespectful manners like hurry or indifference find their way into it? The thought or nearness to God and frequently presenting oneself before Him will constitute a check against many sins. This is supported by the Quran which says : "And establish regular prayers at the two ends of the day and at the approaches of the night for those things that are good remove those that are evil. Be that the word of remembrance to those who remember (their Lord)".

—(Q : 11 : 114)

Hazrat Abdullah bin Amr bin Al-A'as says that once the Prophet (SAW) while talking on the subject of prayers said, "One who observes prayers it will become for him on the Day of Judgement, a light, a pleading and salvation. But one who does not observe it there will be no light or pleading or salvation for him and on the Day of Judgement his destiny will be in common with Korah, Pharaoh, Haman and Ubay bin Khalaf, i.e. with disobedient and rebellious men.

—Ahmed, Darimi, Al Baihiq

When an employee performs the prayer carefully with all its essentials fully understanding the meaning of the words he is reciting, avoiding indifference, fatigue and lack of attention to enter into it, then such prayer is externally and internally correct and will be his light in this world and salvation in the next. Such prayer will not let him stray from the right path and so it is hoped that on the Day of Judgement also the performer of such prayer will be entitled to the Mercy of God and His Benevolence. Thus prayer is all salvation and light. Those who lose it and are indifferent to its proper observance, will not get the inner light in their minds or hearts and when such is the state in this world how can anything better be expected in the next.

> It is reported from Hazrat Ibn Umar that the Prophet had said, "You should offer some parts of your prayers at home also and do not make graveyards of your homes".
>
> —Abu Daud

Due to the importance of congregation the Farz (obligatory) prayers should be offered in the mosques with the congregation. But Nafil (optional) prayers can be better offered at home. Remembrance of God is in fact the light and life of the home and prayer is the most perfect form of remembrance of God. In another report from Hazrat Jabir it is said:

> "When anyone of you offers his prayers in the mosque he should keep part of the prayer to be offered to home as through prayer God grants blessings and prosperity to the home.
>
> —Muslim

> "Prayer is the solace of a Muslim's eye and life of the home. A house where no prayer is offered is deprived of goodness and blessings."

> Hazrat Jabir reports that the Prophet (SAW) had said, "Between man and apostasy is forsaking prayer".
>
> —Ahmed, Muslim

That is, between belief and non-belief there is a stage, which is forsaking prayer. Whosoever gives up prayer is as if hanging between faith and its rejection, one step ahead will lead him to apostasy. Prayer is the pillar of Islam and to abandon it is to give up the path of Islam and adopt the way of the rejecters of faith.

Hazrat Abu Huraira reports that he heard the Prophet (SAW) say: "On the Day of Judgment the first question asked from man will be about prayer. If prayer has been properly offered it will lead to salvation and felicity and if it has not been properly performed it will be a loss and disappointment. If there is shortage in. Farz prayers God will say, "My, servant has Nafl prayers to his credit. If there have been lapses in his farz prayers, let them be made up with his Nafl prayers; and in the same way all his record of actions will be accounted for".

—Abu Daud, Ahmed

This report shows that prayer has basic importance in Islam. "On the Day of Judgment account will be taken of prayers of Muslims. If any one has no record of prayers to his credit, it will mean that he did not try to follow the sacred and desirable path which prayer represents. This report also shows that in the life of a believer, obligatory prayers are not different from optional ones. On the other hand, the second category fills up the gap in the first".

It is reported from Hazrat Ibn Umar that the Prophet (SAW) had said, "The earlier time of prayer is the time of God's pleasure and the later time is that of His forgiveness."

—Tirmizi

Offering prayer in its early time shows that the person has affinity for prayer and does not regard it a burden by offering prayer in its later time. The duty is performed any way but the merit of the early time is lost.

The Prophet (SAW) is reported to have said, "It is the hypocrite's prayer if one continues to sit and wait for the setting of the sun till it becomes pale and the time of the worship of polytheists approaches, he rises and hurriedly offers four Rak'ats (as the fowl pecks at the grain), hardly remembering God in it".

—Muslim, Anas

In this report the difference between the prayer of a believer and that of a hypocrite is indicated. While the believer offers his prayer in its proper time and his heart is devoted to the remembrance of God, the hypocrite not only defers the time of prayer but also indifferently performs its various constituents, bowing and prostration and his heart is devoid of remembrance of God. Although all prayers are important but Fajr (before sun-rise) and Asr (late afternoon) prayers are of particular significance. At the time of Asr people are generally engaged in their business and want to finish their deals before sun-set, and collect together their scattered commodities. So if the believer's mind is not alert the Asr prayer might become endangered. At the time of Fajr men are generally enjoying sound sleep and if faith is not alive in man's heart he is reluctant to sacrifice his sound sleep to remembrance of God.

Hazrat Shaddad bin Ans reports that he heard the Prophet (SAW) say that one who offered prayer for show assigned partners to God and one who kept fast for show committed the same sin, also one who gave charity for show.

—Musnad, Ahmed

According to this report the Prophet (SAW) wants to impress that whatever good act is done it should be to gain the pleasure of God and in compliance with His orders and not to show his piety to others or to please others. Such a show act has no value. Only what is done for God's sake has any value.

Hazrat Abu Zar reports that the Prophet (SAW) had said, "When a man is praying, God necessarily attends to him provided he does not look to his right and left, and when he does that, God's attention is withdrawn". —Abu Daud, Nasai

God's dignity does not tolerate that while He is attentive to his servant the servant's attention is to his right and left. God can only remain attentive with His Mercy so long as the servant maintains the respect due to the Divine Presence. Those who neglect it are not worthy of God's attention.

Hazrat Abu Huraira reports that the Prophet (SAW) had said, "If any one of you leads a congregational prayer he should do it briefly, for in the congregation there are men who are sick or old or weak or those who have to attend to their business. But while praying alone one may prolong it as much as he likes".

—Bukhari, Muslim

Hazrat Anas reports that the Prophet (SAW) had said, "So long as you have interest in prayer and enjoy it you should pray but as soon as you lose interest you should sit down".

—Bukhari, Muslim

God as a hardship does not impose order for prayer on man. On the other hand it is food for his soul and so it should be performed with all interest and alertness in order to gain maximum energy and strength from it and thereby have the fullest benefit out of it.

Hazrat Aqaba bin A'mir says that the Prophet (SAW) had said, "The believer who performs ablution properly and offers two Raka'ts of prayer with full attention and concentration he will ensure paradise for himself". —Muslim

Hazrat Abu Huraira says that the Prophet (SAW) had said that if any one performed ablution and went to the mosque (for prayer) and found on reaching there that the congregation was over, he would nevertheless have the reward equal to those who prayed with the congregation and their reward would not be reduced. —Abu Daud, Nasai

If an employee is regular in his prayers and hardly misses any congregation, but once in a while by accident he fails to join the congregation, God will give him full credit of joining the congregation and the reward of the congregation will not be discounted. In fact, God does not attend to externals but rewards according to intentions and motives. In another report it is said that if any one has been able to join only one Rak'at of congregation he will have the reward of full prayer in congregation provided his motive is pure and unalloyed.

It is reported from Hazrat Ubay bin Ka'ab that the Prophet (SAW) had said, "If a man offers prayer together with another it will be better than his offering prayer alone, and if he joins with two others it will be better than his joining with one, and the larger the number in congregation the greater will be the pleasure of God". —Ahmed, Abu Daud, Nasai

God is pleased with large number of people in congregational prayer and His pleasure increases in proportion spiritual and moral purity will develop. In another report from Hazrat Umar it is said that the Prophet (SAW) had said that performing prayer in congregation has twenty-seven times greater credit than that of praying alone.

It is reported from Hazrat Abu Darda' that the Prophet (SAW) had said, "If in any hamlet or desert there are only three persons and they do not arrange to pray in congregation then Satan gets hold over them. So you should make a rule of praying in congregation, for the wolf eats up only the lone sheep straying from the flock".

This report clarifies by an example how beneficial it is to offer prayer in congregation and to make a rule of it. The strength of congregation helps in reforming a man and keeping him on the right path and saves him from machinations of Satan. Those who find it difficult to offer prayers with regularity congregation will make them regular and a spiritual atmosphere will be created which shall have a salutary effect on the mind and heart.

It is reported from Hazrat Abu Huraira that the Prophet (SAW) had said, "I swear by God in whose hand is my life that I have decided to order that wood is collected and then order for prayer and calling of Azan and appoint a person to lead the congregation and then go to the houses of those who do not join the congregation and set fire to them". —Bukhari, Muslim

The importance of congregational prayer can be well imagined from their report. The intention of giving such a fearful punishment by a person whose mercy and benevolence are testified by God is most significant.

It is reported from Hazrat Abdullah bin Umar that the Prophet (SAW) had said, "You should select the best man from among you to lead the congregation as he is the representative between you and God". —Al-Baihiqi

As stated in the report one who leads the congregation is its representative before God and therefore he should be the best among those gathered? The Prophet (SAW) himself used to lead the congregation but when illness prevented him he appointed the best man of the community, Hazrat Abu Bakr Siddiq to lead.

Hazrat Asma daughter of Yazid says that the Prophet (SAW) had said, "On the Day of Judgement all people will be raised at a time and then a caller will cry, "Where are those people who used to leave their beds to pray at night. Then those who used to offer Tahajjud (early morning) prayer will come forward and collect together and their number will be small. They will be admitted to paradise without taking any account while the account of others will be taken". —Al-Baihiqi

This report throws light on a very important fact. Such persons as keep awake at night and when all the world is enjoying sound sleep they leave their beds and bow prostrate before God, ask forgiveness of their sins and seek the bounty of God. The life of these servants of God is so sanctified that their accounts are adjusted in this world and they do not have any pollution with them when they are presented before God. So they will be admitted to paradise without taking any account.

It is reported from Hazrat Abu Huraira that the Prophet (SAW) had said, "After the Farz prayer the most excellent prayer is that of the middle of the night". —Muslim

It is reported from Hazrat Ibn Abbas that the Prophet (SAW) had said, "Noble men of my community are those who hold on to the Quran and keep awake in the night.

—Al-Baihiqi

Among the followers of the Prophet (SAW) people of pre-eminent and distinctive position are those who recite the Quran and try to mould their lives according to it and those who are prostrating before God seeking His forgiveness and benevolence while others are asleep. Such upholders of the Quran and prayerful at night certainly deserve eminent position.

Hazrat Abu Umama reports that the Prophet (SAW) insisted on waking up at night as this had been the way of godly men before them, the means of approach to God for them, atonement for their evils and restraining from sins. —Tirmizi

II. Fasting

Fasting is a sacred devotional rite and an effective of an employee's moral and spiritual uplift. The real object of fasting is purification of self and restraint as the Quran says : "Oh ye who believe! Fasting is prescribed to you as it was prescribed to those before you that may (learn) self-restraint". —(Q : 2 : 183)

Fasting is the best exercise for self-restraint without which piety cannot be acquired. The angelic qualities given to man are not always at work as sometimes the animal instinct gains control and he loses all thought of God's Greatness and His Omnipresence. Food and sex, which are the most potent demands of animal nature, are restrained for a specified time and turn man's attention to higher realities bringing him nearer to God. This exercise and experience restrains him from becoming disobedient and rebellious to God in the hours of trial so common in life. If this end is not achieved, fasting is useless and reduced to mere starvation for all those who cannot restrain their eyes, tongues and thoughts while those in perfect control of them may be counted as fasting although they may not have stopped eating and indulging in sex.

Fasting not only develops angelic qualities in an employee but even outwardly he acquires qualities of restraint of animal nature and devotion to God in common with angels. Obviously, if one cannot endure the restraint of hunger and thirst and abstention from sins for some time, he will not be able to stand for a moment against the trials and temptations in life and it will be difficult for him to put up with ordinary discipline and order, what to say his trying for any ambitious object and thus he will become an altogether useless an employee.

Fasting is not only a trial of endurance, but also revives in him the sense of thankfulness, for in prescribing fast God has reminded an employee of his very great boon that with His unbounded Grace and Benevolence He made arrangement for their true guidance in the month of fasting, which they could not get otherwise at any cost. On the other hand keeping aloof from the boons and amenities provided by God their importance and value is greatly enhanced and naturally the thought turns towards those who are not very happily placed and feelings of sympathy thus aroused make him attend to the needs of the poor and the helpless, and thereby creating a common bond between them which is the Will and Pleasure of God.

Collective fasting creates a general atmosphere of spirituality and goodness in which evil is suppressed and godliness prospers. Weak and low-spirited employee also gets an opportunity to walk with others on the path of virtue and piety.

If fasting is used to its best advantage, an employee who fasts will be raised to a position in which he will never be oblivious of his responsibilities and his entire lie he will not think of acting in a manner which is displeasing to God or injurious to any creature of God. He will refrain from sinful acts and will devote himself to the service of humanity and will never lose sight of the real aim of life inducing the work life.

It is reported from Hazrat Salman Farsi that the Prophet (SAW) delivered a sermon on the last day of Shaa'ban in which he said, "O my people you are on the threshold of a month of great solemnity and blessings. It is a month whose one night is better than a thousand months. God has prescribed fasting in this month and made Tarawih (early night) prayers optional, but it is pleasing to God. Whosoever willingly and with good intentions does one good act in this month will have the merit of having done an obligatory act of other months and who does a prescribed act in this month it will be equal to seventy prescribed acts of other months. This is the month of endurance and the reward of endurance is paradise and this is the month of sympathy with and care of the poor and needy men of the community".

—Mishkat

This is part of a long report in which the merits of the month of fasting have been explained. The words are quite clear and the excellence of the month is vividly brought forth. Describing the month of Ramazan as the month of endurance implies that in this month, by self-imposed curbs on him for a specified time, every year an employee undergoes training in self-discipline as a preparation for the rest of the eleven months and a zest for obedience to God is engendered in him. A believing employee in the world is like a soldier in the battlefield who has to fight against satanic temptations and forces of evil. If an employee does not possess the power of endurance, he will surrender to the enemy in the very first assault. "Month of sympathy" means those fasting people who have resources should let their poorer brethren participate in their God-given blessing and make arrangements for their Iftar (breakfast) and Sahr (before dawn repast). The word "Muwasat" in original report includes soothing words along with monetary help.

It is reported from Hazrat Abu Huraira that the Prophet (SAW) had said, "The reward of each good act may be ten to seven hundred times, but the reward of fasting is an exception as God says, "Fasting is for My sake and I will reward for it as much as I like". Fasting man gives up food and drink for His sake. He will have two great joys, one at the time of breaking fast and the other on meeting his Lord. Smell of fasting person's mouth is better than that of musk before God and fasting is a shield against evil. A fasting man should not indulge in obscene talk or noisy demonstrations or rioting. If anyone abuses him he should excuse himself from retaliation saying that he is fasting".

—Bukhari, Muslim

God rewards all good acts ten to seven hundred times according to the motive and sincerity in doing it, but the case of fasting is different as it is just for God's sake. Other good acts are somehow brought to the notice of other people but fasting is known only to the man who fasts and to God and no third person, and so its reward also is unlimited. Fasting in the month of Ramazan is a collective virtue in which atmosphere godliness prospers and as much benefit is drawn from fasting and as much sincerity and Taqwa, (fear of God's displeasure) is manifested in it and their effects spread over the remaining eleven months of the year; hence no limits can be placed on the growth of the virtues and their reward. God only can judge it. Other good acts normally do not have this peculiarity.

After enduring the strain of hunger and thirst the joy that is felt on breaking fast with honestly earned sustenance can well be imagined and at that time not only the body is refreshed but the soul is also enriched with the thought that the man has carried out the Divine Behest to the best of his ability. But the joy of meeting the Lord and Sustainer is much more than any joy experienced in this world.

Fast is described as a shield because it provides means of defence against the assaults of Satan. If the spirit of the fast is fully observed and besides the stomach, the mind and heart and the tongue also join in the fast it will become evident how fast becomes a shield against sins and lapses in this world and from the fire of hell in the next, and acts as the means of his salvation as mentioned in the report. If someone in the shape of devil drags him to sinful acts and abuse or a brawl he should excuse himself by taking cover of his fast.

Hazrat Abu Huraira reports that the Prophet (SAW) had said, "Whosoever fasts with firmness of belief and stock taking of his actions, God, will forgive his sins committed before. And whosoever offers Tarawih (early night prayers) with full devotion to faith and constant vigilance as to his accountability, God will forgive all his sins committed before."

Hazrat Abu Huraira reports that the Prophet (SAW) had said, "There is Zakat on everything and the Zakat of the body is fasting".

—Ibn Maja

It is reported from Hazrat Abu Huraira that the Prophet (SAW) had said, "If anyone while keeping fast does not refrain from falsehood or acting on falsehood God does not need his abstaining from food and drink."

—Bukhari

Fasting has another function to perform as a de-stressor. In every culture orgiastic experience is considered as most important de-stressor. That is the reason why in many cultures music, dance, alcoholic drinks, drugs, etc. and other forms of stress relieving techniques are encouraged and rewarded. Without this experience, man will die of stress. Fasting is one of the methods of getting orgiastic experience. The intention of the creator of the mankind is not to make a Muslim hungry for thirteen to fourteen hours. The underlining idea of fasting is to train him to reach a peak experience at the time of breaking of the fast. This tyranny for about a month is believed to be effective for the rest of eleven months in a year for relieving stress.

During the period of thirty days or so a Muslim is given tyranny to reach orgiastic or peak experience. This is the least stress buster.

III. Zakat and Charities

In several places in the Quran offering prayers and paying Zakat is said to be the whole of faith. Prayer represents the one and zakat the other. "And they have been commanded no more than this: to worship God, offering Him sincere devotion, being True (in faith); to establish regular Prayer and to practice regular Charity; and that is the Religion Right and Straight.

—(Q : 98 : 5)

By paying zakat or fulfilling the rights of the fellow-beings an employee not only performs his duty but also provides means to perfect his own personality. This perfection and purification is the main purpose of reducing stress, what is called learning in religion is just training and purifying the self in the light of knowledge and far sight which just means purity and development. By paying Zakat an employee gets rid of the evil traits of his character like selfishness, miserliness and love of money, and gains purity and strength of soul. In the Quran this purifying and training of self is frequently mentioned. Zakat in the Quran is described as means of increasing wealth and on the other hand interest on money is said to leading to loss of wealth, which to a causal observer will appear as a paradox but in fact there is a great secret behind it whose truth will become evident after some reflection. By paying zakat an employee purifies his soul and his wealth.

Payment and collection of zakat should be arranged collectively. An important feature of it is that no one is obliged to another or is tempted by vanity and imposition of obligation. The proceeds of zakat may be utilized in many works of social insurance service of religion and in modern terminology social welfare. The backbone of any Islamic state, which is the model welfare state can be this zakat and charities.

Hazrat Ayesha reports that she heard the Prophet (SAW) say, "If charity is included in any property (not given away) it will destroy the whole of it".

—Musnad Safi's Tarikh Kabir, Bukhari, Musnad Haimidi

If the portion due as zakat is included in any property and is not given away to the deserving, it will destroy the belief and the faith of its proprietor, at the same time the property can also be destroyed on account of this transgression. Non-payment of zakat makes the whole property of an employee unfit for use and what can be more unfortunate than keeping tainted money. In the same way if an undeserving person takes zakat and includes it in his property he makes this property unclean and it may be destroyed also.

Hazrat Abu Huraira reports, "The man whom God gave wealth and he did not pay zakat on it then on the Day of Judgement this property will become an extremely poisonous bald snake and bite him. The snake will have two black spots on its forehead and will entwine it self round his neck and grip his jaws and say: "I am your wealth and your treasure". Then the Prophet (SAW) recited the verse of the Quran: "And let not those who covetously withhold of the gifts which God hath given them of His grace, think that it is good for them; nay, it will be the worse for them; soon shall the things which they covetously withheld be tied to their necks like a twisted collar on the Day of Judgement". —(Q : 3 : 180)

The wealth, which could be the source of one's comfort and ease on the Day of Judgement if zakat were paid on it, would become his curse. The miser and lover of money who sits tight over his wealth like snake and do not allow others to be benefited by it, his wealth will become a snake and bite him. Black spots point out its being highly poisonous.

It is reported from Hazrat Abdullah bin Umar that the Prophet (SAW) had said, "The land watered by rain or a running brook or doing without irrigation because of the proximity of a river, tenth part of its produce will be given in zakat while twentieth part will be given on land for whose irrigation labour has to be employed".

Hazrat Ibn Abbas says that the Prophet (SAW) had made obligatory charity on the Eid day so that any unbecoming or obscene acts which might have been committed while fasting might be atoned and the poor are fed. —Abu Daud

The emphasis laid on the charity of the Eid day is evident from the very word that is purification of fasts and food for the poor.

It is indirectly reported from Hazrat Ata' bin Yasar that the Prophet (SAW) had said, "Acceptance of zakat is not permissible for the rich except in five cases, warriors in the path of God, collectors of zakat, a person indebted and one who has to pay damages and the person who purchases the zakat property from a poor man, or for a person who receives it as a gift from some recipient of zakat". —Malik, Abu Daud

God showers his bounties on those spending on the poor servants of God.

Hazrat Abu Huraira says that the Prophet (SAW) had said, "God ordains, 'O progeny of Adam', spend on poor servants and I will spend on you".

That is, if an employer spends on his employees is wealth on the poor, God will not let him become poor but continue to shower His bounties on him.

It is reported from Hazrat Anas that the Prophet (SAW) had said, "Charity cools the anger of God and guards against evil death". —Tirmizi

If any one by some lapses or sins has put himself in a position that rouses God's anger, charity will cool the God and make him fit to receive God's Mercy and Forgiveness. Besides, the merit of charity prevents bad death and engenders in a person a desire to do well and strengthen and perfect his faith and become stable and firm on the path of truth. So the result of charity is always good. The Quran also says: "But the (fruit of) the hereafter is for righteousness".

Hazrat Musa al bin Sa ad says that Sa'ad considered himself superior to humble men, but the Prophet (SAW) said,

"Men get sustenance from God on account of the poor people".
—Bukhari

To consider oneself superior to his humble fellow-beings is a folly, for God provides sustenance to many on account of and as a result of the blessings from the poor and gives them victory over the enemies of Islam. So it is not proper for the rich to look down upon the poor, rather it is their duty to help the poor and treat them well.

It is reported from Hazrat Ibn Umar that the Prophet (SAW) when he went to the pulpit and spoke on charity and refraining from begging, said, "The upper hand is better than the lower that of the receiver". —Bukhari, Muslim

Hazrat Abu Zar says that once he went to the Prophet (SAW) while he was sitting in the shade of Ka'aba and he called him and said, "By the Lord of Ka'aba they are in great loss." On my enquiry the Prophet (SAW) replied, "They are the wealthy people, excepting those spending (in charity) lavishly, but they are not many". —Bukhari, Muslim

Wealth is a great trial and only such men pass this trial successfully who willingly and generously spend in charities and those who do not do it, wealth for them is a curse, not a boon, and in the end they will be at a great loss.

It is reported from Hazrat Abu Huraira that the Prophet (SAW) had said, "The slave of wealth is accursed". —Tirmizi

There is nothing objectionable in the wealth itself, but what is reproachable is the love and worship of wealth. It is very hard for a worshipper of wealth to spend in the path of God. It is the height of dishonesty and thanklessness not to spend God-given wealth for His pleasure and according to His orders. How can one expect God's Mercy or any reward for such men. They are in fact very far from Divine Mercy. Curse and reproach alone are their lot. Worship of wealth is a very bad habit and this is why acceptance of charity is prohibited for one who is not needy. And even for the needy earning by labour and refraining from acceptance of zakat and charity is preferable as far as possible. Thus in one report it is said that acceptance of zakat and charity is not permissible for the rich or for one who is healthy and strong.

It is reported from Hazrat Abu Saeed Al-Khudri that the Prophet (SAW) had said. "Two characters cannot be consistent with faith, miserliness and discourtesy." —Tirmizi

The evil characters of miserliness and discourtesy are alien to the faith, as faith makes a man large-hearted self-respecting and ambitious while miserliness and discourtesy are products of petty-mindedness and meanness.

It is reported from Hazrat Abu Huraira that the Prophet (SAW) had said, "A generous man is nearer to God, men and paradise and away from hell, while a miser is remote from God, from men and from paradise and nearer to hell. God likes an uneducated generous person better than a prayerful miser".

—Tirmizi

It is reported from Hazrat Abu Masud that the Prophet (SAW) had said, "When a Muslim in the hope of divine reward spends on his wife and children that is also charity".

—Bukhari, Muslim

The real incentive of merit and reward is the pleasure of God which should ever be before a believer's mind. Whether he spends on his own people or on others it is the same trait demonstrated in different aspects of life and in essence all his acts are acts of charity.

It is reported from Hazrat Suria bin Malik that the Prophet (SAW) had said, "Shall I tell you the best form of charity? It is to support your daughter who has been returned to you and has no other supporter except you".

Hazrat Jabir says that the Prophet (SAW) had said: "Every good act is charity and this is also goodness and piety that you meet your brother with smiling face or fill his vessel with your bucket." —Ahmed, Tirmizi

The concept of charity in Islam is very wide and includes every good and pious act and on due consideration it would appear that other acts and deeds-in Islam too have a great value and command a very long range and depth.

It is reported from Hazrat Abu Musa Asha'ari that the Prophet (SAW) had said, "Charity is prescribed for every believer." People asked, "If a man has nothing to give in charity"? The Prophet (SAW) said, "He should earn by his labour, sustain himself and give in charity." People again asked, "If one cannot do this" The Prophet (SAW) said, "He should help a distressed and needy person." People said, "If that too is not possible?" The Prophet (SAW) said, "He should refrain from evil and mischief which is also charity". —Bukhari, Muslim

The wordings of the report are clear enough. What is needed is to feel pleasure in doing anything good, which may take different forms in different circumstances. But total absence of such tendency is a great obstacle in purification of self and that is why it has been made obligatory for every one. Islam has not deprived any one of such opportunities so much so that even taking care that one does not give pain to anyone is also included in the acts of charity.

It is reported from Hazrat Abu Umama that the Prophet (SAW) had said, "O children of Adam, it is better for you to give away in charity what is more than your need and to keep it with you is bad, though it is not reproachable to retain just sufficient for your sustenance and need and to begin with you should spend on those for whom you are responsible." —Muslim

Charity is appreciated in Islam and hoarding of wealth deprecated. By miserliness and greed for wealth on the one hand the circulation of money is blocked which could be of benefit to many and it loses its utility by being locked up in the safe while on the other hand charity develops man's spiritual and moral powers and purifies the soul, and cures him of the greed of wealth and material gains, making him with miserliness and greed. Charity has a great effect on realized by any one who has given thought to religious issues. Most important among persons on whom wealth should be come afterwards. It should not happen that outsiders are benefited generosity and the legitimate demands of the people of house are neglected.

Hazrat Amr bin Sho'aib reports from his father and grandfather that the Prophet (SAW) delivered a public sermon in which he exhorted: "Beware. It you are guardian of an orphan invest his property in trade, lest it should be consumed by zakat." —Tirmizi

It is reported from Hazrat Abu Huraira that the Prophet (SAW) had said, "The deserving man is not one who begs and people give him a piece of bread or a data or tower, but the man who has no means to meet his needs and no one is aware of his poverty to give him something by way of charity and yet he does not beg of anyone." —Bukhari, Muslim

The point emphasized in this report is that the care of such people is necessary who do not let their poverty be known and whose self-respect does not allow then to beg and therefore people do not generally realize their needs. Such people should be helped in a manner that their self-respect is not injured. The Quran also supports this and says: "Charity is for those in need, who in God's because are restrained (from travel), and cannot move about in the land, seeking (for trade or work): the ignorant man thinks because of their modesty that they are free from want. Thou shall know them by their (unfailing) mark. They beg not importunately from all and sundry. And whatever of good ye give, be assured God knoweth it well."

—(Q : 2 : 273)

The Zakat is for such persons who are so helplessly involved in the path of God that they cannot go about to seek their sustenance and because of their avoiding begging people take them for rich. You can read their condition from their faces. They do not pester people to beg and God will reward you for whatever money you spend on them. God knows it too well.

It is reported from Hazrat Abu Huraira that some one asked the Prophet (SAW), "What charity is deserving of greater reward"? The Prophet (SAW) said, "The best charity is one which you give while you are healthy and active and have need and desire for money, are afraid of poverty and hope to become rich. Not that (charity) about which you go on cogitating till your soul is about to depart and you give so much too so and so and so much to another, when to be sure it will be taken by them". —Bukhari, Muslim

It is indirectly reported from Hazrat Hasan that the Prophet (SAW) said, "You should guard your wealth with zakat and treat your sick people with charity and welcome troubles and difficulties with prayer and devotion". —Abu Daud

The point emphasized in this report is that one should keep one's mind above material means. Doctors may be consulted in illness but at no time it should be forgotten that health and disease and life and death are in the hands of God without Whose Will and Orders nothing can happen and in all matter while utilizing material means, help of God should also be sought. And charity is the best means of securing His Pleasure. Praying to God will bring about His help. We should never solely depend on our efforts or material means.

Hazrat Abu Huraira and Hakim ibn Hizam report that the Prophet (SAW) had said, "The best charity is that which leaves a man contented and you should make a beginning from those whose care is your responsibility". —Bukhari, Muslim

Leaving contentment behind means that there are no second thoughts after spending in charity. While giving charity one should be careful not to make himself a destitute in need of charity from others, or that he should be so firm that his poverty does not strain his heart. Hazrat Abu Bakr Siddique brings all his wealth to the Prophet (SAW) that nothing but God and His Prophet (SAW) remain at his home but he is quite content. Yet every one is not Hazrat Saddique and Islam demands from the man only that which he can cheerfully part with leaving himself solvent, and in any case there should be no strain on the heart otherwise the charity will lose all its merit. Another thing to be noted is that only after meeting the needs of his dependents, charity is extended to others, contravention of this is against the very spirit of charity. It must always being at home.

Zakat and charity purges a heart of all impurities such as jealously, misery stringiness, greed and anger. In the act of giving charity a Muslim—an employer and employee finds expression of potency. To give is to love. In the act of loving we feel manliness. Similarly an act of charity gives a feeling of contentment, which acts as a de-stressor. Stress arises from the accumulation of imbecilities of mind such as anger, greed, jealously, fear, etc. when charity is given the fear of becoming poor gets reduced. A man feels happy and contended by giving charity.

IV. Haj

The meaning of Haj is an intention to visit holy places. Haj occupies basic position in religion.

The Quran says: "Pilgrimage thereto (Ka'aba) is a duty men owe to God—those who can afford the journey; but if any deny faith, God stands not in need of any of His creatures."

—(Q : 3 : 97)

To go to perform Haj is in fact responding to the call of God. One who is indifferent to it despite his ability to do it has turned his face away from God, which is to his own detriment and can do no harm to God.

God has made Ka'aba a repository of all good, a blessing and a source of guidance for the whole world. It is the fountainhead of unalloyed unity of God. Prophet Abraham and his son, prophet Ismael, built this house by the order of God and called it His house. God has greatly enhanced it dignity and made it a centre of the world.

God had assigned to Prophet Abraham the leadership of the world and through him proclaimed Haj to all the people of the world, so that the worshippers of one God attach themselves to this centre and collect together once a year to make a round of it, to sacrifice animals, eat their flesh and distribute it to the poor. Ka'aba is on the one hand a real place of worship and a mosque and other mosques are its representatives, while on the other hand the basic purpose of this building is to help and care for the weak and the needy and so it has been made a centre of the faith.

Haj is in a way the greatest devotional rite. Employees for the love and obedience of God leaves his organization, his relatives and friends, undertakes a long arduous journey as if a violent passion is dragging him along with the heart turned to God, with repentance on sins, seeking forgiveness with utmost humility and pledging to keep on the right path in future and praying to God for the courage and strength to live up to it.

The rites of Haj in themselves are impressive in confirming belief in the unity of God. Ahram is a poor man's dress in which there no distinction between the high is and the low and in the house of God all look alike. An employee does not only refrain from evils but even in permissible limits he avoids ostentation. His cry is only "O God, without partner, I am present before you". Walking, sitting, ascending heights and descending, his only call is "I am present" and praising the Almighty he goes ahead kissing the black stone, inoculating the Ka'aba, offering two Raka'ats of prayer at the station of Prophet (SAW) Abraham, ascending the two hillocks of Safa and Marwa and being ever engaged in calling to God, praying, beseeching and seeking His Pleasure; all these rites demonstrate devoted service and obedience which are not met with in other forms of worship throughout one's life. This will reduce stress.

Sacrifice of animals is really in the words of Quran the great sacrifice, which was the atonement of Prophet Ismael. Sacrifice of animals represents sacrifice of one's own life in the path of God and a pledge that it is at His disposal. Otherwise, sacrifice of animals has no significance unless some exalted and sacred sentiment is not at the back of it.

> "It is neither their meat nor their blood that reaches God: it is your piety that reaches Him." —(Q : 22 : 37)

The order of sacrifice is not restricted to Mecca alone, but wherever the Muslims are they should sacrifice animals on this occasion as the Prophet used to do at Medina.

"It is reported from Hazrat Abu Huraira that the Prophet (SAW) had said addressing us: "O people Haj is prescribed for you, so you should perform it." —Muslim, Nasai

"The Prophet (SAW) said that whosoever visited this house (Ka'aba) and did not commit any act of passion or disobedience to God, he would return from there in a state as if he was born anew." (That is, God will forgive all his sins and he will return pure and unpolluted).

The Prophet (SAW) said : "One who, intends to perform Haj should not delay it, for possibly he may fall ill or his she-camel dies (that is the means of travel are blocked or the roads are not safe and travel money saved is spent), and also possibly some urgent business intervenes to make the undertaking of journey impossible." (Therefore, one should hurry otherwise any untoward accident might deprive him of Haj).

—Ibn Maja, Ibn Abbas

It is reported from Hazrat Abu Umama that the Prophet (SAW) had said that one who was not prevented by some urgent need and was not so ill as to be unable to travel nor was he stopped by any tyrant and yet he did not perform Haj and died, it was up to him whether he died as Jew or a Christian.

—Al Baihiqi

Having ability and resources if one refrains from Haj it means that his heart is not with God but elsewhere and the attachment, which he should have to the unity of God and its centre, is not in Him, so God also does not care for such a person and he may die in any condition he likes. Since Jews and Christians did not perform Haj one who abstains from it is likened to them. Indifference to Haj is in fact an attitude of unbelief and so Hazrat Umar had said that he would like to impose Jizia on those who refrain from Haj while in a position to undertake it.

The Prophet (SAW) had said that whosoever starts for Haj, Umra or Jihad and dies on the way, God will reward him as one who performed Haj, Umra or actually joined in the Jihad.

By performing Haj and Umra an employee's heart is purged of all bad-feelings such as desire for power, status, jealously, pride, and animosity to understand this phenomena one should actually performed Haj. After this pilgrimage man's heart does not attached itself to any rewards associated with the mundane affairs. It does not mean that an employee stops working as per the regular schedule. Nay, he works much harder and performs his duties in the best possible way. Excellency will be his hall-mark. However, he is not worried about the rewards associated with hard work. He doesn't compete nor does he feel ill will towards his co-workers, superiors, sub-ordinates, etc. This is really a stress-buster.

V. Reciting the Quran

One of the qualities of reducing the stress in work place is reciting the Quran. By reciting the Quran all the impurities in the heart and mind will be cleaned, an employee feels that the Allah's soul is in his heart an employee will get the closer to the Allah. The Prophet of Allah (SAW) observed: "The servant gets nearest unto Allah by reciting the Quran". —Tirmidhi

An employee should engage in leisure hours the recitation of the Quran and never feel weary of reciting the Holy Book. The Holy Prophet (SAW) said, "Allah has ordained that any man who engages himself in the recitation of Quran so often that he finds no time for supplication I shall provide him more without asking than those who ask". —Tirmidhi

Advising employees to recite the Holy Quran, the Holy prophet (SAW) also said, "The man who has studied the Quran and recite it daily is like a basket fall of musk whose sweet smelt is making the whole atmosphere fragrant. And the man who has studied the Quran but does not recite it is like a bottle full of musk whose mouth has been sealed with a stopper.

—Tirmidhi

Before reciting the Quran, an employee should be completely neat and clean, do ablution and recite it sitting in a clean and tidy place. By doing this his mind and body get purified. All the impurities will go and realize the good things. Thereby it will eliminate the stress. Reciting the Quran with the sole motive of seeking guidance and not for the sake of gaining popularity, or establishing a reputation for good or a name for piety.

The Holy Prophet (SAW) said: "He who recites the Quran will be told on the Day of Judgement. Recite the Quran how in the same clear and distinct manner and in the same harmonious style in which you used to recite it with care and propriety in the world and a reward for the recitation of each verse you shall be elevated one degree higher and your ultimate place is near the end of the final verse.

—Tirmidhi

An employee should recite the Holy Quran with eagerness and favour and put all in the heart and soul in the recitation. Be sure that love of the Quran means love of Allah. The Holy prophet (SAW) said: "The best form of worship for my people is the recitation of Quran".

By reciting the Quran at Tahajjud prayer at dawn, an employee entitles the reward of highest degree and it should be the aspiration of a true employee to attain the appear of excellence in reward for recitation.

"This is a scripture that we have revealed unto thee, full of blessing, that thee may ponder over its revelations, and that men of understanding may get guidance from it" —(Q : 38 : 29)

By reciting the Quran and understanding the meaning an employee will grasp the realities and learn the wisdom contained in it. Hazrat Ikrama (RAA) whenever opened the Quran he often fainted, He used to say: "These are the words of my Great and Glorious Lord".

An employee will feel the full impact of the verses of the Holy book during recitation. Rejoice and feel happy a reading about the narrations of the Divine Mercy, forgiveness and the Everlasting bounties of paradise. On the reading about the narrations of the wrath, anger and the terrific punishment of the Hell, an employee will see his eyes will flow and the heart will melt with the sentiments of repentance and shame.

After reciting the Holy Quran offer a prayer. The words of one of prayers offered by Hazrat Umar (RAA) are as follows, "Allah, whatever my tongue recites from thy book, grant me the fare to reflect upon it. Allah! Bestow upon me the understanding of it vouch safe to me the knowledge of its meaning, and spirit, and the vision to see its pieties. Grand me the favour to act according to its injunctions as long as I live. Your being is without doubt Omnipotent".

Recitation of Quran keeps an employee always in touch with his creator. The believer does not take Quran as any other book. He believes it to be uncorrupted book of God. His belief in the creator gets strengthened when he reads or hears the word of God. This gives him a soothing feeling. There are innumerable verses in the Quran which provide a relief from stress to a Muslim. For example, those who believe in Allah and steadfast in their belief, angels will descend on them and say do not be scared, we with you in this world and in the life hereafter.

VI. Visiting Graveyards

An employee should often visit the graveyard, thereby he realizes that the worldly gains like wealth, power, status, etc. will have lost their value and only his deeds will count. When he realize this, he will not commit any mistake and go for worldly gains. This will reduce his stress.

These visits remind an employee of the life hereafter and induce him to start making preparations for the life after death. The Holy Prophet (SAW) accompanied a funeral procession to the graveyard and sitting down a grave studded so much of tears that the earth becomes wet. Then addressing the companions, the Holy Prophet (SAW) said, Brothers prepare you for this day.

—Ibn Hajah

Once when he was seated near a grave the Holy Prophet (SAW) said "Every grave proclaims in the most terrific voice; O Progeny of Adam! Have you forgotten me? I am the house of loneliness. I am a strange land of wilderness! I am a hole of mites and worms. I am a place of hardship and trial. Save those fortunate one for whom Allah makes me commodious and wide, I am for all other human beings a tortuous place".

In addition, the Holy Prophet (SAW) observed: The grave is either one of the pits of Hell of a small flower –garden out of the gardens of paradise. —Tabarani

An employee will learn a lesson as seeing the graveyard and from the habit of concentrating his work life. Once Hazrat Ali visited a graveyard. Hazrat Kameel accompanied him, on reaching the graveyard, Hazrat looked at the graves and them addressing the inmates of graves, said:

> O inmates of graves, O inhabitants of ruins! O those who like in isolation in a land of wilderness! Say, how you are? As regards conditions over here, the assets left over have been divided, the offspring are rendered orphans the widows have entered into the new marriage contracts. This is the state of affairs in our world. Now tell us what is happening to you". Hazrat Ali then remained silent for some time and then turning towards Hazrat Kameel observed: Kameel, if the inmates of these graves were allowed to speak, they would say piety is the most valuable treasure. Having said this, Hazrat Ali wept and continued to weep for a long time. Later Hazrat Ali remarked: "Kameel, the grave is an enclosure where only deeds matter and as soon as one meets death, he realizes this fact".

From the above, an employee realizes that all the assets will go waste and only the pleasure of God will be useful. An employee should pray Allah for rewards on the death and grant them mercy, whenever he visits the graveyard. Hazrat Sufiyan states "that" just as the living stand in need of eating and drinking, so do the dead stand in dire need of prayers for their salvation.

VII. Sleeping

One of the qualities of reducing stress is sleeping. An employee after doing his work in a day he should sleep at night. This will reduce the stress. Allah has appointed the night-time for peace and rest. He has made the day a time for keeping awake and a time for labour to earn one's living.

"And He it is who created night a covering for you and sleep for response and made the day time waking up".

—(Q : 25 : 47)

"And we made your sleep for repose and we made the night a covering and we appointed the day for livelihood".

—(Q : 86)

"Have they not observed how we have made the night that they may rest therein and the day bright (So that they may strive during its course). No doubt, there are signs in it for a people who believe.

The making of the night dark so as to serve as a time of peace and rest and making the day bright so that an employee should keep a strict schedule of sleeping at night and working hard for earning one's livelihood during the day. In the light of day, an employee should devote his energy to work and make strenuous efforts to earn his living till his faculties and limbs begin to feel tired.

Then in the night when an atmosphere of peace and privacy reigns, repose in bed in a calm and comfortable state. As soon as dawn breaks, arise and involve the blessings of Allah enter into the field of practical endeavour with renewed vigour. Employees who are indolence and lethargy drone a day-time or keep awake throughout night enjoying season's pleasure and making many are guilt of violating the low of nature. They ruin their health and undermine their lives. Those who sleep during the hours of the day not only neglect their daily work but also deprive their body and soul of necessary repose and rest; for sleep during the day cannot serve as an alternative for repose at night in providing rest and nourishment.

The Apostle of Allah (S.A.W) even disapproval of the idea that a man should remain awake all night for offering worship to Allah and thus suffer an unbearable hardship. The Apostle of Allah (SAW) once said to Hazrat Abdullah him. Umar "It is time what I have heard that you regularly keep fast during the day and pass all night in offering prayers? Hazrat Abdullah submitted: I confess this to be time". The Holy Prophet (SAW) observed: "No, don't go on like that keep fast sometimes and eat and drink at other times. Similarly get some sleep and then rise and say prayers. You owe a duty to your eye".

—Bukhari

Recite some portion of the Holy Quran at the time of going to bed. The Holy prophet (SAW) invariably used to recite a portion of the Holy Quran before going to sleep. He has observed: "Allah sends an angel to a man who recites a portion of the book of Allah before going to sleep to protect him from all harm till the time of his rising". —Ahmed

The Holy prophet (SAW) has further observed: "When a man lies down on the bed, an angel and the devil call on him. The angel says to him "Close thy deeds of the day with a virtuous act". And the devil says: "Close thy deeds of the day with an evil act." If that man then recites the name of Allah before going to sleep, the angel stands guard over him all night".

From the above we can understand that the night sleep is a must for all including employees. This will reduce the stress. And after getting from bed, be should offer prayer. All the good work done during the day will be taken into account by the angels and will stand guard over him all night.

VIII. Control of Anger

One of the reasons for stress in work life is anger. When an employee becomes an anger, his health is affected it leads to stress. The following are Islamic solutions for relieving anger.

One of the qualities of conflict is anger. Anger is said to be one of the emotions. When an employee lost his emotion, it becomes anger.

Those who restrain (their) anger and pardon men. And Allah loves the doers of good (to others). —(Q : 3 : 133)

Verily, anger is of Satan. —Abu Dawud

Who do ye imagine to be powerful or strong? Asked the Prophet of his companions. "He who throws people down", they replied. "Nay"? Said the Prophet, "It is he who masters his anger!" —Muslim and Abu Dawud

He is not strong or powerful who throws people down, but he is strong who masters his anger. —Bukhari and Muslim

When one of you is angry while standing, let him sit down; and if his anger subsides, (then, well and good), otherwise let him lie down. —Abu Dawud

A man came to the Prophet, and said: "O Prophet of God! Enjoin upon me a duty, but do not demand much of me, lest I forget (everything)". The Prophet said: "Avoid anger."

—Bukhari and Muslim

A man begged of the Prophet some rule of conduct. 'Avoid anger', said the Prophet. This he repeated several times.

—Bukhari

Narrates Abu Huraira: Once a man asked the Prophet to give him a piece of advice. The Prophet said: Do not fall into anger. The man repeated the question. The same reply was given. The man persisted and asked for yet another advice. The Prophet again said: Do not fall into anger. —Bukhari

"One who subdues anger is really a courageous man," said the Prophet. "A man of strength is not one who overpowers an opponent; but it is he who, in a moment of intense provocations, exercises restraint!"

Said the Prophet: "Anger is roused under the influence of Satan, and Satan was created out of fire and fire is put out by water. So, whenever you fall into anger, wash your face, hands, and feet with cold water."

Said the Prophet; No one has taken a more bitter draught than the subduing of anger for the sake of God.

—Ahmad: Musnad

Hazrat Atiya Sa'adi says that the Prophet (SAW) had said: "Anger is due to satanic influence and since Satan has been created from fire, whenever man feel angry, he should perform ablution". —Abu Dawud

From the above, whenever the man feels anger, he should perform ablution and offer nafil prayer. All the satanic influences from the mind and heart will go, thereby the anger will be relieved.

Hazrat Abu Zhar says that the prophet (SAW) had said,-"If any of you feels angry while he is standing he should sit down". If he subsidies so much the better, otherwise he should lie down.

—Mishkat

If an employee gets anger, he should sit down and if the anger is not controlled, he should lie down.

Hazrat Abu Huraria reports that the prophet (SAW) had said that the strong man was really not one who overcame his opponent in wrestling but one who controlled himself at the time of anger that is reframed from doing anything not liked by God and His prophet (SAW). —Bukhari

An employee should control anger that is his real strength for nearness to Allah.

Hazrat Anas reports that prophet (SAW) had said God would cover up the faults of those who guarded their tongues (from untruth) and put-off punishment of those who controlled their anger and would forgive anyone who asked forgiveness. —Mishkat

An employee should control his tongue (from untruth) in work life, which is the basis of anger. If he controls it, the anger also controlled. The God will give the reward for employees who control the anger.

Hazrat Abu Huraira says that a person (who was probably hot-tempered) requested the Prophet (SAW) to give him advice. The Prophet (SAW) said, "Never be angry". The man repeated his request and every time the prophet gave him the same advice.

—Bukhari

Employees are advised that they should not get angry in their work life.

Hazrat Abu Huraira says that the Prophet (SAW) had said that the Moses had asked God which of His servants was dearest to Him and God had said those who are strong enough to follow forgiveness. —Miskat

An employee should forgive the mistakes committed by their superiors, co-workers, and sub-ordinates for the sake of Allah, and he should not be angry with them.

IX. Patience

One of the qualities for stress is patient. The management, supervisors and employees should be patient in their work life. They should satisfy the Allah (God). There are number of references to patient and perseverance in Islam. Islam asked the people to be steadfast, patient, and to help one another, maintain patience while doing the righteous work. This leads to relieving of stress.

Verily man is in loss. Except such as have faith and do right deeds and join together in the mutual teaching of truth, and of patient and consultancy. —(Q : 103 : 2-3)

The management and also the employees should understand about, the things for which patient is required is an important conditions for controlling stress. This is evident in the following verse

"And how can you have patient
about things about which your
understanding is not complete" —(Q : 18 : 68)

Patience does not only depend on how much people understand the expected reward, but also in how much they believe that they can really attain it.

"Patiently then preserve. For the
promise of Allah is true ......" —(Q : 40 : 55)

In another verse Allah, the All-High,
All Glorious says :
"So persevere in patience, for
the promise of Allah is true". —(Q : 40 : 77)

The management and an employee should depend only on Allah, who gives the reward for patience.

Allah, the exalted has stated patience as a condition for reward. This can be seen as highlighting the importance of patience as well as fact that it is very different to exhibit patience.

Peace be into you for that you have persevered in patience! Now how excellent is the trial home. —(Q : 13 : 24)

From the above it shows that if the management and employees who persevere in this world with patience will be rewarded in the hereafter with excellent homes. This will relieve the stress for them.

"Those who patiently persevere will truly receive their reward without measure". —(Q : 39 : 10)

The above verse shows that the reward for the patient is uncountable.

But those who have been granted (true) knowledge said : Alas for you! The reward of Allah is best for those who believe and work right sources : But this none shall attain except whom stead fast persevere (in good). —(Q : 28 : 80)

From the above it shows that the employees who believe and do righteous work will be rewarded, however one cannot achieve these unless he patiently perseveres.

And none will be granted such goodness except those who exercise patient and self-restraint none but persons of the greatest good fortune. —(Q : 41 : 35).

From the above it shows that if the employees are patient, they have the good fortune.

An employee should be patient whole competing with others. The success depends on patience. For example promotion in the organization may not be forth coming, an employee who is patient keeps his cool.

O' you who believe persevere in patience and constancy; in such perseverance; strong than each other; and fear Allah that you may prosper. —(Q : 3 : 200)

Patience in an organization can be considered as a competitive advantage patient provides necessary strength in one's organizational life.

> "If there are twenty amongst you,
> patient and persevering they will
> Vanquish two-hundred". —(Q : 8 : 65)

> "For the present, Allah has lightened your (task). For He knows that there is a weak spot in you : But (even so) If there are a hundred of you patient and persevering, they will vanquish two hundred". —(Q : 8 : 66)

During stressful work life the employees require a great degree of determination through patience and perseverance.

> "But if you persevere patiently, and guard against evil, then, that will be a determining factor in all attain".
> —(Q : 3 : 186)

The perseverance, patience and persistence of prophet

Mohammad (SAW) and his companions in pursuing a policy of restraint for thirteen years in Makkah are excellent examples, likewise an employee should have it for the sake of Allah in their working life. This will relieve stress.

X. Zikir

One of the qualities of reducing stress at work place by an employee is reciting 'Tasbee'. Tasbee is training given to employees to recite 'subhnallah' thirty three times, 'Allamthulillha' thirty-three times, 'Allah-Akbar thirty-three times and lalilahaillah one time for thanking God. Totally 100 times it has to be recited. If an employee recite this stress at work, it will be relieved. If he recite this, his heart and mind will get purity of things and all the impurities will be removed. He will experience none than the Allah's soul in him.

XI. Believing Taqdir (Fate)

One of the qualities of relieving stress is believing Taqdir or fate. Whatever happens to an employee in organization by nature is the will of God. Employees have to believe it. Fate is the law of life, the decree of God, Taqdir "Whatever suffering ye suffer" points out the Quran, it "is what your own hands have wrought". —(Q : 42 : 29)

Fate or Taqdir is used in the Quran in three broad senses. First the term fate denotes to divine initiative or of the operation of the law of nature. Sign of plan of existence necessarily conceived in advance or pre-determined even as every human plan is pre-determined before it is put into action, with this difference that whereas man's knowledge of the nature of things entering his plan being limited, he changes it as experience warrants him, whereas God's knowledge of everything being perfect, occasion cannot arise to alter the course he adopts, god does not alter his ways or the laws of nature or the fundamental bases of life, of its ebbs and flows from the exclusive domain of divinity, and man as an employee has not valid ground to question them, because he cannot grasp in right perspective the working of these laws or the reality about them. He is simply believe that they are the "laws devised by god", the Lord of compassion, and must necessarily be good. His responsibility lies only in the nature of the use be make of these laws. Every reaction to them is Taqdir (Fate).

Secondly, there is the field of human initiative. "Whosoever followed the right course, he doth so for the good of his own soul, and whosoever followed the wrong course doth so to its own hurt". —(Q : 17 : 16)

"Our own acts" for good or ill, are mightier powers. That too is Taqdir employees here is the maker of his own fate. The balance set in the nature of an employee or the sense of discrimination ingrained in him must, in all circumstances, be the trial guide in distinguish between what he ought and what he ought not to do.

The Quran has laid down certain definite injections touching human conduct, as may easily be endorsed by reason and experience. They denote certain principles of life operating for peace and order, and indicate one has to avoid in life and what to observe. These directions or commandments reflect the principles of harmony subsisting in the world of nature and for that reason may be taken to signify the will of God, and one has to confirm to them also. Conformity with them and non-conformity produce opposite results. Both are called Taqdir.

And lastly, there is the reaction on our life of the deeds of others. Sometimes they bring us joy. The joy may seem unexpected. But an employee to feel the joy proceeding from the good deeds of others is the result of a process of pleasure of God in us. Even that is Taqdir sometimes the deeds of others bring us pain and suffering that is Taqdir.

From the above it has been concluded that the good deeds of an employee and pleasure of God will change our fate. He has to experience and realize it. That will relieve the stress.

Notes and References

1. John, M. Ivancevich, Michael, T. Matteson and Edward, P. Richard III, Who's liable for stress on the job? *Harvard Business Review*, March-April 1985, pp. 60-72.
2. Robert, W. Eckles, Stress-Making friends with the enemy, *Business Horizons*, March-April 1987, pp. 74-78.
3. Keith, Davis and John, W. Newstrom, Human Behaviour at Work, 8th edition, McGraw Hill International Ltd., New Delhi, 1989, p. 482.

4. Resa, W. King Irene Pave, "Stress Claims are Making Business Jumping", Business Week, October 14, 1985, pp. 152-54.
5. Sẹlye, H. (1936). A Syndrome Produced by Diverse Mucous Age, *Nature*, 138, p. 32.
6. Canon, W.B. (1935). Stress and strain, Homeostasis, *American Journal of Medical Science*, 89(1).
7. Lazarus, R.S. Cohen, J.B., Folkman, S. and Schaefer, C. (1980). 'Psychological Stress and Adoption'. Some Unresolved Issues, in H. Selye (Ed.) Selye's Guide to Stress Research, Vol. 1, New York.
8. Jemmot, J.B., J. Boy Senko, M. Boy Senko, D.C. Mc. Cell and R. Chapman, D. Meyer and H.Benson (1983). Academic Stress, Power Motivation, and Decrease in Secretion Rate of Salivary Secretary Immune Globulin, *The Lancet*, 8339, 1400-2.
9. Arsenault, A. and S. Dolan (1983). The role of personality occupation and organization in understanding the relationship between Job-stress, performance and absenteeism, *Journal of Occupational Psychology*, 56, pp. 227-40.
10. Kethleen Anthony and Brain H. Kleiner, "The Price of Success", Business forum, Spring 1987, pp. 10-13; Saroj Parasuraman and Joseph Parasuraman, A. Alutto, "An examination of the organizational antecedents of stressors at work", *Academy of Management Journal*, March 1981, pp. 48-67.
11. Arthur, P. Brief and Jeniffer, M. Atich, "Studying Job Stress : Are we making Mountains out of Molehills?" *Journal of Occupational Behaviour*, April 1987, pp. 115-26.
12. Pareek, U. (1993). Making Organizational Roles Effective, New Delhi, Tata McGraw Hill.
13. John, H. Howard, David, A. Cunningham and Peter A. Rechnitzer, "Role ambiguity, Type A behaviour, and job satisfaction. Moderating effects a cardiovascular and biochemical responses associated with coronary risk", *Journal of Applied Psychology*, February 1986, pp. 95-101.
14. Susan, E. Jackson, Richard, L. Schwab and Randall, S. Schuler, "Towards an understanding of Burnout phenomenon", *Journal of Applied Psychology*, November 1986, pp. 630-40.
15. Janis, I.L. (1982). Decision-making under Stress in L. Goldberger and S. Breznitz (Eds.) *Handbook of Stress : Theoretical and Clinical Aspects*, London, MacMillan.
16. Cameron, R. and D. Meichenbaum (1982), The Nature of Effective Coping and the Treatment of Stress-related Problems : A Cognitive-Behavioural Perspective, in L. Gold Berger and S. Breznitz (Eds.) *Handbook of Stress : Theoretical and Clinical Aspects*, London : MacMillan.

7

Conflict and their Resolution in Islam

After the chapter stress, the conflict management becomes an important part of the study of quality of work life. It can certainly hurt an organizational performance as well as lead to the loss of many good employees. The word 'conflict' means different meanings to different persons. There are plethora of definitions of conflict.[1] Conflict can range from a minor difference of opinion to war between nations. This study examines the conflicts among the members of the organization, given the mature, adult-human-being and the nature of bureaucratic, formal organization conflict is inevitable.

Conflict is a process that begins when one party perceives that another party has negatively affected, or is about to negatively affect something that the first party cares about.[2] One survey reported that managers spent an estimated twenty percent of their time dealing with conflict[3].

EFFECTS OF CONFLICT IN ORGANIZATIONS

Conflict is often seen by on organization as destructive. In fact one observer said that "by adeptly avoiding conflict with co-workers, some executives eventually wreak organizational havoc".[4] Conflict is not all bad, but rather may result in either productive or non-productive outcomes. The conflict is bad when it is lasts a long period of time or becomes too intense. At the interpersonal level, cooperation and teamwork may deteriorate. Distrust may grow among people who need to coordinate their efforts. For employees, some may feel defeated, while the self-image of others will decline. The motivation level of some employees will be reduced. It is important for managers to be aware of the potential for interpersonal and intergroup conflicts, to anticipate their likely outcomes and to use appropriate conflict resolution strategies.

CONFLICT THOUGHTS

One school of thought has argued that conflict must be avoided that it indicates a malfunctioning within the group. This is called traditional view. Another school of thought, the human relation view, argues that conflict is a natural and inevitable outcome in any group and that it need not be evil, but rather has the potential to be a positive force in determining group performance.

The third, integrationist approach, in that can be a positive force in a group but argues that some conflict is absolutely necessary for a group to perform effectively.

(a) The Traditional View

According to the traditional view of conflict, it is a belief that all conflict is harmful and must be avoided. This view was consistent with the attitudes that prevailed about group behaviour in the 1930's and 1940's. Conflict was seen a dysfunctional outcome resulting from poor communication, a lack of openness and trust between people, and the failure of managers to be responsive to the needs and aspirations of their employees.

The view that all conflict is bad certainly offers a simple approach to looking at the behaviour of people who create conflict. Since all conflict is to be avoided, we have to look at the causes of conflict and improve the organizational performance.

(b) The Human Relations Approach

The human relations position argued that conflict was a natural occurrence in all groups and organizations. Since conflict was inevitable, the human-relation school advocated acceptance of conflict. There are even times when conflict may benefit a group's performance. The human relations view dominated conflict theory from the late 1940's through the mid-1970's.

(c) The Integrationist View

While the human-relations approach accepted the conflict, the integrationist approach encourages conflict on the grounds that a harmonious, peaceful tranquil, and cooperative group is prone to become static, apathetic and non-responsive to needs for change and innovation. The major contribution of the interaction approach is encouraging group leaders to maintain an ongoing minimum level of conflict-enough to keep the group viable, self-critical and creative.

FUNCTIONAL AND DYSFUNCTIONAL CONFLICT

Gibson *et. al.*[5], classified conflicts into functional conflicts and dysfunctional conflicts. A functional conflict is one that enhances the performance of an organization; this conflict usually arises when different groups within an organization agree about achieving a certain goal but differ as the means to achieve it. This conflict can motivate the different groups to improve their methods when the conflict is settled, the goal can be achieved in the most effective manner. A dysfunctional conflict is usually one that individuals and groups take personal Kelly[6] notes that conflict occurs when the group faces a novel problem of task when new values are imported from the social environment into the group; or when member extra-group roles are different from their intra-group roles.

...Groups require disharmony as well as harmony, dissociation as well as association, and conflicts within them are by no means altogether disruptive factors. Group formation is the result of both types of process. Far from being necessarily dysfunctional a certain degree of conflict[7] is necessary.

The organization will benefit from the functional conflict after it is settled demonstrates that the effect of a conflict depends primarily on the way it is managed. If it is not well managed it becomes dysfunctional one that hinders operation of an organization. There is a line between functional and dysfunctional conflicts. Managers make sure that this line is not crossed. It usually depends on the group's culture, tolerance and ability to take stress.

The positive view of conflict found in-group process can also be found in an individual when analyzing conflict from the perspective of individuals and organizations. There are two types of conflict namely.

(a) Intra-Individual conflict, and
(b) Inter-personal conflict.

(a) Intra-Individual Conflict

Every individual within there are usually a number of competing needs and roles, a variety of different ways that drives and roles, can be expressed. Many types of barriers which can occur between the drive and goal and both positive and negative aspects attached to the desired goals. These complicate the human adaptation process and often result in conflict. Intra-Individual conflicts are frustration, goal conflict and role conflict.

Frustration

Frustration is a result of a motivation (drive) being blocked to prevent one from reaching a desired goal. If you are trying to finish a report by quitting time in the afternoon, and one interference after another develops to require your time, then by the middle of the afternoon, when you see that your goal for the day may not be reached, you are likely to become frustrated. You may become irritable, develop an uneasy feeling in you as defence mechanisms, because you are trying to defend yourself from the psychological effects of the blocked goal.

The example given is merely a one-day frustration that probably will be overcome tomorrow, but the situation is more serious when there is a long-run frustration, such as a blocked opportunity for promotion. Then you have to live with the frustration day after day. It begins to build emotional disorders that interfere with your ability to function effectively.

Types of Reactions

One of the most common reactions to frustration is aggression. Whenever people are aggressive, it is likely that they are reflecting frustrations that are upsetting them. Additional reactions to frustration include goals. We can illustrate them by continuing the story of the blocked promotion. Suppose that you think your supervisor is blocking your promotion. The blockage may be real or only a result of your imagination, but in any case it is real to you. As a result of your frustration, you may become aggressive by demanding better treatment and threatening to appeal to higher management. Or you may do almost the reverse and become apathetic, not responding to your job or associates. Another reaction is withdrawal, such as asking for a transfer or quitting your job. Regression to less mature behaviour also is possible, such as self-pity and pouting.

If there is a fixation, perhaps you constantly blame your supervisor for the both your problems and the problems of others, regardless of the true facts. You also may develop a physical disorder such as an upset stomach or choose a substitute goal such as becoming the leader of a powerful informal group in office politics. All of these are possible reactions to frustration. It is evident that they are not usually favourable, either to the individual or to the organization, so it is desirable in organizational behaviour to reduce frustrating conditions.

Sources of Frustration

Although the example that was discussed concerns management as the source of frustration, management is only one of several sources. Another major source is co-workers who may place barriers in the way of goal attainment. Perhaps they delay work inputs to you, thereby delaying your work. Or their poorly done inputs prevent you from doing quality work. You can also be frustrated by the work itself, such as a part that does not fit or a machine that breaks down. Even the environment, such as a rainy day, may prevent you from doing the work you intended.

Research suggests that it is the little things, called hassles, rather than major life crises, that produce frustration. These hassles are conditions of daily living that are perceived to threaten one's well-being. They have been found to be related to both symptoms of ill-health and level of absenteeism.[8] The most frequent hassles include too many things to do, losing items, interruptions, and unchallenging work. Some of the hassles with the greatest average severity were related to both the job and the environment, such as problems with aging parents, prejudice and discrimination, and insufficient personal energy.

1. Approach-Approach Conflict

Where the individual is motivated to approach two or more positive but mutually exclusive goals. This type of goal conflict has the least impact an organizational behaviour. "The choice between two positive goals naturally becomes more difficult and takes longer when they are seen of equal value, but in any case it remains relatively easy to make a selection".[9]

2. Approach-Avoidance Conflict

This type of goal conflict is most relevant to the analysis of organizational behaviour. Normally, organizational goals have both positive and negative aspects for organizational participants. The organizational goal may arouse a great deal of conflict within a person and may actually cause indecision, ulcers and even neurosis. Such conflict and its aftermath are very common among decision-makers, complex goal of organization.

3. Avoidance-Avoidance Conflict

Where the individual is motivated to avoid two or more negative but mutually exclusive goals. This type of conflict does not have a great deal of impact an organizational behaviour. Avoidance conflict is usually resolved. An employee faced with two negative goals may not choose either of than and simply may leave them.

(b) Interpersonal Conflict

Besides the intra individual aspects of conflict, the interpersonal aspects of conflict are also important for quality of work-life. Kelly[10] notes "Conflict situations inevitably are made up of at least two individuals who hold polarized points of view, who are some what intolerant of ambiguities, who ignore delicate shades of gray, and who are quick to jump to conclusions".

Interpersonal conflicts are a serious problem to many employees because they deeply affect a person's emotions. There is need to protect one's self-image and self-esteem from damage by others. When these self-concepts are threatened, serious upset occurs and relationship deteriorates. Sometimes the temperaments of two employees are incompatible and their personalities clash. Conflicts may develop from failures of communication or differences in perception.

Baron and Greenberg[11] cited four major factors behind inter-personal conflicts, namely, lasting grudges, faulty attribution, faulty communication, and destructive criticism.

ROLE CONFLICT

Roles such as assembly-link worker, clerk, supervisor, salesperson, engineer, system analyst, department head, vice-president, and chairperson of the board often carry conflicting demands and expectations.

CONFLICT RESOLUTION IN WESTERN THOUGHT

One of the methods of resolving conflict is through "Transactional Analysis". When the employees interact in assertive or non-assertive ways, there is a social transaction in which one person responds to another. The study of these social transactions between people is called transactional analysis (TA). Eric Berne developed transactional analysis for psychotherapy in the 1950's. Its application to ordinary transactions soon was apparent and was popularized by Berne's book Games play (1964) and by Harris, Jongeward, and others.[12] The objective of TA is to provide better understanding of how employees relate to each other, so that they may develop improved communication and human relationships.

EGO STATES

According to Berne, employees interact with each other from one of three psychological positions, known as ego states. These ego states are called parent, adult and child, and a person can operate from any one of the three. Employees whose parent ego state is in control may be protective, controlling, nurturing, critical or instructive.

The adult ego state will appear as rational calculating, factual and emotional behaviour. It tries to upgrade decisions by seeking facts, processing data, estimating probabilities and holding factual discussions.

The child ego states reflect the emotion developed in response to childhood experience. It may be spontaneous, dependent, creative or rebellious. Like an actual child, the child ego desires approval from others and prefers immediate rewards. It can be identified by its emotional tone, as when an employee comments to the supervisor, "you're always picking on me!".

TYPES OF TRANSACTIONS

Transactions may be complementary or non-complementary. They are complementary when the ego states of sender and receiver in the opening transactions are simply reversed in the response. For example, the supervisor speaks to an employee as parent to child and the employee responds as child to parent. If a superior initiates a transaction in a parent-child pattern, the employee tends to response from a child state. A supervisor-subordinate relationship tends to parent child transaction, especially when instructions are given or appraisals are conducted. If the supervisor's behaviour is dominated by this pattern, it may lead to reduce interpersonal and group effectiveness.

Non-complementary transactions or cross-transactions happened when the supervisor tries to deal with the employee on an adult-to adult basis, but the employee responds on a child-to-parent basis. The important point is that when crossed transactions occur, communication tends to be blocked and a satisfactory transaction is not accomplished. Conflict often follows soon afterward.

In general, the transaction that is likely to be most effective at work is that of adult to adult. This kind of transactions encourages problem-solving treats employees as reasonably equals, and reduced the probability of emotional conflicts between employees. However, other complementary transactions can operate with acceptable success. For example, if the supervisor wants to play the parent role and the employee wants the role of child, they may develop a working relationship that is reasonably effective. In this situation, however the employee fails to grow, mature and learn how to contribute ideas. The conclusion is that, although other complementary transactions do work, the one with best result and least chance of problems at work is adult-to-adult transaction.

One study assessed the use of humour in management as it relates to ego states.[13] Some interesting patterns emerged from an assessment of thirty-six different functions played by humour in superior subordinate relations. Most harmless humour at work was seen as stemming from the playful child ego state, for example announcing it's a playtime. The parent state also uses humour, but more often to ridicule, express disapproval or maintain social distance. There is limited use of humour from the adult, but it can be used to create social cohesion, break down pretences, or even introduce change non-disruptively. The most positive uses are by the "I am o.k.—you are o.k." individual, who is likely to use humour is facilitate self-disclosure, create spontaneity, or relieve tension. This study illustrates just one of the many applications of TA in work situations.

STROKING

Employees seek stroking in their interaction with others.[14] It applies to all types of recognition, such as physical, verbal and eye contact between employees. In most jobs, the primary method of stroking is verbal. For example of physical strokes are a pat on the back and a firm handshake.

Strokes may be positive, negative or mixed. Positive strokes feel good when they are received and contribute to an employee's sense of being o.k. Negative strokes hurt physically or emotionally and make us feel less o.k. about ourselves. Mixed strokes are the combination of positive and negative strokes.

The supervisor normally secures a better result by avoiding the punishing parent-to-child approach and initiating an adult-to-adult communication.

BRAIN STORMING

Brainstorming is a popular method of encouraging creative thinking.[15] Its main advantage is deferred judgement, by which all ideas-even unusual and impractical ones—are encouraged without criticism or evaluation. Ideas are recorded as fast as they can be suggested: then they are evaluated for usefulness at a later time. The purpose of deferred judgement is to encourage employees to propose bold, unique ideas without worrying about what others think of them; this approach typically produces more ideas than the conventional approach of thinking and judging concurrently. Brain storming sessions last from ten minutes to one hour and require no preparation other than general knowledge of the subject.

Other advantages of brainstorming are enthusiasm, broader participation, greater task orientation, building upon ideas exchanged, and the feeling that the final product is a team solution.

DELPHI DECISION-MAKING

In Delphi decision groups, a series of questionnaires are distributed to the respondent, who does not need to meet face-to-face. All communication typically is in writing. Members are selected because they are experts or have relevant information to share. They are asked to share their assessment of a problem or predict a future state of affairs. Explanations of their conclusions also can be shared. Replies are gathering from all participants, summarized and fed back to the members for their review. Then they are asked to make another decision based on the new information. The process may be repeated several times until the responses converge satisfactorily.[16]

Success of the Delphi process depends on adequate time, participant expertise, communication skill and the motivation of members to immerse them in the task. The major advantages of the process are :

- Elimination of interpersonal problems.
- Efficient use of experts' time.
- Adequate time for reflection and analysis.
- Diversity and quality of ideas generated.
- Accuracy of predictions and forecasts made.

ISLAMIC THOUGHT AND CONFLICT

"Praise be to Allah
The cherisher and sustainer of the worlds
Most Gracious, Most Merciful
Master of the Day of Judgment
Thee do we worship
And Thine aid we seek". —(Q : 1 : 1-5)

In the first sura Al-Fatheha it is stated that if the praise to Allah is from our inmost being, it brings us closer to Allah. Then our eyes see all good, peace and harmony. Evil, rebellion and conflict are purged out. They do not exist for us, for our eyes are lifted above them in praise. Then we see Allah's attributes better. This leads us the attitude of worship and acknowledgement.

According to Islamic theology, a conflict arose when Satan tempted the first man, i.e. Adam to transgress the limits of Allah. From this episode, it is clear that the route cause of conflict is Satan, who is always on the look out for creating the situation in which human being transcend the instructions of God.

"Recite to them the truth
Of the story of the two sons
Of Adam, Behold! They each
Presented a sacrifice (to Allah) :

It was accepted from one,
But not from the other,
Said the latter : "Be sure
I will slay thee" "Surely"
Said the former, "Allah
Doth accept of the sacrifice
Of those who are righteous".

"If thou dost stretch thy hand
Against me, to slay me,
It is not for me to stretch
My hand against thee
To slay thee : for I do fear
Allah the cherisher of the worlds".

"For me, I intend to let
You draw an thyself
My sin as well as thine,
For thou wilt be among
The companions of the fire,
And that is the reward
Of those who do wrong".

"The (selfish) soul of the other
Led him to the murder
Of his brother : he murdered
Him, and became (himself)
One of the lost ones".

"Then Allah sent a raven,
Who scratched the ground,
To show him how to hide
The naked body of his brother.
"Woe is me!" said he;
"Was I not even able
To be as this raven,
And to hide the naked body
Of my brother?" Then he became
Full of regrets".

—(Q : 5 : 27-31)

The above verses contain the story of Adam's sons : The two sons of Adam were Habil (Abel) and Qabil (Cain). Cain was the elder and Abel the younger, the righteous and innocent one. Presuming on the right of the elder, Cain was puffed up with arrogance and jealousy, which led him to commit the crime of murder of Abel. This was the first conflict between the two-humans arose when the two sons of Adam fought over the sacrifice made by them. Arable and Cain made sacrifice. Allah accepted Label's sacrifice. The sacrifice of Cain was rejected. Enraged by the rejection Cain killed his brother. This is the first report of conflict in the Quran. The root cause of this conflict anger and jealous feeling created by Satan. The following verse only from Quran and Hadeeth illustrates the role of Satan in creation of conflict situation.

The prophet (S.A.W) said :

> "All creatures of God form the Family of God: and he is the best loved of God who loved best His creatures.
>
> —Baihaqi-Kitab-al Iman Shu'ab-ul Iman

> Respect the ways of God, and be affectionate to the family of God. —*Ibid.*

> O ye mankind! Surely we have created you a male and female, and made you tribes and families that you may recognize each other, surely the noblest of you in the sight of God is the one among you most mindful of his duty. God is knowing, fully awake. —*Ibid.*

The best way of resolving conflict in the organization is through love and affection. Love of man is love of God said prophet. The entire organization is said to the family of God. Therefore, it is the duty of every member of the organization to show love and affection to each other. This quality of work-life is for the pleasure of Allah. This way will resolve the conflict in the organization.

The Quran clearly said that Allah created male and female and it is our duty that we have recognize each other and we have to do our work to the satisfaction of him. He knows our intention well. We should fully follow the ways of God like faith, prayer, fasting, Zakat and Haj in our work life. The following are some of the conflict thoughts.

The above approaches are temporary, but the new Islamic approach, which is said to be Divine law approach, is to be a permanent, since God has created it.

ISLAMIC APPROACH

It is said to be Divine Law approach since God creates it. This approach is based on Quran and Hadeeths, which are Divine sources. They are permanent and said to be ever lasting. If organizations adopt this approach it will successful a d conflict will be resolved. The best way of resolving conflict is through love and affection. Loving man is said to be love of God. Since all are created from same family as male and female, we have to live each other as brothers and sisters.

UNITY EMPHASIZED

Islam emphasis on the unity of mankind. The concept of unity arises when the fact that all human beings are from one family, i.e. that Adam Eve. God also emphasizes on his omnipresence and He belongs neither to West and nor to East. He is creator of all human beings. Any kind of bias, prejudies, on the basis of status, caste, community, race, colour, ethnography, etc., is abhorred. Individual should be respected only on the basis of piety. —The Holy Quran

Even among the Muslim ummah (community) unity is stressed. The following verses and Hadeeth enjoin Muslim to be united. In an organization all the members should be united. In a Muslim organization unity is emphasized.

The God said noble person is one who loves his duty and organization. God knows the intention of all. —*Ibid.*

> "O men! Be mindful of your lord, who hath created you of one man and of him created his wife, and from the twain hath spread abroad so many men and women. Verily is God watching over you". —(Q : 4 : 1)

The following are some of the Hadeeth related to family of God:

1. Said the prophet: O Lord! Lord of my life and of everything in the Universe! I affirm that all human beings are brothers into are another".

   —Baihaqi, Kitabul-Iman, Shu'ab-Iman

2. All creatures of God form the family of God and he is the best loved of God who loved best His creatures.

   —Baihaqi, Kitabul-Iman, Shu'ab-Iman

3. Respect the ways of God and be affectionate to the family of God.

   —Baihaqi : Kitabul-Iman, Shu'ab ul-Iman

4. Mankind is a fold every member of which is a shepherd unto every other, and will be accountable for the welfare of the entire fold.

   —Bukhari, Kitabul-iman

5. Islam demands a united life for man.

   —Kunuzul Haqaiq

6. Said the prophet: Unity is bliss: Disunity is misery.

   —Kunuzul-Haqaiq

7. The Muslim who lives in the midst of society and bears with patience wrongs done to him is better than one who shuns society and cannot bear any wrong done to him.

   —Tirmizi

8. In living devotion to God, lives a united life as brothers unto each other.

   —Kunuzul Haqaiq

9. One believer is for another believer what one part of the foundation of a wall is to another, each holding strength to the other. Then joining the fingers of both his hands in a grip said: 'they are joined together like this'.

   —Bukhari, Kitab al-Adab

10. Said the prophet: 'You will find all believers in God as firm and united together in ties of love and kindness as the limbs of a body. If one part of it gets pain, all other parts feel affected in sympathy.

    —Bukhari, Kitab al-Adab

11. Dissensions ruined the people who lived before you.
—Kunuzul Haqaiq

LOVE OF HUMANITY

As was pointed out earlier, the basic cause of stress according to Islamic theology, loneliness and anxiety felt by human being. Because of the burden of being man, there are several ways of getting rid of loneliness. Domination, oppression, injustice, aggression, alcoholism, drugs addiction, etc. are different ways of reducing one's loneliness. A person can mitigate his aloneness by dominating and apprising other human being.

Similarly alcoholism, drug addiction, are the inferior means of reducing one's loneliness and anxiety. Islam does not approve of these methods. Instead, it advocates love of humanity. According to Islam, this is the best way of reducing the burden of human being. In the following Hadeeths love of humanity is emphasized, needless to say this approach minimises conflicts everywhere including the business organization.

1. *Said the prophet* : whosoever loves another for the sake of God in reality has expressed his love for God.
—Ahmed, Musnad
2. *I have heard the prophet saying*: "God says : it is obligatory on me to love those who for my sake love each other and meet together and spend on each other out of what they have.
—Malik : Muatta
3. *God says*: If you wish to receive graciousness from me, show graciousness to those whom I have created.
—Kunuzul Haqaiq
4. Treat kindly the dwellers of the earth and God will treat you kindly.
—Bukhari, Kitab al-Adab
5. *Said the prophet*: A believer is truly the centre and embodiment of love and affection. There is no

goodness in him who does not show affection for others and for whom others do not show affection.

—Musnad and Baihaqi

6. "God says", related the prophet, "Love becomes obligatory on my part who for my sake love one another, and live together and who for my sake greet each other with a goodly cheer, and who for my sake spend of what they earn for the food of one another".

—Malik : Muatta

7. None among you is a believer in God unless he wishes for his brother what he wishes for himself.

—Bukhari : Kitab al-Iman

8. *Said the prophet*: Be faithful to God and be brothers to one another.

—Bukhari

9. *Said the prophet*: Of all human actions, the one which pleases God is that expression of love which is expressed for the sake of God and than expression of dislike which is expressed for the sake of God.

—Abu Dawud

10. He who, for the sake of God, has loved another human being, that person verily has extolled the glory of God.

—Ahmed : Musnad

11. Ma'ad bin Jabal asked of the Prophet what form of faith is good or by what kind of action is such a faith acquired? Said the prophet in reply : "Your likes and your dislikes should be for God only; and every moment of your life, you should feel you are living in the presence of God". Ma'ad asked : what else? The prophet continued, "and wish for others what you wish for yourself and dislike for others what you dislike for your own self"

—Ahmed : Musnad

12. He who loves or hates, offers favours or withholds them, and whatever he does, so for the sake of God, he perfects his faith.

—Bukhari; Muslim, Abu Dawud

13. *The prophet once said* : On the day of judgement, God will address a particular individual. "O Son of Adam! I was sick, but you did not attend on the". Bewildered,

this individual will say : How is that possible? You are after all the Supreme Lord of al the Worlds (and cannot fall sick). God will reply : "Do you not remember that so and so among my servants was ill and lying close to you and you did not turn to him in sympathy. If you had but gone near him, you would have found me beside him". In like manner, God will address another individual : "O son of Adam! I had asked of you a piece of bread; but you would not give it to me". The individual will submit : "How is that possible? Could God feel hunger and need bread?" God will reply : "So and so among my servants had in a moment of hunger asked of you bread, and did you not refuse to give it to him? If you had given him food, you would have found me beside him". Similarly, God will turn to yet another and address him : "O son of Adam! I was thirsty and I asked of you a cup of water, but you did not give it to me". The individual will cry out : "How is that possible? How can God feel thirsty?" God will reply : "So and so of my servants who was thirsty asked of you water, but you did not give it to him. If you had given it to him, you would surely have found me beside him".

—Muslim

14. These three things also enter faith—to help others even when one is himself economically hard pressed; to pray ardently for the peace of all mankind, and to deal justice to one's own self.

    —Amar bin Yasir Bazzar

15. Faith expresses itself in numerous ways. Humility is one of them. The highest form is admission in spirit of the truth that there is none worthy of worship except God. And the most ordinary is to remove any obstacle lying across a wayfarer's path.

    —Abu Huraira (Agreed)

WORKING FOR THE PLEASURE OF GOD

Another way of reducing the pangs of separation of man from nature is to relate him with outside world by productive work. This productive work should be done exclusively to please Allah. He should not have any motive other than seeking the pleasure of God. The following verses from the Hadeeths emphasis this aspect of RAZA-YE-ILAHI (to seek pleasure of God).

1. *Said the prophet*: Shall I tell you what type of charity is most pleasing to God? It is to restore peace where peace is distributed.

   —Kunuzul Haqaiq
2. *Said the prophet* : Shall I tell you what is better than prayer and fasting and the highest form of charity? It is to resolve internal dissensions and bring about concord between contending parties. It is internal dissension that primarily ruins a society.

   —Ibn Maja, Tirmizi, Ahmed
3. There is no good in the company of the man who does not wish for thee what thou desired for him.

   —Kunuzul-Haqaiq
4. Live together do not turn against each other, make things easy for the other and do not put obstacles in each other's way.

   —Kunuzul-Haqaiq
5. It is narrated by Abu Shari that the Apostle of God (peace be on him) emphatically exclaimed; "He is not a believer in God". The question was asked : "O Apostle of God! Who is he?" He declared : "He whose neighbour does not feel secure on his account".

   —Bukhari
6. Abu Huraira narrates that the Apostle of God said : "He who believers in God and the Day of recompense will never harm his neighbour, will be hospitable to his guests, and speak to others in a gentle tone or remain silent".

   —Bukhari
7. The believer in God is he who is not a danger to life and property of any other.

   —Tirmizi, Nisai and Bukhari
8. A true believer in God does not curse others or counts

at them; nor does he indulge in slander or abusive language. —Tirmizi, and Bukhari

9. Wisdom lies in loving each other without depriving the other of his rights.

—Kunuzul Haqiaq

10. The disposition and the very nature of a believer can contain all qualities except dishonesty and falsehood.

—Musnad and Baihaqi

11. The Apostle of God said: Tenderness always lends beauty to one who displays it in one's relations with others. On the other hand, a lack of it lends ugliness.

—Taisirul Usul: Kitabur Rifaq

12. He who accompanies a wicked person in order to help him in his wicked designs, and knows that the persons whom he has agreed to help in his designs is a wicked person. Straightaway ceases to be a believer.

—Baihaqi

In an organization all are said to be brothers and sisters. Their aim to get the pleasure of God. By having love and affection to each, they fulfil the pleasure of God. It is best way of resolving conflict.

FAITH IN GOD

Faith in God by employees will give hope. This is the belief that should be entrenched by employees. It gives full explanation. Once this belief has established itself, the heart is purified of all falsities and impurities and it is released from all ties except those of one and Unique Being who alone possesses the reality of being and who is the only effective power in this world. An employee's heart is then released from bondage to anything in this world, the real being is that of the Divine Being and the truly effective-power is the Divine will.

When an employee's heart releases itself from believing in anything but the one Truth, the Truth of Allah, and upholds this everlasting Truth, it liberates itself from all shackles, false ideas, evil desires, fear of earthly powers and from the confusion that mislead in this life. For when an employee's heart finds Allah, it benefits and loses nothing. So why should it desire anything since there is no absolutely effective power but that of Allah.

When a conception that sees nothing in the world but the reality of Allah establishes itself in the worker's mind and heart, it is accompanied by the vision of this genuine, permanent reality in every other being that has sprung from it. This is the stage at which the heart feels the hand of Allah in everything and beyond which it feels nothing but Allah in the whole Universe. There would be no other reality to be felt.

The Qur'an takes great care to establish this truth in the concept of faith. It has always put aside apparent causes and associated events directly with the will of Allah. It says :

> "When you threw (a hand feel of dust) it was not your alt, but Allah's. —(Q : 8 : 17)
>
> 'There is no triumph except that given by Allah'. —(Q : 8 : 10 and Q : 3 : 126)
>
> "You have no will except as Allah's wills". —(Q : 76 : 30)

By disregarding all apparent causes and connecting matters directly with the will of Allah, a feeling of relief gently penetrates the worker's heart so that it knows the only saviour from whom it cark ask whatever it wishes and by whom it is rescued from all it fears. It become unimpressed by the apparent influences, reasons and causes that bear no reality or true existence in themselves.

By attributing every happening in his personal and organizational life, to the hidden hand of Allah, the real doer, real mover, the real decision-maker, an employee gets rid of feeling of frustration, animosity, jealousy, etc. This leads to internal tranquillity and this tranquillity makes him pacifists.

ROLE CONFLICT

The Islamic way of resolving role conflict of an employee is to trust in Allah who is the only one who will deliver the outcomes. Putting the trust in Allah is called tawakkul. Making tawakkul is a sign of belief in Allah. It is a sign of belief in the unseen that is controlled by Allah. Tawakkul is the reliance of the heart on, and its confidence in Allah. An employee make tawakkul in performing their roles believing that Allah is the most merciful and most graceful, the exalted in might, the one with absolute knowledge, wisdom and justice. Tawakkul gives employees a sense of optimism that can encourage them to avoid excessive risk. Tawakkul does not mean that an employee does not do what is necessary to achieve in his role but expects Allah to grant him success. Tawakkul comes after one does his role.

Tawakkul comes from belief in Allah and His attributes. It is evident from the following verses:

> "And put your trust on the exalted in might, the merciful".
> —(Q : 26 : 217)

> "You say: Indeed this affair is wholly Allah's".
> —(Q : 3 : 154)

> And the sun, the moon and the stars (all) governed by laws under His command. Is it not His to create and to govern "Now shall they compass ought to of His knowledge expect as He wills". —(Q : 2 : 255)

> "If any trust in Allah, behold! Allah is Exalted in might, wise". —(Q : 8 : 49)

From the above it is clear that an employee can perform their multiple roles, believing Allah. This type of work-life will not experience any type of conflict in the organization. The aim of performing different role is to get the pleasure of God.

I. Lasting Grudges

Lasting grudges could be due to deep anger with an employee or group of employees that have or are perceived of having badly hurt the subject. The Quran says that this factor can be dealt with the value of justice. The Allah said :

> "Allah commands justice the doing of good deeds, and liberality to kith and kin, and He forbids, all shameful

> deeds, and injustice, and transgression, He instructs you that you may receive admonition". —(Q : 16 : 90)

Further, the Quran command forgiveness and linked it to the forgiveness of Allah.

> "Let them forgive and overlook, do you not wish that Allah should forgive you, for Allah is oft forgiving, most merciful". —(Q : 24 : 22)

In another verse Allah, the Almighty, called upon His messenger (SAW) to forgive his followers.

> "So forgive them and ask for (Allah's) forgiveness for them". —(Q : 3 : 159)

Allah considered forgiveness as an attribute of the believers who will be greatly rewarded in the hereafter.

> "Those who avoid the major sons and shameful deeds, and when they are angry even then forgive". —(Q : 42 : 37)

Forgiveness is not always easy and not everybody is expected to forgive, but for the sake of Allah. Allah, the exalted said.

> "Let not the hatred of other people to you swerves you to wrong and make you unjust. Be just it is closer to piety." —(Q : 5 : 8)

II. Faulty Attribution

One of the qualities for Interpersonal conflicts is faulty attribution, which is the negative interpretation of other's behaviour. It is a sort of suspicion and conjecture that is rejected in Islam.

> "O you who believe avoid suspicion as much (as possible): for suspicion is in some cases of sin". —(Q : 49 : 12)

Allah prohibits passing judgment based on suspicions and conjecture.

> "And pursue not that of which you has no knowledge; for every act of hearing, or of seeing or of (feeling) of the heart will be inquired into". —(Q : 17 : 36)

Faulty attribution can also be due to deliberate misinformation. Allah says to verify the information they receive before passing judgment. Hasty judgments without the verification of the information on which the judgment is made may lead to future regrets.

> "O you who believe! If a wicked person comes to you with any news, ascertain the truth, lest you harm people unwittingly, and after that become full of regret for what have done". —(Q : 49 : 6)

III. Faulty Communication

One of the factors for interpersonal conflicts is faulty communication. It is due to when employees, willingly or unwillingly, communicate with others in a way that disturbs or angers them. The Quran warned against this problem and praised the good manure communication indication that it is a always fruitful.

> "Say to my slaves to say those things that are best, for Satan sows dissensions among them". —(Q : 17 : 53)

> See you not how Allah sets forth a parable? A goodly word like a good tree whose root is firmly fixed and its branches reach the heavens. It brings for its fruits at all times by the leave of its Lord. So Allah set forth parables for people in order that they may receive admonition. And the parable of an evil work is that of any evil tree. It is torn-up by the root from the surface of the earth; It has no stability.
> —(Q : 14 : 24-26)

IV. Destructive Criticism

One of the reasons of interpersonal conflict is a destructive criticism. It is a feedback delivered in a manner that angers the receiver rather than helps them. Islam discouraged advices that can hurt or embarrass the recipient and encouraged employees to first advice one another in a more private fashion.

Hazrat Abu Umama reports that the Prophet had said that for anyone who did not indulge in controversy, although he was in the right, he guaranteed a house he was in the right, he guaranteed a house in a corner of paradise and for anyone who did not tell a lie even in fun he guaranteed a house in the middle of paradise and for anyone who embellished his manners, he guaranteed a house in the most prominent part of paradise. —Abu Dawud

LOVE AND AFFECTION

> "The believing men and believing women are protecting friends of one another." —(Q : 9 : 71)

The Holy Prophet (SAW) used to cherish deep feelings of affection for all his illustrious companions (RAA) so each one of them entertained the happy thought that the Holy Prophet (SAW) loved him more than any one else.

Hazrat 'Amr b.al-As (RAA) reports: "The Holy Prophet (SAW) used to converse with me with such deep attention and sincerity and lavished such great care on me that I came to believe myself to be the best person among my people. And one day I submitted to the Holy Prophet (SAW): "O Prophet of Allah (SAW): Who is better—Me or Abu Bakar?" The Holy Prophet (SAW) observed: "Abu Bakar is the better one. "I submitted again: "Who is better—Me or 'Umar (RAA)?" The Holy Prophet (SAW) affirmed: "Umar is better." I submitted once more: "O Prophet of Allah (SAW): Who is better—Me or 'Uthman (RAA)?" The Prophet of Allah (SAW) observed: "Uthman is better than you." I then requested the Holy Prophet (SAW) to explain the real matter in detail whereupon the Holy Prophet (SAW) told me the plain truth. I felt greatly ashamed of myself and wondered what impelled me to ask such questions!

Love your friends for the sake of Allah. The favourites of Allah are those who join together on the basis of Allah's religion and struggle shoulder to shoulder with perfect unity of mind and soul to discharge their obligation of establishing the religion of Allah and stand like a solid wall in defence of their creed.

The Holy Qur'an affirms:

> "Lo! Allah loved those who battle for His cause in ranks as if they were a solid structure." —(Q : 61 : 4)

And the Holy Prophet (SAW) has affirmed:

> Allah will ordain on the Day of Judgment: Where are those people who used to love their fellows for my sake only. I shall place them under My own shadow." —Muslim

> "Lo! Verily the friends of Allah are (those on whom fear (cometh) not, nor do they grieve." —(Q : 10 : 62)

> Hazrat Abu-Darda (RAA) states that the Holy Prophet (SAW) observed: "Some people shall be raised from their graves on the Day of Judgment in a state that their faces will be glowing with radiant light. They shall be seated on pulpits made of pearls. Other people shall envy their elevated state. These dignified people, however, will neither include Prophets nor martyrs." The companions submitted: "O Prophet of Allah (SAW)! Who are these people? Tell us their distinguishing qualities." The Holy Prophet (SAW) observed: "These are the people who love each other for the sake of Allah only."
>
> —Tabrani

Consider the love of pious people as a source of salvation in the eternal life and a means of winning the favour of Allah. Pray to Allah to bless you with the love of righteous people and beseech. His favour to admit you to the ranks of the pious. Hazrat 'Abdullah ibn Mas'ud (RAA) narrates: "A person came to the presence of the Holy Prophet (SAW) and submitted: "O Prophet of Allah (SAW), a person, loves a pious man for his piety, yet himself does not emulate the good deeds of this pious man; how shall he be treated in the next world?"

The Prophet of Allah (SAW) affirmed: "It does not matter at all. Man shall find himself in the company of that person whom he loves.

—Bukhari

One night the Holy Prophet (SAW) was blessed with the vision of Allah. Allah said to the Holy Prophet (SAW): "Ask what thou wilt?" Thereupon the Holy Prophet (SAW): said this prayer.

"Allah! I beseech Thy favour to perform good deeds and avoid evil deeds and I seek the love of the poor and Implore Thee to grant me forgiveness and show me Thy Mercy. When you wish to send a calamity over a people, lift me in a state in which I may enjoy Your protection from the calamity. I implore Thy love and I beseech Thee to grant me love of that person who loves Thee and grant me the favour to perform deeds which may serve as means of obtaining nearness to You."

Hazrat Mu'adh ibn Jabal (RAA) states that the Holy Prophet (SAW) affirmed: "Allah ordains that I owe love to those people who develop links of love and friendship among themselves for My sake and assemble at one place to recite My name and meet each other for the love of Me and show good treatment to each other in order to win My favour.

—Ahmad, Tirmidhi

If you love someone, you must express your love to that person. Its psychological effect on that person will be that he will develop a sense of nearness to you. The exchange of feelings and passions on both sides will augment love and sincerity to an extraordinary extent. Love then will no longer be merely a feeling confined within the heart but will begin to play a potent role in practical life. Thus people will have an opportunity of taking deep interest in the individual lives of each other and coming nearer to each other.

The Holy Prophet (SAW) has affirmed: "Any person who cherishes in his heart sentiments of love and sincerity for his brother, he should express these sentiments to his brother and tell him clearly that he holds him in love and affection".

—Abu Dawud

On one occasion a man passed in front of the Holy Prophet (SAW). Some people were at that time in attendance on the Prophet (SAW). One of them submitted; "O Prophet of Allah (SAW)! I love this man for the sake of Allah alone". On hearing this Holy Prophet (SAW) enquired form him: "Have you told this to the man?" The man submitted: "No, I have not." Thereupon the Holy Prophet (SAW) urged the man: "Go and tell the man that you love him for the sake of Allah. "The man stood up at once and approaching the passer-by expressed to him his sentiments. The passer-by made the answer: "May Allah love thee for whose sake you entertain feelings of love for me."

The Holy Prophet (SAW) enjoined: "in their sense of mutual love and affection and perception of common distress, you will find Muslims as one body; if one organ of this body is afflicted; the whole body is affected by fever and sleeplessness."

—Bukhari, Muslim

CAUSES OF CONFLICT

The following are some of the factors, which create conflict in the organizational life.

(A) Back Biting

One of the reasons of conflict in the organization is backbiting. It is naturally that in-order to satisfy the employer, an employee will do backbite of another employee. Islam prohibits the back-biting. Backbiting is most heinous sins.

Hazrat Abu Huraira says that the Prophet (SAW) asked: "Do you know what is back-biting? People said, "God and His prophet know best". The talk about your brother in terms that he does not like". People asked, "If the man actually has the defect pointed out, will it still be backbiting? The prophet said, "If a man actually has the defect you talk about then it will be backbiting, but if he does not have that defect it will be calumny". —Mishkat

Hazrat Abu saeed and Hazrat Jabir report that the Prophet (SAW) had said that backbiting was greater sin than adultery. Those present asked how it was a greater sin and the Prophet (SAW) said that if a man committed adultery and asked forgiveness of God, God would forgive him, but God would not forgive a backbiter unless the man whom he maligned behind his back forgave him. —Miskat

Hazrat Anas reports that the Prophet (SAW) had said: Atonement for backbiting is to pray for forgiveness of the sins of the man you have talked ill about behind his back and say: "O God, forgive my sins and his". —Miskat

Hazrat Ayesha says that the Prophet (SAW) had said, "Do not talk ill of the dead as their record has been closed".

—Bukhari

"A back-biter will not be able to enter heaven".

—Bukhari

(B) Obscene Language and Abusiveness

Another reasons for conflict in an organization is obscene language and abusiveness. The language used by an employee should be pleased and it should not hurt others.

Hazrat Abu Darda reports that the Prophet (SAW) had said that the weightiest thing that would be put in the scale of a believer on the Day of Judgment would be his good manners and God very much disliked the man who used observe language and was abusive. —Tirmizi

Hazrat Ali ibn Abu Talib says that the Prophet (SAW) had said that one who used obscene language and one who propagated it were both equally sinners. —Mishkat

(C) Double-Dealing

One of the reasons of conflict is double-dealing. Islam prohibits the double-dealing by the person or group of persons who create conflict among the employees.

Hazrat Abu Huraria says that the Prophet (SAW) had said that on the Day of Judgment they would find that the worst man was one who had two faces in the world, meeting one person with one face and another person with a different face.

—Unanimous

When there is a conflict between two employees or two groups, some persons who come forward to visit both the parties and creating their enmity. This is most objectionable. There are some employees who express great familiarity on the face but speak ill behind the back. This is also double-dealing.

Hazrat Ummer says that the Prophet (SAW) had said that one who had been double-faced in the world would have two tongues of fire on the Day of Judgment. —Abu Dawud

The employee who has two tongues, on the Day of Judgement will emit fire from his mouth, which burnt mutual relationship.

(D) Rumour-Mongering

Rumour mongering is one of the reasons for conflict. Employees are directed to refrain from saying anything without confirming it as it may be that the employee who reported it may be Satan himself. Spreading unconfirmed rumours may cause a lot of mischief and conflict in the organization.

Hazrat Abdullah bin Masud says that the Prophet (SAW) had said Satan works in the shape of man and goes about among the people telling those lies, then people dispense and one of the men says he had heard such and such thing from a person whom he knows by the face but does not know his name. —Muslim

(E) Fault-finding

At another reason for conflict is faultfinding of others. This quality leads to conflict in the organization. Usually the superior will find the fault of his sub-coordinated and similarly the sub-ordinate will find the fault of his superior and his colleagues. In Islam it is prohibited.

Hazrat Ayesha says that once she mentioned the defects of Hazrat Safia (that she is short statured, which is a great defect). The prophet (SAW) said, "O Ayesha, you have spoken such a filthy work that if it is mixed with an ocean it will pollute the whole of it". —Mishkat

(F) Nepotism

Nepotism is one of the reasons for conflict in an organization. If any of the relatives or friends and his caste people of superior are working in an organization the superior will show his favour to them. This will create conflict among the employees of the organization. In Islam God dislikes it.

Hazrat yazid bin Abu sufian says that when Hazrat Abu Bakar sent him as a commander to Syria he advised him, "O yazid, you have some of your relatives there and it is possible you give them preference in appointing to responsible posts and this is my greatest fear about you. The Prophet (SAW) had said that if any one was made to rule over Muslims and made responsible for their collective affairs and he appointed any officer merely an account of his relationship or friendship then

God's curse be upon him and He would accept no apology from him till he is cast into hell.

—Kitabul Khiraj, Imam Abu Yusuf

CONFLICT RESOLUTION MECHANISM IN ISLAM

The following are the Islamic mechanism by which conflict will be resolved. These methods based on Quran and Hadeeths.

I. Responsibility of Conflict Resolution

The Muslim ummah and the business organization in the Islamic framework are responsible to resolve conflicts. Be the individual or organizational, it is obligatory. The holy Quran says:

> "The believers are but a single brotherhood: So reconcile between your contending brothers; and fear Allah, that you may receive mercy". —(Q : 49 : 10)

Reconciling conflicting parties is something ordained by Allah. Use of authoritative command can be very efficient in arbitration. However, if it is not coupled with justice and a clear explanation of the reasons behind the authoritative decision, it will only work in the short run. Authoritative command is needed when conflicts persist and start hurting the organization, or when one party is determined to be right while the other is at fault. In fact, if one party has transgressed upon another. Muslims are ordained to firmly stop this transgression. Once this aggression is stopped, Muslims have to reconcile between the two parties. Allah, the Exalted, said:

> "But if one transgresses beyond bonds against the other then fight you against the one that transgresses until it complies with the command of Allah, but if it complies, then make peace between them with justice, and be fair for Allah loves those who are fair". —(Q : 49 : 9)

II. Shura (Mutual Consultation)

If any conflict arises between the two individuals or groups it can be resolved through shura system.

It is a mutual consultation among the employees or group of employee to discuss the problem and take a decision for the pleasure of God. The Quran has made it clear that leaders are obligated to consult those who have knowledge or those who can provide sound advice. The holy Quran says:

> "More enduring is a portion with God whose affairs are guided by mutual counsel". —(Q : 42 : 36)

> And those whose answer the call of their Lord and establish prayer, and who conduct their affairs by consultation and spend out of what we bestow on them for sustenance. —(Q : 42 : 38)

The Prophet (SAW) himself was directed by the Quran to consult his companions.

> It is part of the Mercy of Allah that you do deal gently with then. Were you severe or harsh-hearted, they would break away from about you. So pass over (their faults) and ask for (Allah's) forgiveness for and consult them in affairs (of moment). Then, when you have taken a decision, put your trust in Allah. For Allah loves those who put their trust (in Him). —(Q : 3 : 159)

> The community which regulates its affairs by counsel will prosper. —Kunuz-Ul-Haqaiq

The above verses and Hadeeth clearly state that any conflict can be resolved through mutual consultation, any organization, which goes through counsel, will prosper.

The. practice of shura enables the employees of the organization to participate in resolving conflicts. At the same time, shura serves a check on the conduct of employees in case he deviates from the aim of the group.

III. Freedom of Thought

Freedom should be given to employee or group employees to express their thoughts or view about their problem. Addressing a gathering during his last Haj, said the Prophet

(SAW): O people! Your God is but one, and the rather of each one of you is but one. The Arab has no superiority over a non-Arab the fair coloured over the black coloured or the black coloured over the fair coloured, except by the righteousness he displays in life. —Ahmed, Musuad

All are equal before the Lord, each employee has the freedom to express his views about the problem in the organization. If employees express their view, the problem can be known; thereby the conflict can be resolved. The management should create an atmosphere of freethinking, healthy exchange of ideas, and mutual advice so that the employees feel very comfortable in discussing matters of interest to the groups.

IV. Justice

One of the basis of resolving conflict is justice. The management of an organization must establish an internal judiciary or arbitration committee to settle any dispute or grievance within the group or among the employees. The members of such a committee must be selected from among the knowledgeable, pious and wise people.

The management should deal with the people justly and fairly regardless of their race, colour, national origin or religion. The Quran says that every one should be fair even when dealing with those opposed to them.

> "Surely Allah enjoins justice and the doing of good (to others) and the giving to the kindred, and He forbids indecency and evil and rebellion. He admonishes you that you may be mindful". —(Q : 16 : 90)
>
> "O you who believe, be upright for Allah, bearers of witness with justice, and let not hatred of a people incite you not to act equitably. Be just that is nearer to observance of duty. And keep you duty to Allah. Surely Allah is aware of what you do". —(Q : 5 : 8)
>
> "O you who believe, be maintainers of justice, bearers of witness for Allah, even though it be against your own selves or (your) partners or near relations. Whether he is rich or poor, Allah has a better right over them both. So follow not (your) low desires, best you deviate. And if you

distort of turn away from (truth), surely Allah is ever aware of what you do". —(Q : 4 : 135)

From the above, verses, it is clear that justice should be established by the management to the employees in the conflict should get pleasure of God.

V. Self-restraint and Forgiveness

One of the methods of resolving conflict in Islam is self-restraint and forgiveness. An employee or group of employees who are in the conflict should follow the same for the pleasure of God. The following are related to the same.

"Who master their anger, and forgive other God loved the doers of good". —(Q : 3 : 133)

"Moreover, good and evil are not to be treated alike. Turn away evil by what is better, and lo! He between whom and thyself was enmity, shall be as though he were a warm friend. But none attain to this save men steadfast in patience and none attain to it except the most highly favoured". —(Q : 41 : 32-25)

If you at all retaliate, then retaliate to the same extent that he were injured; but if ye can endure patiently, best will it be for those who patiently endure.

"Endure then with patience. But thy patient endurance must be sought in none but God". —(Q : 16 : 126-127)
"And whose beneath wrongs with patience and for gives—this verily is high-mindedness". —(Q : 40-42)

And who, when a wrong is done them, redress themselves: Yet let the recompense of evil be only a like evil- but he who forgives and is reconciled, shall be rewarded by God himself; for He loved not those who act unjustly.

And there shall be no way open against those who unjustly wrong others, and act insolently on the earth in disregard of justice. These! A grievous punishment doth await them.

"And whose beneath wrongs with patience and forgives, this verily is (a bounden duty); a high resolve".

—(Q : 42 : 37-41)

Verily, it is better that the leader should be on the side of forgiveness rather than on the side of retaliation.

—Tirmizi

Moses said, "O my Lord! Who is the most honoured of Thy servants in Thy sight?" God said: "He who pardons when he has the power (to avenge himself)." —Baihaqi

Narrates Abdullah bin Abbas: The Prophet (SAW) once addressing a tribal chief remarked: Two of your qualities are pleasing to God. One is your sense of self-restraint; the other is your disinclination to act hastily. —Muslim

Said the Prophet (SAW): Considerate action is godly in quality and a hasty one satanic. —Tirmizi

Said Prophet (SAW): An upright character and a balanced disposition form two of the 24 elements, which constituted the equipment of a prophet. —Tirmizi

From the above verses and Hadeeths it is clear that every member of a business organization is enjoin to practice self-restraint and forgiveness. Justice is not at the end of the organization. If all the members of an organization keep an harping and their rights and obligations of others, the organizational climate will become bureaucratic; where everybody be—management or employees—think only about their authority and duties of others. It will take away the friendly and caring spirit of an organization. It will be a machine and not body of human beings. The over-emphasis of formalization of rationality, rules and regulations, rights and duties by Max-Weber has lead to bureaucratic culture in western organization. Muslims blindly copied this form of structure and try to transplant in their countries. The net result is that Muslim organizations are neither here nor there. Islam emphasizes on mutual tolerance, and forgiveness, justices, bureaucracy, rationality, rules and regulations are only for people who are operating at baser levels. For members who have risen themselves above this level need an organization culture, with love, affection, care, mercy, forgiveness, etc. which are enjoin in the above quoted words of the creator of the universe and the words of the last Prophet (SAW) make an organization a humanistic and Islamic. It is this culture in which self-actualization process reaches it pinnacle, organizational growth will be at its peak, business performance will be at its highest level.

V. Providing an Expert Opinion

Conflicts between groups can be caused by different perception of the reality or by different understanding of some matters. On many occasions, the groups involved in the conflict do not have enough knowledge to judge which view is right or which view is best. Jawdat Sa'eed[10] said, "The judge of a conflict is only knowledge". To support his opinion, Sa'eed quoted the following Qur'anic verse:

> "....Say: Have you any (certain) knowledge? If so, produce it for us. You follow nothing but conjecture: you do nothing but lie". —(Q : 6: 1-18)

If there is a conflict in an organization, it is best to bring an outside expert who will be able to deliver judgment on the issue. The outside expert should be able to win the trust of the conflicting groups, and should possess the necessary professional credibility. The expert shall make a professional judgment and shall be able to convince both parties. Convincing both parties about the experts' judgment is instrumental in the settlement of the conflict.

VI. Negotiation

Negotiation is the bargaining between the two parties that have recognized their conflict. Representatives of the conflicting groups can handle it. This negotiation process is very efficient when there is a tendency for reconciliation or agreement. It is not an effective when the settlement will require judging in favour of one side. Allah, the All-High, said regarding marriage conflicts:

> "If you fear a breach between them twain, appoint two arbiters, one from his family and the other from hers; if they wish for reconciliation, Allah will cause their

reconciliation. For Allah has full knowledge, and is acquainted with all things". —(Q : 4 : 35)

McKensie[11] stated that negotiators could view a win-lose situation where gains by one party mean losses by the other. Negotiations can also be viewed as a win-win situation where the interest of both parties can be maintained. This situation appears to be unrealistic, however, there is usually an innovative potential solution that offers greater joint benefits than compromise. These solutions are termed integrative agreements.

VII. Arbitration

As the degree of communication between conflicting group's decreases., the need for arbitration becomes urgent. Delays in arbitration can worsen the conflict. Arbitration can take various forms. An accepted neutral person or arbitrators have to show knowledge of the issue, understanding of the overall interest of the organization and especially impartiality and justice. Allah, the All-High, All Glorious, said:

"Allah does command you to render back your trusts to those to whom they are due; and when you judge between people, that you judge with justice: verily how excellent is the teaching which He gives you! For Allah is He Who hears and sees all things". —(Q : 4 : 58)

In another verse Allah, the Exalted, ordained His messenger (Blessings and Peace be upon him) to judge with equity.

"If you judge, judge in equity between them, for Allah loves those who judge in equity". —(Q : 5 : 42)

We should stress here that judgments rendered by the arbitrators should be with equity and justice.

Arbitration should involve conflict smoothing by emphasizing their differences. Allah has ordained Muslims to reconcile the differences between one another, emphasizing the bonds of brotherhood that exist among them. Further, because ego and grudge usually accompany conflicts, Allah, the Almighty, has coupled reconciliation with belief and awareness of Allah. Allah, the All Merciful, said:

> The fact that a dysfunctional conflict started to have its tolls on an organization proves that the latter is failing at directing and motivating its members towards achieving a desired goal. Therefore, the organization has to develop or to redefine its objective and goals in such a way that they transcend conflicts. That is, these goals shall be appealing and should only be feasible through the cooperation of all groups. From an Islamic perspective, the feedback between the actions of a group during conflict, and the objective of entering Paradise can smooth conflicts. Further, the compatibility between the general objective of Muslims and their goals at their organization shall make the latter more appealing.

Groups tend to unite and to focus on their activities during inter-group conflicts. Similarly, organizations can also unite and overlook their internal differences when faced by a common enemy. While internal unity is needed for an organization, which is faced with a common enemy, this internal unity shall not transform into 'group think'. The organization shall try to avoid all the negative behavioural consequences of conflicts. Further, the fact that dysfunctional conflicts can close the ranks of an organization does not justify creating them. Creating an enemy can go out of control. Emphasizing a common enemy is only recommended when one really exists. Islam commanded Muslims to be united together because there was a real danger in their disunity, while the pagans were united in fighting them.

Allah, the Almighty, All Merciful, said:

> "And fight the pagans all together as they fight you all together". —(Q : 9 : 36)

The above verse shows an example where a real enemy exits and is thus emphasized and the Muslims are urged to unite against this common enemy.

This danger is not confined to Muslims rather it is threatening the whole world. Allah, the Exalted, said:

> "The unbelievers are protectors one of another: Unless you do this (protect one another), there would be tumult and oppression on earth and great mischief". —(Q : 8 : 73)

On the other hand, the unity of Muslims is a mercy for mankind. Allah, the All-High, All Glorious, said:

> "We sent you not, but as a mercy for all creatures". —(Q : 21 : 107)

In another verse Allah, the All-Merciful, said:

> "And it (the Quran) certainly is a Guide and a Mercy to those who believe". —(Q : 27 : 77)

Finally, emphasizing organizational super-ordinate goals and common enemies can help settle conflicts in the short-term but as soon as the goals are achieved or the enemy disappears, the internal conflicts are likely to re-emerge. One way of dealing with this problem could be to keep identifying new challenging goals. Creating enemies is not acceptable, for we are created to know one another and to cooperate together, rather than to become enemies.

VIII. Faith

Faith on Allah who is the creator and creatures of the entire world. Once this belief has become clear and that explanation has established itself in the employees mind, the heart is purified of all falsities and impurities and it is released from all ties except those of the one and unique being who along possesses the reality of being and who is the only effective power in this world.

The employer's heart is then released from bondage to anything in this world. It has one Truth, the Truth of Allah and upholds this everlasting Truth, it liberates itself all shackles false ideas, evil desires, and fear of earthly powers and from the confusions that mislead in the working-life.

When the employee's heart finds Allah, it benefits and loses nothing. So why should it desire anything but the pleasure of Allah. This attitude will minimize the chances of conflict in the organization.

IX. Prayer

"And establish regular prayer at the two ends of the day and at the approaches of the night for those things that are good remove those that are evil. Be that the work of remembrance to those who remember (their Lord)".

—(Q : 11 : 114)

An employee who follows regular prayer five times a day will have purity of heart and mind. This will help him know the reality of things. Thereby he will not go for any conflict in the organization but seeks the pleasure of Allah.

Hazrat Abu Huraira says that he heard the Prophet (SAW) asked whether any dirt would be left as his body if any on them took a bath five times a day in a steam flowing by his house. (The companions) replied in the negative, saying that nothing of dirt would be left. The Prophet then said that five times of prayers were just like that and that God removes the filth of sins by them. —Bukhari, Muslim, Tirmizi, Nasai, Ibn Maja

X. Fasting

The real objective of fasting is purification of self and restraint as the Quran says:

"Oh ye who believe! Fasting is prescribed to you as it was prescribed to those before you that ye may (learn) self-restraint". —(Q : 2 : 183)

Fasting is the best exercise for self-restraint, through which conflict will be resolved. The angelic qualities given to employee are all not work as some times the animal instinct gains control and he loses all thought of God's Greatness and His Omnipresence.

Food and sex, which are the most potent demands of animal nature are restrained for a specific time and turn man's attention to higher realities bringing him near to God. This experience and exercise restraint employees from conflict in the organization.

> Hazrat Abu Huraira reports that the Prophet (SAW) had said, "Whosever fasts with firmness of belief and stock taking of his actions, God will forgive his sins committed before. And whosoever offers Tarawih (early night prayers) with full devotion to faith and constant vigilance as to his accountability, God will forgive all his sins committed before.
>
> —Unanimous report

XI. Sincerity

Sincerity is one of the qualities required for minimizing conflict in an organization. Sincerity is the freeing of one's intentions from all impurities in order to come nearer to Allah. It is to ensure that the intentions behind all acts and deeds are exclusively for His pleasure.

> "And they have commanded to worship
> only Allah, being sincere towards
> Him in their deen and true" —(Q : 98 : 5)

Abu Umama has related that a man once came to the Prophet (SAW) may Allah bless him and grant him peace, and said "what a man who joined us in the fighting, his intention being for fame and booty? The Prophet said, "He receives nothing. The man repeated the question three times and each time the Prophet said, "he receives nothing". Then he said, "Allah only accepts actions that are intended purely for His pleasure".

Notes and References

1. C.F. Frik, "Some conceptual difficulties in the theory of social conflict", Journal of Conflict Resolutions, Dec. 1968, pp. 412-60 and J.A. Wall Jr. and R.R. Callister, "Conflict and its Management", *Journal of Management*, Vol. 21, No. 3, 1995, pp. 515-58.
2. K.W. Thomas, "Conflict and Negotiation process in organizations" in M.O. Ounnette and L.M. Hough (ed.) Handbook of Industrial and Organizational Psychology, 2nd ed., Vol. 3 (Palo Alto, CA: Consulting Psychologists Press, 1992), pp. 657-717.

3. Kenneth Thomas and Warren H. Schmidt, "A survey of Managerial Interests with Respect to Conflict", *Academy of Managerial Journal*, June 1976, pp. 315-18. A measurement Instrument is described in Boris kabanoff, "Predictive validity of the MODE conflict Instrument, Journal of Applied Psychology, February 1987 pp. 160-63.
4. Chris Argyris, "Skilled incompetence", *Harvard Business Review*, September-October 1986, pp. 74-79.
5. Gibson *et. al.*, "Organizations" Business Publications Inc, Houston, p. 295 (1985).
6. Joe Kelly, Organizational Behaviour, rev-ed., Richard D. Irurin inc.... and The Dorsey Press, Home wood ... 1974, p. 565.
7. Lewis coser: The Functions of Social Conflict. The Free Press, Glencoe, 1956, p. 31.
8. John M. Ivancevich, "Life Events and Hassles as Predictors of Health Symptoms, Job-performance, and Absenteeism, *Journal of Occupation Behaviour*, January 1986, pp. 39-51, Also see Richard S-Lazarus, "Little Hassles can be Hazardous to your Health", *Psychology Today*, July 1987, pp. 58-62.
9. Bernard Berelon and Gary A. Steiner, Human Behaviour, Harcourt, Brace & World Inc., New York, 1964, p. 271.
10. Kelly, *op. cit.*, p. 563.
11. Baron, R.A., Greenberg, J., "Behaviour in Organizations", Allyn and Bacon, pp. 376, Boston, (1989).
12. Eric Berne, Transactional Analysis in Psychotherapy, New York : Grove Press, Inc. 1961 : Eric Berne, Games people play, New York : Grove Press, Inc., 1964; Thomas A. Harris, I'm o.k.—you're o.k. : A Practical Guide to Transactional Analysis, New York : Harper & Row Publishers, Inc. 1969. Dorothy Jongeward, Everybody Wins; Transactional Analysis Applied to Organization Reading, Mass : Addison-Wesley Publishing Company, 1973.
13. William, P. Galle, Jr. "Transactional analysis as a tool for Humor Applications in Management", in James O. Smith and Carl into Gooding (Eds.), 1985. *American Institute for Decision Sciences Proceedings*, Vol. 2, Las Vegas, Nov. 11-13, 1985, pp. 193-95.
14. David, J. Cherrington and B. Jackson Wtixom, Jr., "Recognition is still a top Motivator", *Personnel Administrator*, May 1983, pp. 87-91.
15. Brain storming was developed by Alex F. Osborn and is Described in his book Applied Imagination, New York; Charles Scribner's Sons, 1953. See also Stephen, R. Grossman, "Brain Storming Updated", *Training and Development Journal*, February 1984, pp. 84-87, and Tony Proctor, "Brain": The Computer program that Brain-storms "Simulation and Games", December 1986, pp. 485-91.
16. Robert, C. Erffmeyer and Others, "The Delphi Technique : An Empirical Evaluation of the optimal number of rounds", *Group and Organizational Studies*, March-June 1986, pp. 120-28.

8

Summary and Conclusions

The following are the summary and conclusions :

I. IMPACT OF TAWHEED ON QWL

The belief 'LA ILAHA ILLALHA' brings forth the following characteristics in the Muslim employees for their successful working lives:

- An employee who believes in this kalmia can never be narrow minded in outlook. He believes in God who is the creator of the heavens and the earth, the Master of the East and the West and sustainer of the entire universe. He looks upon everything in the universe belongs to same Lord.
- This belief produces in an employee highest degree of self-respect and self-esteem. The employee knows that Allah alone is the possessor of all power, and none besides Him can benefit or harm a person or provide his needs or gives and takes away life or wields authority or influence. This makes him an independent and fearless, never bows, his head nor stretches his hand before anyone else.

- This belief generates in the employee a sense of modesty and humbleness.
- It makes him unostentatious and unpretending. The boisterous pride of power, wealth and worth has no room in his heart.
- This belief makes the employee virtuous and upright and has the conviction that there is no other means of success and salvation for him except purity of soul and righteousness of behaviour.
- The employee does not became dependent and broken heart, and has firm faith in God who is the master of all treasures of the earth and heavens, whose grace and bounty have no limits and whose powers are infinite.
- This belief produces in the employee a very string degree of determination, patient perseverance and trust in God, and devotes his resources to fulfil the divine commands in order to serve God's pleasure.
- The employee knows that his life and property and everything belongs to God. He is ready to sacrifice everything for His pleasure.
- This belief creates in the employee an attitude of peace and contentment, purges the mind of the subtle passions of jealousy, envy and greed and keeps away the unfair means of achieving success. If He wills to give, no power in the world can prevent Him from doing so and if He does not will it, no power can force Him to give.
- This belief makes the employee sure that God knows everything hidden or open and is nearer to him than his own jugular vein. He knows our thoughts and intentions, bad or good.
- It brings the employee's elevation above greed for worldly gains and the choice of Allah's richer, ever lasting reward for which all the employees to elevation, purification and cleaning of their souls.
- Tawheed gives us meaning of life and boredom. It gives full and complete meaning of work. The heart is purged of all impurities, except those of the one and unique being.

- When the heart releases itself, all shackles, false ideas, evil desires, and fear of earthly powers will go.
- When this stage is reached, the employee attributes every moment of his life to the first cause event, i.e. Allah, apparent causes do not disturb him. The mind is released of all anxieties and tensions associated with the apparent causes. "When you threw (a handful of dust) it was not your act, but Allah's".
- He is real and permanent being and whose will is the only effective power in the world. From Him Muslims receive beliefs, outlook, values, criteria, legislation, institutions, systems, ethics and traditions.
- It creates love, brotherhood, mutual sympathy and responsiveness between all beings and an individual hearts.
- In present days, employees face the problem of meaning of life and meaning of quality of work life. They became cynical, feel bore because they have lost the meaning of work life. Tawheed gives the meaning of life and enriches them their experience about working life. It gives them purpose of life personal, which includes them meaning of work life.
- Tawheed makes them do the work not for external motivators like money, fear of supervisions, working conditions, fringe benefits, recognition, autonomy, but to please his creator, seeking the pleasure of the God. It is the summom bonum of their work life.
- The employee who is infused by Tawheed is worried about taste autonomy, task significance, task variety which the luxuries. He works whatever be the type of work, for him work is ordained by God.

II. MOTIVATION BASIS IN ISLAMIC PARADIGM

- In Islamic framework motivation stems from the need of the man to seek RAZA-YE-ILLAHI (pleasure of Allah). It is an internal state, which makes an employee to seek 'Raza' (pleasure) of Allah.
- Mundane needs have to be taken care by the human beings. Islam does not advocate complete asceticism.

- ❑ Human needs should be controlled according to the requirements of Sharia. Unbridled human needs will lead to misery in this world.
- ❑ Man has got inherent tendency to seek the pleasure of God. This is the ultimate need of a man. This need has to be realized in this life in his/her mundane life.
- ❑ According to Islamic theology, there are four lives of human beings: Alame–Arwah (spiritual life before birth)
  - Alame-Duniya (earthly life)
  - Alame-Barzakh (spiritual life after death)
  - Alame-Akhirath (life after death)
- ❑ Though, mundane life is important, mundane needs such as sex, wealth-seeking behaviour, need for accumulation of money/wealth are necessarily only to the extent they do not come in the way of the ultimate need of human being, i.e. seeking pleasure of God.
- ❑ A Muslim employee who has internalized this absolute and ultimate value of seeking pleasure of God always strives towards this goal in all aspects of his/her behaviour, be it in relationship with his subordinates, colleagues, company policies and work itself. He has acquired meaning of work; work is a way of seeking the pleasure of God. This galvanizes him/her to exert utmost. In fact, this is called Jihad-e-Akbar. Jihad, which has been translated as Holy war in English, does not convey the true shade of meaning. Jihad means exerting one's utmost in his/her endeavour.
- ❑ This conceptualization of RAZA-YE-ILAHI (pleasure of God) is superior to self-actualization of western theories. Self-actualization for what? The Islamic theory of work motivation answers the question that self-actualization is for RAZA-YE-ILAHI (pleasure of God), for it is an inborn urge of human beings.

III. STRESS INOCULATION IN ISLAM

Concept of Stress in Islam

- ❑ Islamic theology does not subscribe to the theory of evolution. Allah created man. Man was totally regulated by nature in initial stages of his creation. His instinct, desires will, was regulated by nature. He was in paradise and he was not aware of his life. Allah decided to give him a limited freedom and sent Adam to earth. The life, which was totally regulated by natural laws, was given freedom. By sending Adam to earth, Allah created a life, which is aware of it. A life which knows that it has freedom, a life which knows that it can create, a life which knows that it can produce, a life which has been given the faculty of reasoning. This life is also aware that it is not completely free from nature. In spite of separation from the nature it is dominated and regulated by nature to a limited extent. This life is aware that there is an end to itself in the form of death. Man knows that there are natural calamities such as floods, typhoons, Tsunamis, earthquake and diseases over which he has no control. He is not totally part of nature nor can he transcend or dominate nature. This dualism is the root cause of stress in Islamic thought. Man knows that he has the productive capacity to build two hundred story building. But at the same time he knows that this building may fall down due to earthquake. He has invented medicines for thousands of diseases, he can reduce pain, he can control diseases but also aware that a diseases called death for which there is not medicine. This dualism is the root cause of anxiety.

- This anxiety produces loneliness. When he was in paradise there was no loneliness. When Allah sent Adam to earth he felt lonely. Therefore, man must relate himself to this society to the nature and to his creator to get rid off his loneliness, anxiety and stress.
- The Quran forbids the drinking of alcohol by employees, which leads to stress.

"O ye true believers, come not to prayer when ye are drunk, but wait till ye can understand what ye utter".

—(Q : 4 : 46)

"O ye who believe! Forbid not the good things which God

has made lawful for you go not beyond this limit. God loved not those who out step it".

> "And eat of what God hath given you for food, that which is lawful and wholesome, and fear God, in whom ye believe". —(Q : 5 : 87-88)

> "O believers! Surely wine and games of chance, and statues, and the diving arrows, are an abomination of Satan's work!. Avoid them that ye may prosper".
> "Only would Satan sow hatred and strife among you by wise and games of chance, and turn you aside from the remembrance of God, and from prayer, will ye not, therefore, abstain from them? Obey God and obey the Apostle, and be on your guard: but it ye turn back, know that our Apostle is only bound to deliver a plain announcement". —(Q : 5 : 92-93)

Stress Coping Mechanism in Islam

Prayer (Salah)

- The word 'salah' refers to 'remembrance' of God. Whatever we do in this world should be the law of God. Our work, our relationship with superiors, subordinates and co-workers should be the law of God.
- This continuous remaining is necessitated by the fact that man's 'nafs' is a satan who continuously instigates him by saying 'you are my slave', employee reminds himself several times in a day that he is not slave of satan but of God. It reminds us five times during the day. The Quran has made to this remembrance.
  "And when the salah is ended then disperse in the land and seek of Allah's bounty (i.e. exert yourself in search of lawful means of sustenance), and remember Allah profusely, so that ye may gain success and well-being". —(Q : 62 : 10)
- Salah makes us the practice of obedience. Employees are tested in obeying the commandments of God in their working life. It is said in the Quran.

"And truly it (salah) is hard save for the humble minded". (Q : 2 : 45)

- Prayer makes the fear of God which is necessary to be kept alive in the heart uninterruptedly. If an employee believes that God is aware of every of his action, even in the darkness and when he is alone, all the time at every place. He will not commit any mistake and he will try to satisfy the God. This leads to free of tensions. It is possible to hide one-self from the whole world but it is impossible to hide from God. It leads to stress free life.

  Salah prevents man from evil and lewdness.

  —(Q : 24 : 25)
- Prayer is offered when an employee is clean and have done Wudu (ablution).

Loneliness

- One of the reasons for stress is loneliness. Prayer can relieve this loneliness. In prayer all employees are united and standing in front of God and all are equal. This type of prayer removes loneliness.
- Prayer is the divine injunction; it keeps alive in the employee's mind the fear of God, the belief in His Omni-science and Omni-presence and the conviction that he is accountable before Him.
- Prayer creates a purpose assembly. Through prayer employees meet each other recognize each other and come to know each other. This kind of attachment that all Muslims are one community, they are all soldiers of the same army. This type of feelings creates a related mind and reduces stress.
- By prayer an employee attaches himself to the almighty. This attachment gives him the feeling of sufficiency. An employee being finite human being, by attaching himself with almighty. Finite being become infinite or at least comes closer to it. This feeling of infinity gives him a strong courage. An employee with all his limitations as a human being gets rid of the

burden of being man by attaching himself with the Supreme Being.

- That is the reason why the Prophet (SAW) has asked a Muslim to offer prayer as if he is seeing God. If he cannot do that at least he should feel that Allah is watching him. Stress is burden of being man. Proximity to the Supreme Being reduces the stress. A gentle feeling of peace and tranquillity descends a him.

Fasting .

- Fasting is a sacred devotional rite and an effective of employee's moral and spiritual uplift. Its aim is purification of self and restraint.
- "O ye who believe! Fasting is prescribed to you as it was prescribed to those before you that may (learn) self-restraint".

  —(Q : 2 : 183)
- Food and sex are the most potent demands of animal nature are restrained for a specified time and turn employee's attention to higher realities bringing him nearer to God. This helps him to restrain eyes, tongues, and thought.
- Fasting is a trial of endurance and the sense of thankfulness. God has reminded an employee of his very great boon that with His unbounded grace and Benevolence.
- Employee will refrain from sinful acts and will devote himself to the service of humanity and will never lose sight of the real aim including the work life.
- Fasting has another function to perform as a de-stressor. In every outcome orgiastic experience is considered as the most important de-stressor. That is the reason why in many cultures music, dance, an art, alcoholic drinks, drugs, etc. and other form of stress relieving techniques are encouraged and rewarded. Without this experience, man will die of stress. Fasting is one method of getting orgiastic experience. The intention of the creator of the mankind is not to make a Muslim hungry for thirteen to fourteen hours. The

underlining idea of fasting is to train him to reach a peak experience at time of breaking of the fast. This tyranny for about a month is believed to be effective for the rest of eleven months in a year for relieving stress.

- During the period of thirty days or so a Muslim employee is given tyranny to reach orgiastic or peak experience. This is best stress buster.

Zakat and Charity

- By paying 'zakat' or fulfilling the rights of the fellow-beings an employee not only performs his duty but also provides means to perfect his own personality. This perfection and purification is the main purpose of reducing stress.
- "And let not those who covetously withhold of the gift which God hath given them of His grace, think that it is good for them; nay, it will be the worse for them; soon shall the things which they covetously withheld be tied to their necks like a twisted collar on the day of judgment". —(Q : 3 : 180)
- Zakat means an increasing of wealth by paying it; an employee purifies his soul and his wealth. An important feature of it is that no employee is obliged to another or is tempted by variety and imposition of obligation. The proceeds of zakat may be utilized in much social welfare.
- The miser and lover of money who sits tight over his wealth like snake and does not allow others to be benefited by it his wealth will become a snake and bite him, black spots point out its being highly poisonous.
- If an employer spends his wealth on his employees God will not let him become poor but continue to shower His bounties on him.
- It is the height of dishonesty and thanklessness not to spend God given wealth for His pleasure and according to His orders.
- Zakat and charity purges a heart of all impurities such as jealousy, misery, stringiness, greed and anger. In the

act of giving a charity a Muslim—an employee and employee, finds expression of potency. To give is to love. In the act of loving we feel manliness. Similarly an act of charity gives a feeling of contentment, which acts as a de-stressor. Stress arises from an accumulation of imbecilities of mind such as anger, greed, jealously, fear, etc. When charity is given, the fear of becoming poor gets reduced. An employee feels happy and contended by giving charity.

Haj

Hay is an intention to visit holy places. The Quran says :

"Pilgrimage thereto (kaaba) is a duty men owe to God—those who can afford the journey; but if any deny faith, God stands not in need to any of His creative".

—(Q : 3 : 97)

- To perform Haj is responding to the call of God.
- God has made Ka'aba a repository of all good, a blessing and a source of guidance for the whole world.
- Employees for the love and obedience of God leaves his organization, his relatives and friends, undertakes a long odorous journey as if a violent passion is dragging him along with the heart turned to God, with repentance on sins, seeking forgiveness with utmost humility and pledging to keep on the right path in future and praying to God for the courage and strength to live up to it.
- Sacrifice of animals represents sacrifice of one's own life in the path of God and pledge that it is at His disposal. "It is neither their meat nor their blood that reaches God : it is your piety that reaches Him".

  —(Q : 22 : 37)
- By performing Haj and Umra an employee's heart is purged of all bad feelings such as desire for power, status, jealousy, pride, animosity. To understand these phenomena one should actually performed Haj. After this pilgrimage, man's heart does not attach itself to any rewards associated with the mundane affairs. It

does not mean that an employee stops working as per the regular schedule. Nay he works much harder and performs his duties in the best possible way. Excellency will be his hallmark. However, he is not worried about the rewards associated with hard work. He does not complete nor does he feel ill-will towards his co-workers, superiors, etc. This is really a stress buster.

Reciting the Quran

- One of the qualities of reducing the stress in work place is reciting the Quran. By reciting the Quran all the impurities in the heart and mind will be cleaned, an employee feels that the Allah's soul is in his heart and closer to Allah. The Prophet (SAW) said :
"The servant get nearest into Allah by reciting the Quran". —Tirmizi
- Recitation of Quran keeps an employee always in touch with his creator. The believer does not take Quran as any other look. He believes it to be uncorrupted book of God. His belief in the creator gets strengthened when he reads or hears the word of God. This gives him a soothing feeling. There are innumerable verses in the Quran, which provide a relief from stress to a Muslim. For example, "Those who believe in Allah and stead fast in their belief, angles will descend on them and say do not be sacred, we are with you in this world and in the life hereafter".

Visiting Graveyards

- An employee should after visit the graveyard, thereby he realizes that the worldly gains like wealth, power, status, etc. will have lost their value and only his deeds will count. When he realizes this, he will not commit any mistake and go for worldly gains. This will reduce his stress.
- These visit remind an employee of the life hereafter and induce him to start making preparations for the life after death.

Sleeping

- One of the reasons of reducing stress is sleeping. An employee after doing his work in a day he should sleep at night. Allah has appointed the night time for peace and rest. He has made the day time for keeping awake and for labour to earn one's living.
- "And he it is who created night a covering for you and sleep for response and made the day time waking up".
- In the night when an atmosphere of peace and privacy reigns, repose in bed in a calm and comfortable state. As soon as down breaks, arise and involve the blessings of Allah enter into the field of practical endeavour with renewed vigour.

Controlling of an Anger

- One of the symptoms of stress in work life is anger. The Prophet (SAW) said : "Anger is due to satanic influence and since satan has been created from fire, whenever a person feels angry, he should perform ablution".

  —Abu Dawud
- Whenever an employee feels anger he should sit down, otherwise he should lie down.
- The God will give the reward for the employee who controls his tongue, which leads to anger.
- Employees should forgive the mistakes committed by their superiors, co-workers and subordinates for the sake of Allah, and they should not be angry with them.

Patience

- One of the solutions for stress is patience. The management, supervisors and employees should be patient in the work life. Islam asked the people to be steadfast, patience, and to help one another, maintain patience while doing the righteous work. This leads to relieving of stress.

  "Patiently then preserve. For the promise of Allah is true". —(Q : 40 : 55)

- During stressful work life, the employees require a greater degree of determination through patient and perseverance.
- "But if you persevere patiently, and guard against evil then that will be a determining factor in all attain".
—(Q : 3 : 186)
- An example is Prophet (SAW) and his companion in pursuing a policy of restrain for thirteen years in Makkah"

Zikir

- One of the reasons of reducing stress at work place is reciting "Tasbee". Tasbee is training given to an employee to recite 'subhanallah' by thirty-three times, 'Alhamthulillha' thirty-three times, Allah-u-Akber thirty-three times and 'LA-ILAHA-ILLALAHI' one time. Totally one hundred times it has to be recited. If an employee recite his heart and mind will get purity of things, and he will experience none other the Allah's soul in him.

Believing Taqdir (Fate)

- Believing Taqdir is one of the quality of relieving stress. Whatever happens to an employee in the organization by nature is the will of God.
- "Whatever suffering ye suffer".
- "It is what is your own hands have wrought".
—(Q : 42 : 29)
- "Whosoever followed the right course, he doth so for the good of his own soul, and whosoever followed the wrong course doth so to its own hurt"
—(Q : 17 : 16)
- Our own acts for good or bad are might powers. It is Taqdir. The good deeds of on employee and pleasure of God will change our fate.

TYPES OF STRESS AT WORK

Role Stress

- Each employee from the time of birth plays a variety of roles such as son/daughter, brother/sister, student/teacher, husband/wife, father/mother, boss/subordinate/peer mate, etc. Each of these positions/role occupied by an employee is connected by set of norms a guidelines for appropriate behaviour. These guidelines are devised by society from religious values.
- Each of these position or role called for different types of behaviour after causing problem. Thus ensuring stress. Role stress is when an employee plays multiple roles.

Tawakkul

- The better way of relieving role stress is to trust in Allah who is the only one who will deliver the outcomes. Putting the trust in Allah is called tawakkul. It is a sign of belief in the unseen that is controlled by Allah. Tawakkul is the reliance of the heart on, and its confidence in Allah. An employee should make tawakkul in performing their roles believing that Allah is the most merciful, the most graceful, and the exalted in might, the one with absolute knowledge, wisdom and justice. Tawakkul comes after one does his role.

Decision-making Stress

- One of the important types of stress in organization occurs as a result of making difficult decisions.
- Islam advocates that the decision-making can be done through consultation, which by consensus. If a consensus is not reached, it concludes by voting. The following are some of the verses from Quran.
- "Say : O people of the Book! Come to common terms as between us and you: that we worship none but Allah! That we erect not from among ourselves : Lords

and patrons other than Allah. It them they turn back, say Ye. Bear witness that we are Muslims (submitting to the will of God). —(Q : 3 : 64)

- The culture of the companions of the Prophet (SAW) can also be described as a culture of a dialogue or consultation. All members of the society irrespective if their age, gender, race, or ethnic origin shared the value of dialogue. Any decision taken by a manager in an organization is for the benefit of employees and pleasure of Allah. Before it he should consult with all the employees. This type of decision-making will not experience any type of stress.

Relationship at Work

- The work life in an organization consists of interpersonal relationship, they are
    - Relationship with employer,
    - Relationship with subordinates, and
    - Relationship with colleagues.
- These relationships may cause frictions and leads to stressful work life.
- The human life according to the Quran is to express itself a system of activity promoting peace and harmony in work life.
- "Oh no soul do we lay a responsibility greater than it can bear". —(Q : 2 : 286)
- An employee has a dual responsibility to discharge. One is in relation to God, i.e. Pleasure of God (RAZA-YE-ILAHI) the other is in relation to his external world, i.e. relation to superior, relation to subordinate, relation to co-workers. The two types of responsibilities are one and the same attitudes towards working life.

IV. CONFLICT

Islamic Thought and Conflict

- According to Islamic theology, conflict arouse when satan tempted the first man, i.e., Adam to transgress the limits of Allah. From this episode, it is clear that the root cause of conflict is satan, who is always on the look-out for creating the situation in which human being transcend the instructions of Allah.

- The first conflict between the two humans arose when two sons of Adam fought over the sacrifice made by them. Jabil made sacrifice Allah accepted Jabil sacrifice. The sacrifice of Cain was rejected. Estranged by the rejection Cain killed his brother. This is the first report of conflict in the Quran. The root cause of this conflict is anger and jealous feeling created by satan.

The following verse from Quran and Hadeeths illustrates the role of satan in creation of conflict situation.

- "Those who restrain (anger) and pardon men and Allah loves the does of good to others".—(Q : 3 : 133)
- "Verity, anger is satan". —Abu Daud
- Hazrat Atiya sa' adi says that prophet (Saw) said: "Anger is due to satanic influence and since satan has been created from fire, whenever a person feel angry, he should perform ablution". —Abu Daud
- Hazrat Abu Zhar says that the Prophet (SAW) said : If any of you feels angry while he is standing he should sit down. If he subsidies so much the better, otherwise he should lie down". —Mishkat
- Hazrat Abu Huraria reports the Prophet (SAW) had said that the strong man was really not one who overcome his opponent in wrestling but one who controlled himself at the time of anger that is refrained from doing anything not liked by God and His Prophet (SAW). —Bukhari
- Hazrat Anas reports that Prophet (SAW) had said God would cover-up the faults of those who guarded their tongues (from truth) and put off punishment of those who controlled their anger and would forgive anyone who asked forgiveness. —Mishkat
- Hazrat Abu Huraira says that a person (who was probably hot tempered) requested the Prophet (SAW)

to give him advice. The Prophet (SAW) said, "Never be angry". —Bukhari

- Hazrat Abu Huraira says that the Prophet (SAW) said that the Prophet Moses had asked God which of his servants was dearest to Him and God has said those who are strong enough to follow forgiveness. —Miskat

Causes of Conflict

The following are some of the factors, which create the conflict in the organizational life.

Backbiting

- One of the reasons of conflict in the organization is backbiting. It is naturally that in order to satisfy the employer, an employee will do backbite of another employee. Islam prohibits the backbiting. Backbiting is most heinous sins.
- "A backbiter will not be able to enter Heaven". —Bukhari
- Hazrat Abu Saeed and Hazrat Jabir reports that the Prophet (SAW) had said that backbiting were greater than adultery. Those present asked how it was a greater sin and the Prophet (SAW) said that if a man committed adultery and asked forgiveness of God, God would forgive him, but God would not forgive a backbiter unless the man who he maligned behind his back forgive him. —Miskat

Obscene Language and Abusiveness

- Another reason for conflict in an organization is obscene language and abusiveness. The language used by an employee should be pleasing and it should not hurt others.
- Hazrat Ali Ibn Abu Talib says that the Prophet (SAW) had said "that one who used obscene language and

one who propagated it were both equally sinners".

—Miskat

- Hazrat Abu Darda reports that the Prophet (SAW) had said "that the weightiest thing that would be put in the scale of a believer on the day of judgment would be his good manners and God very much dislike the man who use obscene language was abusive. —Tirmizi

Double Dealing

- Double-dealing is one of the factors for conflict in the organization. Islam prohibits the double-dealing by an employee or group of employees who create conflict among the employees. When there is a conflict between two employees or two groups, some persons who come forward to visit both the parties and creating their enmity. This is most objectionable. There are some employees who express a great familiarity on the face but speak ill behind the back. This is also double-dealing.
- Hazrat Ummer says that the Prophet (SAW) had said "that one who had been double-faced in the world would be two tongues of fire on the day of judgment.

  —Abu Dawud
- An employee who has two tongues on the Day of Judgment will emit fire from his mouth, which burns mutual relationship.

Rumour-Mongering

- Rumour mongering is another reason for conflict in an organization. Employees are directed to refrain from saying anything without confirming it as it may be that an employee who reported it may be satan himself. Spreading unconfirmed rumours may cause a lot of mischief and conflict in the organization.
- Hazrat Abdullah Bin Masood says that the Prophet (SAW) had said "satan was in the shape of man and goes about among the people telling them lies, then people disperse and one of the man says that he had

heard such thing from a person who he knows by the face. But does not know his name". —Muslim

Fault Finding

- At another reason of conflict is fault finding of others. Usually the superiors will find the fault of his subordinates and similarly the subordinate will find the fault of his superior and his colleagues. It is prohibited in Islam.
- Hazrat Ayesha says that "once she mentioned the defects of Hazrat safia (that she is short statured, which is great defect). The Prophet (SAW) said "O, Ayesha you have spoken such a filthy work that if it is mixed with an ocean, it will pollute the whole of it". —Mishkat

Nepotism

- Nepotism is another reason for conflict in an organization. If any other relatives or friends and his cast people of superior are working in an organization, the superior will show his favour to them. This will create conflict among the employees of the organization. In Islam God dislikes it.
- The Prophet (SAW) had said "that if any one was made to rule over Muslims and made responsible for their collection affairs and be appointed any officer merely on account of his relationship or friendship then God's cense be upon him and He would accept no apology from him till he is cast into hell". —Imam Abu Yusuf

Conflict Resolution Mechanism in Islam

The following are the Islamic method by which conflict will be resolved. These methods are based on Quran and Hadeeths.

Responsibility of Conflict Resolutions

- The Muslim Ummah and the business organization in the Islamic framework is responsible to resolve conflict. Be the individual or organization it is obligatory. The Holy Quran says :
- "The believes are but a single brotherhood: So reconcile between your contending brothers; and fear Allah, that you may receive mercy". —(Q : 49 : 10)
- The conflict parties should be reconciled as ordained by Allah. In the case of arbitration, use of authoritative command can be very efficient. Authoritative command is needed when conflicts persist and start hurting the organization, or when one party is determined to be right while the other is at fault. In fact, if one party has transgressed another. Muslims are ordained to firmly stop this transgression. Allah, the Exalted said :
- "But if one transgresses beyond bonds organist the offer, then fight you against the one that transgresses until it complies with the command of Allah, but if it complies then make peace between them with justice, and be fair for Allah loves those who are fair".
  —(Q : 49 : 9)

Shura (Mutual Consultation)

- If any conflict arises between the two individuals or groups it can be resolved through shura system. It is a mutual consultation among the employees or group of employees to discuss the problem and take a decision for the pleasure of God. The Quran has made it clear that leaders are obligated to consult those who have knowledge or those who can provide sound advice. The Holy Quran says :
- "More enduring is a portion with God whose affairs are guided by mutual counsel". —(Q : 42 : 36)
- "And those whose answer the call of their Lord and establish prayer, and who conduct their affairs by consultation and spend out of what we bestow on them for sustenance". —(Q : 42 : 38)

- The community which regulates its affairs by counsel will prosper. —Kunuz-ul-Haqaiq
- The practice of shura enables the employees of the organization to participate in resolving conflicts. At the same time, shura serves a check on the conduct of employees in case be deviates from the aim of the group.

Freedom of Thought

- Freedom should be given to an employee or group of employees to express their thoughts or view about the problem.
- Addressing a gathering during his last Haj, said the prophet (SAW) : "O people! You God is but one, and the rather of each one of you is but one. The Arab has no superiority over a non-Arab the fair coloured over the black coloured or the black coloured over the fair coloured except by the righteousness he displays in life". —Ahmed : Musnad
- Before Lord all are equal, each employee has freedom to express his views about the problem in the organization. The management should create an atmosphere of freethinking, healthy exchange of ideas, and mutual advice so that the employees feel very comfortable in discussing their matters.

Justice

- One of the basis of resolving conflict is justice. The management of an organization should establish an internal judiciary or arbitration committee to settle any dispute or grievance among the employees.
- The members of such a committee should be selected from among the knowledgeable, pious and wise people.
- The management should deal with employees justly and fairly regardless of their race, colour, national origin or religion. The Quran says that :
- "Surely Allah enjoins justice and the doing of good (to

others) and the giving to the kindred, and the forbids indecency and evil and rebellion. He admonishes you that you may be mindful". —(Q : 16 : 90)

- "O you who believe, be upright for Allah, bearers of witness with justice, and not hatred of a people incite you not to act equitably. Be just that is nearer to observance of duty. And keep you duty to Allah. Surely Allah is aware of what you do". —(Q : 5 : 8)
- "O you who believe, be maintain of justice, bearers of witness for Allah, even though it be against your own selves or (your) partners or near relations. Whether he is rich or poor, Allah has a better right over them both. So follow not (your) low desires, best you deviate. And if you distort of turn away from (truth), surely Allah is ever aware of what you do". —(Q : 4 : 135)

Self-restraint and Forgiveness

- One of the methods of resolving conflict in Islam is self-restraint and forgiveness. An employee or group of employees who are in the conflict should follow the same for the pleasure of God. The following are some of verses from Quran and Hadeeths
- "Who master their anger, and forgive other God loved the doers of Good". —(Q : 3 : 133)
- "Endure then with patience. But thy patient endurance must be sought in none but God". —(Q : 16 : 12)
- "And whose beareth wrongs with patience and for gives this verily is highly mindedness".—(Q : 40 : 42)
- "Abdullah bin Abbas said that the prophet (SAW) once addressing a tribal chief remarked : Two of your qualities are pleasuring to God. One is your sense of self-restraint; the other is your disinclination to act hastily". —Muslim
- Moses said, "O my Lord! Who is the most honoured of thy servants in Thy sight? God said : He who pardons when he has the power (to avenge himself).—Baihqai
- From the above, it is clear that every member of a business organization is enjoin to practice self-restraint and forgiveness. Justice is not the end of an

organization. If all the members of an organization keep an harping on their rights and obligations of others, the organizational climate will become bureaucratic; where everybody be management or employees, think only about their authority and duties of others. If will take away the friendly and caring spirit of an organization. It will be a machine and not body of human beings. The over-emphasis of formulation of rationality, rules and regulations, rights and duties of Max Weber has lead to bureaucratic culture in western organization. Muslims blindly copied this form of structure and try to transplant in their countries. The net result is that Muslim organizations are neither here nor there. Islam emphasis on mutual tolerance and forgiveness. Justice, bureaucracy, rationality rules and regulations are only for people who are operating at baser levels.

- For members who have risen themselves above their baser level need our organization culture, with love affection, care, mercy, forgiveness, etc. which are enjoin in the above quoted words of the creator of the universe and the words of last prophet (SAW) make an organization a humanistic, and Islamic. It is this culture in which self-actualization process reaches pinnacle, organizational growth will be at its peak, business performance will be at its highest level.

Providing an Expert Opinion

- Conflict between employees can be caused by different perception of the reality or by different understanding of same maters. On many occasions, the employees involved in the conflict do not have enough knowledge to judge, which view is right or which view is best.
- Jawdat Sa'eed said, "The judge of a conflict is only knowledge".
- Say : Have you any (certain) knowledge? If so, produce it for us. You follow nothing but conjecture : you do nothing but lie". —(Q : 6 : 18)

- If there is a conflict in the organization it is best to bring an outside expert who will be able to deliver a judgement on the issue. The expert shall make a professional judgement and shall be able to convince both the parties. This is instrumental in the settlement of the conflict.

Negotiation

- Negotiation is the bargaining between the two parties that have recognized their conflict. Representatives of both the parties can handle it. This negotiation process is very efficient when there is a tendency for reconciliation or agreement. Allah, the All high said regarding marriage conflicts.
- "If you fear a breach between them twain appoint two arbiters, one from his family and the other from hers; if they wish for reconciliation, Allah will cause their reconciliation. For Allah has full knowledge and is acquainted with all things. —(Q : 4 : 35)

Arbitration

- When the degree of communication between conflicting groups decreases, the need for arbitration becomes urgent. Delays in arbitration can worsen the conflict. Arbitration can take various forms. An accepted neutral person or arbitrators have to show knowledge on the issue, understanding of the overall interest of the organization and especially justice.
- "If you judge, judge in equity between them, for Allah loves those who judge in equity". —(Q : 5 : 42)
- "Allah does command you to render back your trusts to those to whom they are due; and when you judge between people, that you judge with justice : verily how excellent is the teaching which He gives you! For Allah is He who hears and sees all things". —(Q : 4 : 58)

Faith

- Faith on Allah who is the creator and creatures of the entire world will resolve conflict in the organization. Once this belief has become clear and that explanation has established itself in the employees mind, the heart is purified of all falsities and impurities and it is released from duties except those of the one and unique being who alone possess the reality of being and who is the only effective power in their world.
- When the employee's heart finds Allah, it benefits and loses nothing. So why should it desire anything but the pleasure of Allah. This attitude with minimizes the chances of conflict in the organization.

Prayer

- An employee who follows regular prayer five times a day will have purity of heart and mind. This will help him know the reality of things. Thereby he will not go for any conflict in the organization but seeks the pleasure of Allah.
- "And establish regular prayer at the two ends of the day and at the approaches of the night for those things that are good remove those that are evil. Be that the work of remembrance to those who remember (their Lord). —(Q : 11 : 14)
- Hazrat Abu Huraria says that "he heard the Prophet (SAW) asked whether any dirt would be left as his body if any of them took a bath five times a day in a stream flowing by his house. The companions replied. in the negative saying that nothing of dirt would be left. The Prophet (SAW) than said that five times of prayers were just like that and that God removes the filth of sins by them". —Bukhari, Muslim

Fasting

- The real objective of fasting is the purification of self and restraint. It is the best exercise for self-restraint, through which conflict will be resolved. The angelic quality given to an employee is all not work as some times the animal instinct gains control and he loses although of God's greatness and His omnipresence. Food and sex, which are the most potent demands of animal nature, are restrained for a specific time and turn man's attention to higher realities bringing him near to God. This experience is restraint employees from conflict in the organization.

- The Quran says : "Oh, Ye who believe! Fasting is prescribed to you as it was prescribed to those before you that ye may (learn) self-restraint". —(Q : 2 : 183)

Sincerity

- Sincerity is one of the qualities required for minimizing conflict in an organization. Sincerity is the freeing of one's intentions from all impurities in order to come nearer to Allah. It is to ensure that the intentions behind all acts and deeds are exclusively for His pleasure.
- "And they have commanded to worship only Allah, being sincere towards Him in their deen and true".
—(Q : 98 : 5)
- Abu Umama has related that a man once came to the Prophet (SAW) may Allah bless him and grant him peace, and said, "what a man who joined us in the fighting, his intention being for fame and booty? The Prophet said, "He receives nothing. The man repeated the question three times and each time the Prophet said, "he receives nothing". Then he said, "Allah only accepts actions that are intended purely for His pleasure".

Other Good Qualities of Work Life

- The prophet (SAW) is reported to have said that he had been sent with the mission of elevating good manners to the level of perfection.
—Moatta Imam Malick

- The prophet (SAW) prepared a list of good manners from his life and sayings and implemented it in his whole life with its various aspects, and directed all to live by them.
- Hazrat Abdullah Bin Mubarak has defined good manners as a smiling face, spending money on the poor and never to hurt anyone.
- Hazrat Abdullah bin Amr Ibnul Alas says that the prophet (SAW) never uttered an obscene word all his life, nor indulged in any obscene act, nor spoke ill of anyone and used to say that the best men among them were those whose manners are good.

  —Bukhari, Muslim
- The employer of an organization should also possess the good manners.
- Hazrat Mo'as says, "The last advice which the prophet (SAW) gave me at the time of mounting my horse while sending me to Yeman (as governor) so that I should have full regard for good manners in dealing with the people. —Mo'atta Imam Malik

Simplicity and Cleanliness

- The employees of an organization should be simple and clean. It is one of the qualities of work life.
- Hazrat abu Umama reports that the Prophet (SAW) had said that simplicity in life was part of the faith.

  —Abu Dawud
- A muslim employee who have faith so much for the better part of his life in the next world and does not run after the good things in life.
- Hazrat Ata'bin yasar says that once while the Prophet (SAW) was sitting in the mosque a man came whose hair was unkempt. The Prophet (SAW) pointed at him with his hand which was meant to direct him to go and have his hair combed. The man went out and returned with hair properly arranged and Prophet (SAW) said, "Is it not better than disarranged hair giving one the appearance of satan". —Mishkat

- Hazrat Abu Ahwas reports from his father who went to the Prophet (SAW) in inferior and cheap dress and the Prophet (SAW) asked him if he had no worldly possessions. Father said, "Yes". The Prophet asked, "What possessions"? Father said, "God has given me wealth in cows, sheep, horses and slaves". The Prophet (SAW) said, "The mark of the benevolence of God should be visible on your body". —Mishkat
- It means that when God has given an employee everything he should eat and dress according to his status and not that he should look like a man of no means, which was being ungrateful to God.

Salutation

- The employee of an organization should respect and salute to the employer. Hazrat Abdullah bin Umar reports that a person asked the Prophet (SAW) which act was best in Islam and the Prophet (SAW) said to feed the poor and to salute everyone whether acquainted with him or not. —Bukhari, Muslim

- Salutation creates mutual affection and sympathy, between employer and employee. Hazrat Abu Huraira reports that the Prophet (SAW) had said, "You cannot be admitted to paradise, cannot be true believers, unless you have affection for one another". Then he asked if he would tell them how to have affection among themselves. It was by popularizing salutation. —Muslim

Guarding the Tongue

- Guarding the tongue and private parts is one of the qualities of work life. Hazrat Sahl bin Sa'ad reports that the Prophet (SAW) had said that whosoever assured him of his guarding the tongue and that between his two legs he (the Prophet) would guarantee paradise for him. —Bukhari

- These two are the most vulnerable parts in the human body through which satan can easily assault. If anyone has succeeded in guarding these parts from satan he will certainly have his abode in paradise.
- Hazrat Abu Huraira says that the Prophet had said, "Man utters certain words and does not attach much importance to them but God advances his position through them. In the same way, man sometimes carelessly utters something displeasing to God, which takes him to hell. —Bukhari
- The employee should not leave his tongue uncontrolled but should think before he speaks and should not say anything, which may lead to hell.

Secrecy

- Secrecy is one of the essential qualities for success in work life. Hazrat mo'az bin Jabal reports that the Prophet had said that for success in your efforts you should practice secrecy, as there are people envious of the prosperous men. —Al-Mo'jam-us-Saghir Tabrani
- The employee should not be so shallow minded as to make public the aims and intentions as in that case he will not be safe from envy and machinations.
- A secret will not remain secret if revealed to another employee. It is reported from Hazrat Amr ibnul A'as that the Prophet had said that he was surprised to find anyone flying from his destiny as destiny was sure to overtake him, and one who saw the straw in another's eye and not the log in his own, and one who was anxious to remove malice from another and himself fostered in him enmity and ill-will. And he further said that it had revealed his secret to another and then blamed him for its being divulged. "How can I accuse another for revealing a secret which I myself could not keep", he said. —Al-Adabul-Mufrad

Humility and Modesty

- Humility and modesty is one of the reason of work life.

It is reported from Hazrat Umar that once while delivering a sermon from the pulpit he enjoined upon people to take to humility and modesty as he had heard the Prophet say that one who humbled himself before God. He exalted his position and while he though himself to be humble he was exalted in the public eye and the proud man was humbled in the public eye although he regarded himself great, till he came to be regarded lower than pigs and dogs.

—Mishkat

- Hazrat Abdullah bin Umar reports that he never found the Prophet reclining while taking food or walking ahead of even two persons, following behind.

  —Miskhat, Abu Dawud

- The Prophet was so modest that he never reclined while taking food, nor walked ahead of people following behind, as these two practices are signs of pride and superiority.
- It is reported from Hazrat Umme Salma that the Prophet saw a slave named Aflah that when prostrating in prayer he blew away the dust. The prophet called him and said, "O Aflah, let your face be covered with dust. —Tirmizi, Mishkat
- Hazrat Abu Umama reports that the Prophet had said, "Do you not listen, do you not listen: Simplicity is without doubt a symbol of faith, simplicity is without doubt a symbol of faith".
- Simplicity is meant avoiding with one another in ostentation. Islam does not prohibit well and trimming. But what is prohibited is the excess of it and spending too much on it and thus leaving nothing for other useful works such as helping the poor and looking after their needs.

Cost Efficiency

- The companions were taught by their leader, the Prophet (SAW) to be cost efficient. The Prophet's teaching to his companions is that they should use the minimum amount of water necessary even if they are taking their ablution in the river.

- Luxury was not part of the life of the companions of the Prophet (SAW). Many of them could not afford it, and those who could, were not interested in indulgence. Islam encourages moderate spending for ones comfort. Extravagance is strongly condemned in Islam. Allah, the Exalted says :
- "Verily spendthrifts are brothers of satan and satan is to his Lord ungrateful". —(Q : 17 : 27)
- Since the companions lived in the desert, they were not used to the comfort of urban Rome, or Persia. The difficulties they experienced in their daily lives made them capable of enduring hardship. It also fostered in them strength, patience, and perseverance. These qualities contributed in making the companions great soldiers.
- An employee should realize the importance of the cost spend by the organization for the manufacture of a product or service rendered. An employee should not waste the cost same.

Time Efficiency

- While time means money in the West, it means "Life" in Islam. Whatever time we lose is from our limited for which we are accountable. The Prophet (SAW) said :
- "Man will be asked about his life, how he spent it, his youth, how he used it and his money, how he earned it and how he spent it". —Tirmidhi
- "Take advantage of fire before death : Your youth before your aging, your health before your sickness, your wealth before your poverty, your free time before your busy time, and your life before your death". —Tirmidhi
- The sahaba (companions) hardly had free time during their lives. Their life was a continuous jihad (struggle). Their descendants, the tabey'een. The tabey'een were known for scheduling their time effectively between

three main activities, seeking knowledge, formally worshipping Allah and working.

- From the above, it is clear that an employee should realize the importance of time in their working life. They should not waste it. They are responsible for the use of the time.

RAZA-YE-ILAHI (pleasure of God) alone becomes sum mum bonum of an employee's life.

Bibliography

I. Books

Abu Ameenah Bilal Philips, *The Fundamentals of Tawheed (Islamic monotheism),* AHYA publications, Mumbai, 1999.

Ahmad Farid, *"The Purification of the Soul",* Al-Firdous Ltd., London, 1998.

Ahmad Von Denffer, *Research in Islam,* Islamic foundation, United Kingdom, 1996.

Al. Twaheed, *Its Implications for thought and Life by Ismail Raji al Faruqui,* International Institute of Islamic Thought, Herndon, Virginia, U.S.A. 1995.

Alderfer, C.P., *"An Empirical Test of a New Theory of Human Needs",* Organizational Behaviour and Human Performance, May 1969.

Al-Quran, *English translation,* The presidency of Islamic Research, IFTA, 'Saudi-Arabia'.

Al-Qushayri, *Translated by with an introduction by Hamid Algar,* B.R. Von Schlegell, Principles of Sufism, Islamic book trust, Kualalumpur, Malaysia, 2004.

Amarchand, D. and Jayaraj, B.J., *Corporate Culture and Organizational Effective,* New Delhi : Global Business Press, 1992.

Anderson, R. Carl, *Management Society Function and Organization Performance,* 2nd End., Bostaw : Allyn of Bacon Inc., 1988.

Andrella, H. and Rumbold, B., *Organizational Development in Action,* Melbourne Producing Promotion Council of Australia, 1974.

Arnold, H.J., *"Effects of Performance Feedback and Extrinsic Reward upon High Intrinsic Motivation"*, Organizational Behaviour and Human Performance, Dec. 1976.

Arrygis C., *Integrating the Individual and the Organization,* New York, Wiley, 1964.

Asha Bhandarkar, *Motivational Research in India,* A Literature Review, Unpublished paper Prepared for ICPE, Yugoslavia, 1988.

Aurobindo, Sri, *The Message of the Gita,* Sri Aurobindo Ashram, Pondichery, 1977.

Azami, M.M., *Studies in Hadith Methodology and Literature,* Islamic Book Trust, Kualalumpur, 1977.

Baron, R.A., Greenberg, J., *"Behaviour in Organizations"*, Allyn and Bacon, Boston, 1989.

Barow Roben, E.A., *Behaviour in Organization Understanding and Managing the Human Side of Work,* 2nd Edn., Masschusetts?, Allyn and Bacan Inc., 1986.

Bennis, W.G., *Changing organization,* New Delhi, Tata McGraw Hill Publishing Company.

Bernard Berelon and Gary, A., *Steiner,* Human Behauin, Harcourt, Brace & World Inc., New York, 1964.

Bhave, Vinoba:, *Talks on the Geetha,* Sarva Seva Sangh Prakashan, Varanesi, 1974. Vikarma or mind and heart applied to external action is necessary to convert Karma into akarma or pure, Unsullied action.

Blake, R.R., Moutor, J.S., *The Managerial Grid* : Key Orientation for Achieving Production through People, Houston Gulf Publishing Co. 1964.

Branda, Lee, *Work and Workers—A Sociological Analysis,* Robert, Florida, Erkriga Publishing Company, 1883.

Buhler, G., *'The laws of Manu,* Clarendon Press, Oxford, 1986.

Cameron, R. and D. Meichenbaum, *The Nature of Effective Coping and the Treatment of Stress Related Problems:* A Cognitive—Behavioural Perspective, in L. Gold Berger and S. Breznitz (Eds.) Handbook of Stress : Theoretical and Clinical Aspects : London : MacMillan, 1982.

Campbell, J.P., Duwette, M.D., Lawler, E. III and Weick, K.E., *Managerial Behavioural Performance and Effecting,* New York, McGraw Hill, 1970.

Carl, W. Ernst, *Sufism,* South Asia Editions, New Delhi, 1997.

Carvell, Fred J., *Human Relations in Business,* London : Courier, MacMillan, 1970.

Casus, Wayne F., *Managing Human Resources, Productivity QWL and Profits,* McGraw Hill International, 1989.

Chakaraborty, S.K. , *"Managerial Effectiveness and Quality of Work Life"*, Indian Insights, Tata-McGraw Hill Publishing Company Ltd., New Delhi, 1996.

Chaudhury, *et. al., Change through Team Work,* New Delhi : Century Business, 1993.

Crossby, B. Philips, *Quality is free : The Art of Making Quality Certain,* New York, Penguin Books, 1980

Daniel, A. Ondrack and Martin, G. Evans, *Job Enrichment and Job Satisfaction in Greenfield and Redesign QWL sites"*, Group and Organization Studies, March 1987. A Greenfield site for a quality of Worklife program is a location where an organization constructs a totally new operation and therefore it has no prior job designs or systems in place.

Daniel, C. Feldman, Hugh Arnold, *Managing Individual and Group Behaviour in Organizations,* Tokyo : McGraw Hill International, 1983.

Daniel Quisner Milb, *Labour—Management Relation,* New York, McGraw Hill. 1986.

David, A. Nadler and Edward, E. Lawler IV, *"Quality of Worklife : Perspectives and Directions"*, Organizational Dynamics, Winter 1983.

David McClelland, *The Achieving Society,* Van Nostrand Reinhold, New York, 1961. J.W. Atkinson and J.O. Raynor, Motivation and Achievement (Washington, D.C., Winstow, 1974); D.C. McClelland, Power: The Inner Experience (New York: Irvington, 1975); and M.J. Stahl, Managerial and Technical Motivation: Assessing Needs for Achievement, Power and Affiliation, Praeger, New York, 1986.

Davis, K., *'Human Relations at Work'*, McGraw Hill, New York, 1962.

Davis, Kerith and William G. Scott, *Human Relations and Organizational Behaviour,* New York, McGraw Hill Book Company, 1969.

Davis, L.E. and Cherns, A.B., *The Quality of Working Life,* Free Press, New York, 1975.

De Nitish, R., *Organization Scanning,* New Delhi : Prentice Hall, 1991.

De, Nitish R., *New Forms of Work Organization in India,* Geneva, Conations of Work Life Branch, INC, 1976.

Delamotte, Yuves and Shri Incr Takezawa, *QWL in International Prospective:* ILO, 1984.

Drucker, Heter R., *People and Performance,* New Delhi : Allied Publisher Pvt. Ltd

Dyer, J.S. and Hoffenberg, M., *"Evaluating the Quality of Working Life"* in the Quality of Working Life.

Elton Mayo, *A detailed account of these experiments is available in several books:* The human problems of an industrial civilization, New York: The MacMillan Company, 1933. T.N. Whitehead, The industrial worker, Cambridge, Mass : Harvard University Press, 1938.

Eric Berne, *Transactional Analysis in Psychotherapy,* New York : Grove Press, Inc. 1961 : Eric Berne, Games people play, New York : Grove Press, Inc. 1964; Thomas A. Harris, I'm o.k. – you're o.k. : A Practical Guide to Transactional analysis, New York : Harper or Row Publishers, Inc. 1969. Dorothy Jongeward, Everybody Wins; Transactional analysis applied to organization reading, Mass : Addison-Wesley Publishing Company, 1973.

Fazl Ahmed, *Four companions,* Idara Isha'at-e-Diniyat (P) Ltd., New Delhi, 1993.

Food Robert N., *Motivation through the Work itself,* New York, AMA, 1969.

Frank Blacker and Sylvia Shinemin, *Applying Psychology in Organization,* New York : Methods Inc., 1984.

Fraser, John, *Making Work Face more Satisfying,* Tripartie Steer Group on Job-satisfaction, London.

Fromm, Erich, *Man for himself : An Inquiry into the Psychology of Ethics,* New York, Hott, Richart and Wistom, 1861.

Gibson *et. al., "Organizations",* Business Publications Inc., Houston, 1985.

Goodman, P.S, *"An Examination of Referents used in the Evaluation of Pay",* Organizational Behaviour and Human Performance, October 1974.

Green, Francis, *Demanding Work,* University of Kent, 2003.

Hadi-Hussian M. Imam Abu Hanifah, *Life and Work,* Indara Ishaal-e-Diniyat (P) Ltd., New Delhi, 1995.

Hans Selye, *The Stress of Life,* Rev. Ed. New York : McGraw Hill Book Company, 1976.

Herrick, N.Q. and Maccoby, M., *Humanizing Work :* A Priority Goal of the Seventies in the Quality of Working Life.

Herzber, F., *Work and the Nature of Man,* London : Campton Printing Ltd., 1971.

Herzberg, F. *et. al., Job Attitudes :* Review of Research and Opinions, Pittsburgh : Psychological Service, 1957.

Herzberg, F., Mausher, B. and Synderman, B., *The Motivation to Work,* John Wiley, New York: 1959.

Herzberg, F. Pernard Manscher *et. al., The Motivation to Work,* London : The Mac William Collier Ltd., 1970.

Hnikle, L.E., *The Concept of Stress in the Biological Sciences,* Stress, Man and Medicine, 1973.

Hoppock, R., *Job Satisfaction,* New York : Harper and Brother, 1985.

Iqbal, A. Ansari, *"Concept of Man in Comparative Perspective",* Institute of Objective Studies, New Delhi, 1997.

Ismail Raji al Frauqi, *"Al-Tawhid",* Its Implications for thought and Life, International Islamic Publishing House, and the International Institute of Islamic thought, Virginia, USA, 1995.

Jack Hawley, *"Reawakening The Spirit in Work",* The power of Dharmic Management, Tata McGraw Hill Publishing Company Ltd., New Delhi, 1994.

Janis, I.L., *Decision-making under Stress,* In L. Goldberger and S. Breznitz (Eds.) Handbook of Stress : Theoretical and Clinical Aspects : London, MacMillan, 1982.

Jemmot, J.B., J. Boy Senko, M. Boy Senko, D.C. Mc. Cell and R. Chapman, D. Meyer and H. Benson, *Academic Stress, Power Motivation, and Decrease in Secretion Rate of Salivary Secretary Immune Globulin,* The Lancet, 8339, 1400-2, 1983.

Joe Kelly, *Organizational Behaviour,* rev. ed., Richard D. Irvin Inc.... and The Dorsey Press, Homewood, 1974.

John, A. Subhan, Sufism, *Its Saints and Shines,* Indigo Books, Cosmo Publications, New Delhi, 2002.

John Mac Donald and John Piggott, *Global Quality : The New Managerial Culture,* New Delhi : Viva Books Private Ltd., 1992.

Keith Davis and John, W. Newstrom, *Human Behaviour at Work,* 8th edition, McGraw Hill International Ltd., New Delhi, 1989.

Khandwalla, Pradeep W., *Organizational Designs for Excellence,* New Delhi : Tata McGraw Hill, 1992.

Khurram Murad, *Way to Quran,* The Islamic Foundation, United Kingdom,, 1985.

Lazarus, R.S. Cohen, J.B., Folkman, S. and Schaefer, C., *'Psychological Stress and Adoption',* Some Unresolved Issues, in H. Selye (Ed.) Selye's Guide to Stress Research, Vol. 1, New York, 1980.

Lewis Coser, *The functions of Social Conflict,* The free Press, Glencoe, 1956.

Locke, E.A., *"Toward a Theory of Task Motivation and Incentives",* Organization Behaviour and Human Performance, May 1968.

Low A. Zen, *'The Art of Creative Management' (play boy paper backs),* New York, 1976.

Maccoby, M., *Emotional Attitudes and Political Choices,* Politics and Society, 2(2), 1972.

Martzomey, Leslive Lynn, *Improving Productivity and Quality of Worklife: An Impact and Study on Work Design at Infocorp,* Harvard University, 1986.

Maslow, A., *Motivation and Personality,* Harper & Row, New York, 1954.

Maulana Fazul-Ul-Kavin, *Imam Gazzalis Ihya Ulum-id-Din,* Kitab Bhavan, New Delhi, 1982.

Maulana Muhammad Zakariyya Kaandhlauri, *Stories of Sahaabah Farid,* Book Depot (Pub.) Ltd., New Delhi, 2000.

Maurice Bucaille, *What is the Origin of Man?* Islamic Book Service, New Delhi, 2001.

Mc Gregor, D., *The Human side of Enterprise,* McGraw-Hill, New York, 1960. For an updated Analysis of Theory X and Theory Y constructs, see R.J. Summbers and S.F. Cronshaw, "A Study of Mc Gregor's Theory X, Theory Y and the Influence of Theory X, Theory Y Assumptions on casual Attributions, for Instances of Worker Poor Performance", in S.C. McShare (ed), Organizational Behaviour, ASAC 1988 Conference Proceedings, Vol. 9, Part 5, Halifax, Mova Scotia, 1988.

Michael, A. Campion and Paul W. Thayer, *Four different Job design,* Approaches for different Situations are Described in Job Design : Approaches, outcomes and Trade-offs, Organizational Dynamics, Winter 1987.

Mohammad Marmaduke Pickthall, *The Cultural Side of Islam,* Islamic Book Trust, New Delhi, 1982.

Mohammad Nejatullah Siddiqui, *Economic Enterprise in Islam,* Markazi Maktaba, Islamic, New Delhi, 2000.

Morse, Nancy C., *Satisfaction in the White-collar Job.* Ann Arbos : University of Michigen, Institute for Social Research, Survey Research Centre, 1953.

Muhammad Yusuf Islahi, *"Etiquette of life in Islam",* Markazi Maktaba Islamic Publishers, New Delhi, 2000.

Naceur Jabnoun, *Islam and Management.* International Islamic Publishing House, Riyadth, Saudi-Arabia, 2001.

O'Plahery, W.D., *'The Rig Veda',* Penguin, Harmondsworth, 1981.

Osborne, A., *Ramana Maharishi and the Path of Knowledge,* B.I. Publications, New Delhi, 1979.

Pareek, U., *Making Organizational Roles Effective,* New Delhi, Tata McGraw Hill, 1993.

Pradip, N. Khandwalla, *Organizational Designs for Excellence,* New Delhi, Tata McGraw Hill, 1993.

Prasad, L.M., *Principles of Practice of Management,* Sultan Chand and Sons Publications, New Delhi, 2004.

Radhakrishna, S., *The Bhagavad Gita, Blacke,* Bombay 1976.

Rahm Ali Al-Hashmi, *A Guide to Moral Rectitude,* The Board of Islamic Publications, New Delhi, 2000.

Richard, T. De George, *Business Ethics,* New York : MacMillon Publishing Company, 3rd Ed., 1990.

Robert, C. Erffmeyer and Others, *"The Delphi Technique : An Empirical Evaluation of the Optimal Number of Rounds",* Group and Organizational Studies, March-June 1986.

Robin Fincham and Peter, S. Rhodes, *The Individual, Work and Organization,* George Weldenfeld Nicolson Ltd., London, 1993.

Rockeach, M., *The Nature of Human Values,* New York : Free Press, 1973.

Sangeeta, J., *Quality of Work Life,* Delhi : Deep and Deep Publications, 1981.

Savall, Henri, *Work and Evaluation of Job Enrichment,* Oxford : Calendar Press, 1981.

Sayles and Straus, *Human Behaviour in Organizations,* London : Prentice Hall, 1966.

Sayyid Abul A'a Mawdudi, *The Islamic Way of Life,* Markazi Maktaba Islami Publications, New Delhi, 2000.

Sayyid Qutb, *In the Shade of the Quaran,* Vol. 30, Crescent Publishing Company, Aligarh, 2000.

Seashore, S.E., *Defining and measuring the QWL* in Davis, L.E. and Chen, A.E., QWL, New York, 1975.

Selye, H., *History and Present Status of the Stress Concept* in L. Gold Berger and S. Brezcitz (Eds.) Handbook of Stress : Theoretical and Clinical aspects, London; Macmillan, 1983.

Shaykh Saleem al-Hilaalee, *Love and Hate for Allah's Sake,* Al-Hidaayah Publishing Company, Kingdom, 1999.

Sheikh 'Abdul Rauf', *Muslim Way of Life,* Idara Ishaat-e-Diniyat (P) Ltd., New Delhi, 2002.

Singh, I.P., *The Gita—A Workshop on the Expansion of Self,* Somaiya, Bombay 1977.

Singh, R., *Participation and Consultative Mechanics QWL,* Quality of Work Life and Productivity, New Delhi, NPC 1991

Stanley, Dennis, *Quality of Worklife in India: Its Development and Psychometric Validation,* The University of Aaron, 1986.

Staw, B.M., *"Motivation in Organizations: Toward Synthesis and Redirections"* in B.H. Staw and G.R. Salancik (eds.) New Directions in Organizational Behaviour (Chicago: St. Clain, 1977).

Stephen, P. Robbins, *Organizational Behaviour,* Prentice Hall of India, New Delhi, 1998.

Stephen, R. Corey, *The Seven Habits of Highly Effective People : Powerful Lessons in Personal Change,* London : Simmon and Schurstafied, 1989.

Sultan Ahmed Qureshi, *Letters of the Holy Prophet Muhammad (SAW),* Idara Ishaat-e-Diniyat (P) Ltd., 2000.

Suri, G.K. Ajit Singh, Syed Akbar, *Quality of Worklife and Productivity,* New Delhi, NPC, 1991.

Syed Abdul Latif, "*Bases of Islamic Culture*", Idarah-I Adabiyat-e-Delhi, New Delhi, 1977.

Tennings, Sandra Arun Ruff, *An Investigation of Employee Responses to QWL issue : A Demographic Analysis,* The University of Oklahoma, 1985.

Thomas, G. Cummings, Edman, S. Molloy, *Improving Productivity and QWL,* New York : Praeger Publishing, 1977.

Thomas, K.W., "*Conflict and Negotiation Process in Organizations*" in M.O. Ounnette and L.M. Hough (ed.) Handbook of Industrial and Organizational Psychology, 2nd ed., Vol. 3, (Palo Alto, CA: Consulting Psychologists Press, 1992).

Vroom, V.R., *Work and Motivation,* New York : Wiley, 1964.

Wahba, M.A. and Bridwell, L.G., "*Maslow Reconsidered : A Review of Research on the Need Hierarchy Theory,* "Organizational Behaviour and Human Performance, April 1976.

Walton, R.E., *Improving the QWL,* HBR and Management, Vol. 1, Perennial Library, New York : Harper and Row Pub. Inc. 1985.

Wanous, J.P. and Zwany, A., "*A Cross Sectional Test of Need Hierarchy Theory*", Organizational Behaviour and Human Performance, May 1977.

Weber, Max, *Protestant Ethics and the Spirit of Capitalism,* New York : Scribner, 1930.

William H. Whyte Fr., *The Organization Man,* New York : Simon and Schuster, 1956.

Journals

Ahmed, D., Quality of Work Life : A Need for Understanding, *Indian Management,* 20(1), 1981.

Ajit Singh, Status of Quality Circles in India, *Productivity,* Vol. 29, No. 4, Jan.-March 1989.

Alex Carey, "The Hawthrone Studies : A Radical Criticisms", *American Sociological Review,* June 1967.

Anderson, G., 'The Quality of Work Life', Seminar on Worker Participation in Australia, South Australian Development, *Department of Legal Studies and Industrial Relations Programme,* University of Melbourne, Melbourne, Australia, 1975.

Arsenault, A. and S. Dolan, The role of personality occupation and organization in understanding the relationship between Job-stress, performance and absenteeism, *Journal of Occupational Psychology*, 56, 1983.

Arthur, P. Brief and Jeniffer M. Atich, "Studying Job Stress : Are we making mountains out of Molehills?" *Journal of Occupational Behaviour*, April 1987.

Asha Bhandarkar, Motivational Research in India. *A Literature Review, Unpublished Paper Prepared for ICPE*, Yugoslavia, 1988.

Augenblick, Lynw, Barriers to Quality, *Personnel*, Journal, May 1990.

Bandyopandhyay, P.K., 'Quality'—A Way of Work Life, *Personnel Today*.

Barry Wilkinson, Technology and Quality of Working Life, *Singapore Management Review*, Vol. 8, July 1986.

Bellman Geoffrey, M., Balancing your Work in your Life, *Training and Development*, Journal, Dec. 1990.

Bennet, S.N. *et al.*, Quality and Quality of Work in Rows and Clan Room Group, *Educational Psychology*, 1983, Vol. 3(2).

Blucstare, Implementing QWL Programs, *Management Review*, July 1977.

Bradley, K. Hills, Quality circles and managerial interests. *Industrial Relations*, Berkeley, 26(1), Writer 1987.

Brain Storming was developed by Alex, F., Osborn and is described in his book Applied Imagination, New York; Charles Scribner's Sons, 1953. See also Stephen R. Grossman, "Brain Storming updated", *Training and Development*, Journal, February 1984 and Tony Proctor, "Brain": The Computer Program that Brainstorms" Simulation and Games, December 1986.

Breaugh, J.A., Measurement of Work Autonomy, *Human Relations*, New York, 38(6), 1985.

Calder, B.J. and Staw, B.M., "Self-Perception of Intrinsic and Extrinsic Motivation", *Journal of Personality and Social Psychology*, April 1975.

Campagna, Franco, Japan's Example in Training in Quality Control, *Personnel Today*, Jan.-Mar. 1980.

Canon, W.B., Stress and Strain, Homeostasis, *American Journal of Medical Science*, 89(1), 1935.

Chans, A., Political Dimensions of QWL, *International Journal of Manpower,* (Bradford), 7(4), 1986.

Charles, Weaver, N., What Workers want from their Jobs? *Personnel,* May-June 1976.

Chichester, Clark Robin, In the QWL, *Personnel Management,* Nov., 1973.

Chris Argyris, "Skilled incompetence", *Harvard Business Review,* September-October 1986.

Cox, Martha Glenn and Brown, QWL, Another Fad or real benefit, *Personnel Administrator,* 27(5), 1983.

Cracer, R.F., QWL Experiment, A Practical Case Study. *Management Review,* June 1983.

Crick, Lydan, QWL and Productivity : The Australian Approach, *Productivity,* 22(4), Jan.-March 1982.

David, J. Cherrington and B. Jackson Jr., "Recognition is Still a Top Motivator", *Personnel Administrator,* May 1983.

De, Nitish R., Inter Linkage between Quality of Life and Productivity, 1982, 22(4).

De, Nitish, R., Towards an Appreciation of Quality of Life and QWL, *Economic and Political Weekly,* 19(20-21), 1984.

De, Charms, R., Personal Causation; *The Internal Affective Determinants of Behaviour Academic Press,* New York, 1968.

Declamotte, Yures Walker, Kenneth, F., Humanization of Work and the Quality of Working Life in Trends and Issues. *International Institute for Labour Studies Bulletin,* (11), 1975.

Delbert, C. Mill and William H. Form, Industrial Psychology, New York, Harper and Row, 1951.

Earley, P.C., Wojnaroski, P. and Prest, W., "Task planning and Energy Expended: Exploration of How Goals Influence Performance, *Journal of Applied Psychology,* February 1987.

Edward, E. Lawler III and Richard Hackman, Corporate Projects and Employees Satisfaction: Must they be in Conflict? *California Management Review,* Fall 1971.

Edward, E. Lawler III, Showed the Quality of Work Life be Legislated? *Personal Administration,* Jan. 1976.

Elizur, Dov., 'Quality Circle and Quality of Work Life', *International Journal of Manpower,* Year 1990, Vol. II, No. 6, MCBUP Ltd., Israel.

Ellen, L. Maher, "Burnout and Commitment : A Theoretical Alternative", *The Personnel and Guidance Journal,* March 1983.

Erwin, L. Malone, A Discussion of this Early Failure is Presented in "The Non-linear System Experiment in Participative Management", *The Journal of Business,* January 1975.

Eugene Ramdseep, Team Work into Work Teams, *Personal Today,* Jan.-March, 1990.

Frenden Berger, H.J., Staff Burnout, *Journal of Social Issues,* 1974.

Frik, C.F., "Some Conceptual Difficulties in the Theory of Social Conflict", *Journal of Conflict Resolutions,* Dec. 1968 and J.A. Wall Jr. and R.R. Callister, "Conflict and its Management", *Journal of Management,* Vol. 21, No. 3, 1995.

Gallie, Duncam, The Quality of Working Life : Is Scandinavia Different? *European Sociological Review,* 19(1), 2003.

Ganquly, O.N. and Joseph, J.S., Quality of Working Life : Work Prospects and Aspirations of Young Employees in Air India, *Central Labour Institute,* Mumbai, 1976.

George Bursetin, "Enhancing the Quality of Worklife", *Business Forum,* California State University, Los Angeles, Winter 1987.

Ghosh, Subash, Quality of Working Life in two Indian Organizations, Implications of Case Studies, *Decision,* Vol. 19, No. 2; April-June, 1992.

Glaser, E.M., Improving the QWL, Los Angeles, *Human Interaction Research Institute,* 1974.

Glasier, E.M., State of Art Questions about the Quality of Worklife, *Personnel,* Nov.-Dec. 20, 1976.

Goel, S.S., Quality of Worklife Programmes, *Personnel Today,* Oct.-Nov. 1988.

Herzberg, F., How do you motivate employees? *Harvard Business Review,* 46(1), 1988.

House, R.J. and Wigdor, L.A, "Herzberg's Dual Factor Theory of Job-Satisfaction and Motivation: A Review of the Evidence and Criticism", *Personnel Psychology,* Winter 1967; D.P. Schwab and L.L. Cummings. "Theories of Performance and Satisfaction: A Review", *Industrial Relations,* October, R. Braito, "A Specification Issue in Job-Satisfaction Research", *Sociological Perspectives,* April 1998.

James, W. Thacker and Mitchell, W. Fields, "Union Involvement in Quality of Worklife Efforts", A Longitudinal Investigation, *Personnel Psychology,* Spring 1987.

James, G., QWL and Total Quality Management, *International Journal of Manpower,* 13(5), 1992.

Jerome, M. Rosow, In Karew, E. Debats (ed.), "The Continuing Personnel Challenge", *Personnel Journal,* May 1982.

John, H. Howard, David, A. Cunningham and Peter A. Rechnitzer, "Role Ambiguity, Type A behaviour, and Job satisfaction. Moderating Effects an Cardiovascular and Biochemical Responses Associated with Coronary Risk", *Journal of Applied Psychology,* February 1986.

John, M. Ivancevich, "Life Events and Hassles as Predictors of Health Symptoms, Job-performance, and Absenteeism, *Journal of Occupation Behaviour,* January 1986, Also see Richard S-Lazarus, "Little Hassles can be Hazardous to your Health", *Psychology Today,* July 1987.

John, M. Ivancevich, Michael, T. Matteson and Edward P. Richard III, Who's Liable for Stress on the Job? *Harvard Business Review,* March-April 1985.

Kalleberg, Anne L., Work Values and Job Rewards : A Theory of Job Satisfaction, *American Sociological Review,* Feb. 1977, Vol. 42.

Kenneth, W. Thomas and Warren, H. Schmidt, 'A Survey of Managerial Interests with Respect to Conflict". *Academy of Managerial Journal,* June 1976. A measurement Instrument is described in Boris Kabanoff, "Predictive validity of the MODE conflict Instrument", *Journal of Applied Psychology,* February 1987.

Kethleen Anthony and Brain H. Kleiner, "The price of success", *Business Forum,* Spring 1987; Saroj Parasuraman and Joseph Parasuraman A. Alutto, "An examination of the Organizational Antecedents of Stressors at Work", *Academy of Management Journal,* March 1981.

Korman, A.K., Greenhaus, J.K. and Badin, I.J., "Personnel Attitudes and Motivation" in M.R. Rose and L.W. Porter (eds.), *Annual Review of Psychology,* Palo Alto, CA: Annual Reviews, 1977.

Latham, G.P. and Yukl, G.A., "A Review of Research on the Application of Goal Setting in Organizations", *Academy of Management Journal,* December 1975.

Lawler, III, E.E. and Suttle, J.L., "A Casual Correlation Test of the Need Hierarchy Concept, Organizational Behaviour and Human Performance, April 1972; D.T. Hall and K.E. Nougaim, "An Examination of Maslow's Need Hierarchy in an organization setting", *Organizational Behaviour and Human Performance,* February 1968, and J. Rausehenberger, N. Schmitt and J.E. Hunter, "A Test of the Need Hierarchy concept by a Markor Model of change in Need Strength", *Administrative Science Quarterly,* December 1980.

Lawler III, Edward E., Should the QWL be legislated? *Personnel Administration,* Jan. 1976.

Leonard Schlesinger and Richard Walton, Unpublished background committee, *Harvard Graduate School of Business Administration.*

Milkant, V. and R. Tandon, An Alternative Approach for Improving QWL in India, *PECEE,* New Delhi, 1982.

Monga, R.C., Dynamics of Productivity Management, *Productivity,* Vol. 33, No. 1, April-January, 1992.

Ozley, L.M. and Ball, J.S., QWL : Initiating Successful Effort in Labour Management Organization, *Personnel Administration,* May 1982.

Pascale Carayon, Peter Hoonakker, S. Marchand, Jen Schwarz., Job-characteristics and Quality of Working Life in IT Work Force; the Role of Gender, *Personnel Research Annual Conference,* 2003.

Pehr, G. Gyllenhammar, People at Work, Reading, Mass : Addison-Wesley Publishing Company, 1977; and Pehr G. Gyllenhammar, "How Volvo Adapts Work to People", *Harvard Business Review,* July-August 1977. Recent results are reported in Berth Jonsson and Alden G. Lank, "Volvo : A Report on the Workshop on Production Technology and Quality of Working Life", *Human Resource Management,* Winter, 1985.

Portigal, Alam H., Current Research on QWL, *Industrial Relations,* Oct. 1973.

Rajagopalan, A.V., Role of Quality of Work Life Programmes, *The Hindu,* 27th May 1985.

Randall, B. Dunham, Jon L. Pierce and John W. Newstrom, The need to balance internal and external factors is presented in "Job Context and Job Content: A Conceptual Perspective", *Journal of Management,* Fall Winter, 1983, mixed results from a literature review are in Richard, E. Kopelman, "Job Redesign and Productivity : A Review of the Evidence", *National Productivity Review,* Summer, 1985.

Ranney, J.M., QWL in the Office, *Training and Development*, 36(4), 1981.

Resa, W. King Irene Pave, "Stress Claims are Making Business Jumping", *Business Week*, October 14, 1985.

Rice, R.N. *et al.*, Organizational Work and the Perceived Quality of Life Towards a Conceptual Model, *Academy of Management Review*, April 1985, Vol. 10(2).

Richard, E. Walton, "Improving the Quality of Work Life", *Harvard Business Review on Management*, Vol. 1, New York, 1975.

Ritti, R.R., Under Employment of Engineer, *Industrial Relations*, 9(4), 1970.

Robert, L. Dodson, Speeding the Way of Total Quality, *Training and Development*, June 1991.

Robert Quest, "Quality of Work Life—Learning from Tarry Town", *Harvard Business Review*, July-August, 1979.

Robert, R. Rehder and Marta Medaris Smith, "Kzizen and the Art of Labor Relations", *Personnel Journal*, December 1986.

Robert, W. Eckles, Stress-making friends with the enemy, *Business Horizons*, March-April 1987.

Rosow, J.M., QWL Issues for the 1980s, *Training and Development*, 35(3), 1981.

Rosow, J.M., 'Human Dignity in the Public Sector Work Place', *Public Personnel Management*, Vol. 8(1), Jan.-Feb. 1975.

Sayeed, O.D. and Sinha, P., QWL in Relations to Job Satisfaction and Performance in Two Organizations, *Managerial Psychology*, 2(1), 1987.

Seashore, Stanley E., Accessing the QWL : The US Experience, *Labour and Society*, 1(2), April, 1976.

Sekaran, U., Perceived Quality of Working Life in, Banks in Major Cities in India, *Prajanan*, Vol. 14(3), 1981.

Selye, H., A Syndrome Produced by Diverse Mucous Age, *Nature*, 138, 1936.

Shalala, E. Donna, QWL—Issues United States Department of Health Human Services, Dec. 1996.

Singh and Dewari, Job Satisfaction among Bank Employees, *Indian Psychological Review*, 24(2), 1983.

Singh, J.P., Improving Quality of Working Life in the Indian Context, *Productivity*, 1982.

Sinha, M.K., Banking Industry : QWL, *Economic Research Department*, Bombay, 1992.

Suri, B.K., QWL Domain and its Components, *Quality of Work Life*, Jan.-April 1984.

Susan, E. Jackson, Richard, L. Schwab and Randall, S. Schuler, "Towards an Understanding of Burnout Phenomenon", *Journal of Applied Psychology,* November 1986.

Tenmings Sandra Ann Ruff, An Investigation of Employee Responses to QWL Issue : A Demographic Analysis, The University of Oklawama, 1985.

Thompson, G., Tommy, Secretary, United States Department of Health Human Services (HHS), dated 21.02.2005, Washington D.C. 2001.

Thorsrud, Einar, Quality of Working Life in the First and the Third World, *Productivity*, 1982, 22(4).

Tom Wranlinger and Tom Huberty, Behavioural *verses* Humanizing, *Training and Development*, Dec. 1990.

Trist, E.L., Planning the First Step Towards QWL in a Developed Country. *The QWL*, New York, Vol. 1, Free Press, 1975.

Varma, M.K., Quality Circle : A Catalyst for Motivation, *Personal Today*, Oct.-Nov. 1988.

Vroom, Victor, Ego Involvement, Job Satisfaction and Job Performance, *Personnel Psychology*, Vol. 15, No. 27, Summer 1962.

Waltar, R.E., QWL : What is it? *Management Review*, Feb. 1973.

Waltar, R.E., Improving the QWL, *HBR*, May-June 1974.

Walton, R.E., QWL Indicator : Prospects and Problems, Studies in *Personnel Psychology*, 1974, Spring, Vol. 6(1).

West, M.A., and R. Rushton, Mismatches in the Work Role Transition, *Journal of Occupational Psychology,* 1989.

West, M.A., N. Michoson and A. Rees, Transitions into Newly Created Jobs, *Journal of Occupational Psychology,* 1987.

William, P. Galle, Jr., "Transactional Analysis as a Tool for Humor Applications in Management", in James, O. Smith and Carl into Gooding (Eds.), 1985, *American Institute for Decision Sciences Proceedings,* Vol. 2, Las Vegas, Nov. 11-13, 1985.

Yuves Delamotte and Schi-Ichi-Taaezawa., Quality of Working Life in International Perspective, Geneva, ILO, 1984.

Index